THE COMPLETE GUIDE TO PROPERTY FINANCE

THE COMPLETE GUIDE TO PROPERTY FINANCE

TOOLBOX OF 50+ FINANCING SOLUTIONS BEYOND BUY-TO-LET

RICHARD W J BROWN
THE PROPERTY VOICE

The Complete Guide to Property Finance

ISBN: 978–1-7398320–2-5 (paperback)
ISBN: 978–1-7398320–1-8 (e-book)

A CIP catalogue record for this book is available from the British Library.

Published by The Property Voice
thepropertyvoice.net

Design and Production: Catherine Williams, The BizBook Foundry
Managing Editor: Helen Pollock, The BizBook Foundry

Printed and bound in Great Britain

Foreword

As someone who has worked my way up from running an estate agency at 17 to owning a substantial property portfolio, as well as being a developer and consultant, I am keenly aware of the importance of understanding property investment finance. When I started out, I borrowed some money from my Mum to make my first property investment – and made her a profit. Some 4 decades on, I have my own investment fund, helping newbie developers to get started.

What Richard Brown and I have in common is a desire to share our knowledge and help others. We both have significant experience and success in property investment – in all of its guises – but we both also shun the "guru" tag.

Richard's no-nonsense, straightforward and ethical approach is clear to see in the high-quality resources he makes available through his podcast, *The Property Voice*, his YPN column, and his books, of course.

With admirable honesty about the ups and downs of property investment, as well as in-depth knowledge, Richard is a natural teacher and mentor. In this book, he sets out over 50 different property investment finance strategies. Whether you are a complete novice or have some experience already, there's bound to be something you haven't thought of before.

The Complete Guide to Property Finance does exactly what it says on the tin. It gives investors the financial strategy tools to make sure that they can finance their property deals and developments. Striking the right balance between highlighting opportunities and mitigating risk, this book needs to be on every property investor's bookshelf as a reference guide.

John Howard
Property Expert & Author

Table of Contents

Introduction and Welcome

The realm of property investment and development is an expansive one and so too is the related world of property finance. When I set out to write this book, I was clear and deliberate in my mind that I did not want to write a boring book about Buy-to-Let mortgages! This is a book about property finance with a very broad definition, scope and with **50+ different property finance strategies** shared, hopefully a wider span of interest too.

My definition of property finance is this:

Property finance comprises payment over time and/or a financial contribution and/or control without necessarily ownership of our property investments and developments. Property finance is therefore the combination of the three levers of money, time and control over property assets.

This book will take you on a journey through all the areas of property finance. It is broken down into three main sections, as follows:

- Institutional finance – this is what most people think of when they think about property finance and includes buy-to-let mortgages and commercial loans, bridging finance and development finance and, to a lesser extent, consumer finance.

- Alternative finance – starts to take us into less familiar territory and, includes sources such as crowdfunding, peer-to-peer lending, friends and family, becoming our own bank and broker, private finance (including joint ventures) and then bonds, shares and mezzanine finance and finally grants and soft loans.

- Creative finance – we have certain methods of financing our property acquisitions that might not, at first glance, seem like a property finance source at all. But not in my book! These could include property and land options, sub-lease or rent-to-rent structures, 100% vendor, developer and bank finance, assisted sales, instalment contracts and exchange with delayed completion, along with the wide array we will see in the 'Best of The Rest' chapter, including: adverse possession, assignable off-plan contracts and valuation arbitrage.

There is an argument that this could have been three separate books but, equally, it is not an in-depth tome on each sub-topic either. So, it will cover what you need to know in each of the topics in outline, along with some top tips to add small nuggets of advice from my personal experience intertwined. Consider it a signpost for you to explore each of the topics further, if you would like. It is also intended to form a toolbox comprising the various tools of the property finance strategies and techniques covered. As with any toolbox, there is a tool for every job and every job could lead to using more than one tool. Of course, there are the odd tools in the toolbox that rarely or even never get used – well, there are in my toolbox at home anyway!

In addition, there are a number of extras that make the book even more expansive and comprehensive, which I have chosen to include as Book Bonuses. This includes case studies on many of the property finance strategies, along with additional content and other supporting resources. I would highly recommend that you get a copy of these Book Bonuses to add greater richness and depth to your reading and understanding of the topic. You can get the Book Bonuses here: https://www.thepropertyvoice.net/bookbonus/.

My first book, *Property Investor Toolkit*, sets out the fundamentals of property investment and has been well received and well reviewed too, thankfully. You might like to get a copy of that book to accompany this one, especially if you are new or in the early stages of your property investment activities. *Property Investor Toolkit* does discuss the principles of property as an investment, which is foundational to any form of investment. So foundational that I included a modified excerpt of that section here for you.

Leverage and Cash-on-Cash Return

Leverage is the concept of using somebody else's money to grow the size of our investment fund. The most common example with property investing is a buy-to-let mortgage, where we add funds from a lender to our own deposit to buy a property with the combined fund value.

Our leverage is the ratio by which we increase our own cash investment in relation to the property value. In the case where we can take out a buy-to-let mortgage at 75% of the purchase price (known as the 'loan-to-value'), our leverage would be 4:1 excluding costs (£100,000 purchase price compared to £25,000 of our own cash).

Put another way, we can multiply our investment funds and hence our purchasing power from £25,000 up to £100,000 by using leverage.

Cash-on-cash return (COCR) is the amount of financial return we make on the personal cash funds invested, expressed as a percentage. Some people refer to this as return on capital employed (ROCE) or return on investment (ROI).

Our COCR is the net return on our actual cash invested. So, on a full year basis if our net income return in the example above were say £2,400, then our COCR would be 9.6% (£2,400 / £25,000). However, if we were to pay for that same investment property in full using only our personal cash funds, then the COCR would be 2.4% instead (£2,400 / £100,000).

This is a simple illustration to highlight the point and excludes a number of costs and fees for ease. However, it also demonstrates the power of leverage and how that can increase our investment purchasing power and investment returns. Leverage is another word for property finance in my world and so you could say that this book is really all about how to maximise our leverage and investment returns through property.

Financial Engineering

I like to think about applying many of the concepts within this book as a form of 'financial engineering'. We can engineer a solution for our investment and development activities using elements of property finance outlined within this book. By doing so, we can not only magnify or multiply our investment returns, we can also grow and scale our investment and development reach at the same time. Personally, I have reached the point in my own property journey where I can look beyond myself and my immediate family's needs and plan for my legacy. For me, this is the formation of a foundation that supports causes close to my heart; housing, entrepreneurship, learning and poverty. This spells out the word HELP, of course, so it will be the HELP Foundation. Property finance and the idea of financial engineering have been the means by which I now have this foundation as my life's purpose, along with sharing my knowledge, such as through this book.

However, when I had my 'Eureka moment' in the mid-noughties and discovered all that property investing could offer, I did not set out then to form a foundation. I followed a process of what I now call 'fix and flex', where I set a course to achieve a specific outcome and then when I reached that, flexed it to an alternative, often higher outcome.

I started out by wanting to plug a hole in my rather inadequate pension. Realising that I had in fact fixed this with my very first property investment, I was then able to flex the new outcome to quit my job or achieve financial independence you might say. Then, for my wife to quit her job, although she is very happy with her career and still chooses to work; although we have a nice lifestyle, fortunately. Then it became family legacy, where our three adult daughters would have sufficient means to support their own lifestyle choices. Let's just say that they all intend to pursue a life purpose that is full of meaning and not so full of financial reward. It is our pleasure and wish to support them in their respective worthy quests. After that, it flexed to give back to and support future generations of people from less advantaged positions. That's a personal insight that might help you frame or visualise how the tools shared throughout this book might help you to fix and flex the outcomes and causes in life that are important to you too. I sincerely hope it does.

There are a number of financial terms and concepts that are outlined throughout the book, which I endeavour to explain as we go. Some of the earlier chapters are foundational to many of the principles in the later chapters and so reading them in sequence might help. However, many of the chapters are standalone and can be read in isolation too. So, if you have a good grasp of the Institutional Finance options, for example, you could dive into the more advanced property finance concepts outlined in the Alternative Finance and Creative Finance sections. There are over 50 different property finance strategies covered in this book, so dig in and enjoy them all.

Disclaimer

The strategies and topics covered in this book are financial in nature and can be complex. Everybody's situation is unique and so specific to them. This book is for educational purposes and many of the comments by the author and other contributors are personal opinions or reflect our personal situation. Therefore, I strongly advise that you seek independent professional and tax advice before applying any of the strategies, tools or techniques outlined within this book.

Whilst I attempted to ensure that the content within is accurate at the time of writing, much is subject to change. A lot depends on external third parties, such as national and local government, lenders and the relevant legal, regulatory and tax authorities. In some respects, the book could be out of date or mention policies or products that no longer exist, are no longer available or indeed new alternatives have arisen too. Therefore, please make your own checks and enquiries in terms of relevance and currency of the content before relying too heavily on it.

The information available through this book is for your general information and use and is not intended to address your particular requirements. In particular, the information does not constitute any form of advice, whether financial, tax, legal, regulatory, or otherwise nor any form of recommendation by the author. The content is not intended to be relied upon by readers in making (or refraining from making) any investment decisions.

Acknowledgements and Thanks

A lot of the content has come from publicly available information published on government, regulatory, industry association and individual institutional websites. Some case studies and proofreading suggestions have been provided by friends and members of *The Property Voice* community – thank you kindly.

In addition, I have been supported by a number of people that have added greatly to the publication of this book in a variety of ways. My thanks go to the following people:

Helen Pollock and Catherine Williams from The BizBook Foundry for helping to make sense of my ramblings and present this book in such a wonderful way.

To Mafalda Casanova, who you can find on Linked In for designing the book cover and icons within.

To John Howard, property expert with four decades in the property sector, who provided the foreword to the book. Also, to Jayne Owen, Rupal Patel, Stephanie Taylor and Kemi Egan, who provided some kind words having reviewed the book before publication.

To friends and members of *The Property Voice* community that helped with case studies, proofreading and other notable contributions: Kemi Egan, Alice Williams (Pilot Fish), Sue Whittle, Damien Fogg, Dominick Hardy, Darren Millwood, Richard Corcoran, Martin Hetzel, Richard Parker, Matthew Saunders, Carl Gilbert, Daniel Theo, Lee Hall and Sergio Grande.

To the ever generous Stephanie Taylor, property investor and author of *Rent to Rent Success*, for providing some invaluable pointers on getting the message out about this book.

To the members of the Creative Finance Mastermind Group that was formed several years ago and helped to form some of the foundations and original content contributions upon which this book was built and developed: Kylie Ackers, John Burridge and Sundeep Vaswani. It has changed a lot since then, although you helped to start this off.

To my lovely wife, Catia Porto, who saw me disappear most weekend mornings for around six months to convert a rough draft into 80,000 words of what lies ahead. To our daughters, Natalia, Laura and Jessica for what you are and what you will become, supported by our property adventures.

To the team behind *The Property Voice* that help me to do the stuff that I either can't or don't like to do most of the time, in particular to Karen Tan and Nina Kaminskaya.

To all in my wider social and professional network that supported with likes, shares, words of encouragement and other contributions at various stages throughout this process.

Being of a certain age, there could well be someone that I may have inadvertently forgotten. If so and that's you – thank you sincerely and please forgive me for the unintended omission.

Finally, to you dear reader. Thank you for purchasing a copy of this book. I am very grateful that you did and equally, I hope that you gain great value from your investment in yourself.

I have one small request. If this book has helped you in some way, why not consider 'paying it forward' and gift a copy to someone you know who could benefit by reading it? I will gladly replace your personal copy with a PDF version if you would like to gift your own book and still retain the content. I mentioned my life's purpose with the HELP Foundation, and whilst the odd book royalty would help that cause, perhaps of equal importance is my wish to share my knowledge for others to learn from too. Please help to make that happen, with my sincere thanks and appreciation.

Now, settle down and enjoy the book …

Part One

Institutional Financing

Chapter One

Buy-to-Let Mortgages and Commercial Finance

What You Need to Know

Buy-to-Let (BTL) mortgages are secured loans, provided by mortgage lenders, specifically aimed at enabling the purchase of property that will be let out to tenants. Many property investors use BTL mortgages to grow their property portfolio more quickly. Borrowing large sums of money from a mortgage provider means that available cash can be spread as deposits across several properties rather than investing it in just one.

BTL mortgages are widely available with loan amounts of up to 85% of the purchase price of a property – known as the loan to value (LTV) percentage – in some cases. While 85% LTV mortgages do exist, most investors use 60% to 75% LTV products for the security of having equity in a property and because the interest rates are lower.

BTL mortgages were originally aimed at property investors that bought and rented property in their personal names, whether alone or with up to three others.. However, recently, more landlords and investors are choosing to invest through a limited company or a limited liability partnership (LLP). This trend accelerated markedly following the introduction of restrictions on the ability of individual landlords to reclaim mortgage interest payments as an allowable business deduction for tax purposes, known as 'Section 24 Relief' or 'S24'. Essentially, this makes BTL less profitable for higher-rate tax payers owning property in their individual names. It can be complicated to work it out, but as a rule of thumb, if you are already or will become a higher-rate taxpayer, then the profitability of BTL could be lower owning the property individually versus through a company, where the mortgage interest IS a fully allowable deduction – at the time of writing, at least!

Many lenders will offer BTL mortgages to both individuals and limited companies. However, not all lenders do offer BTL mortgages to limited companies and if they do, they may offer them on different, often less favourable, terms to a mortgage in someone's personal name. The main reason for this is that a company or LLP has limited liability and so the risk of lending to them is higher than lending to an individual. For the most part, we will refer to BTL mortgages as one category, but do be aware that there could be differences between personal and business BTL mortgages.

TPV TIP: When weighing up 'incorporating' a property business, consider your long-term objectives and how professional you intend to be as an investor – not just taxation benefits. Keep in mind that a couple owning BTL properties together would need to earn over £100,000 jointly before they became higher-rate taxpayers, so it's not as straightforward a decision as it might appear. Speak to your accountant and consider both the 'now' and also the 'then' in terms of your plans.

Let's look at a simple example using 75% LTV. Imagine that a property has a purchase price of £100,000. Using a BTL mortgage you could borrow £75,000 (75% of £100,000) leaving a required deposit of £25,000 which you would need to fund from your own cash reserves. If you actually had £100,000 in cash then you could buy four properties of £100,000 in this manner, rather than buy just one property with cash. Please note that this simple example has not taken into account any of the associated costs with buying a property, such as legal fees, Stamp Duty Land Tax (SDLT), broker fees and so on.

The following sections outline the characteristics of BTL mortgages, highlighting important considerations that must be made when choosing a BTL mortgage product.

Mortgage Providers

Typically, BTL mortgages are provided by the major bank and building societies. In addition to these there are many specialist providers who target a niche audience, for example light or heavy refurbishment projects or properties with lease issues. One point of note is that a large number of lenders are members of the Council of Mortgage Lenders or CML. The CML has a code of practice that requires their members to adhere to. Non-CML members are not bound by that code, however. The reason for making this distinction is that sometimes you can agree more flexible terms with a non-CML member than a CML member. One of the most important distinctions is when it comes to arranging refinancing of a property, say after a refurbishment. Most CML lenders won't allow you, nor an incoming buyer of that property if it were a flip for example, to refinance the property for at least six months under the CML code of practice. Non-CML members are not bound by this provision and so could allow a refinancing much more quickly.

TPV TIP: If you are refurbishing a property and want to follow the Buy Refurbish Refinance Strategy or 'BRR', then if you can complete the refinancing after say 3–4 months with a non-CML lender rather than say 6–9 months with a CML lender, then you can recycle your funds under the BRR strategy much more quickly. This would then allow a greater 'deal velocity' or, in plain speak, to do more deals more quickly.

Due to the wide range of providers and products, with over 2,000 different products available at the time of writing, it advisable to consult with a mortgage broker. While you may have to pay a small fee for this specialist advice you often find that a broker is much quicker (it is their job after all) and you gain so much more in terms of a product that suits your own personal circumstances. You will also find that many products on the market are only available via intermediaries, so not consulting with a mortgage broker could actually harm your portfolio.

TPV TIP: Choose a mortgage broker that specialises in BTL mortgages and also has 'whole of market' reach to be able to access all lenders.

Borrowing Criteria

Every mortgage provider has different lending criteria but there are some criteria that tend to be very similar across lenders and products:

- The monthly rental income of the property must cover the monthly mortgage payment. Lenders often use a multiplier of 125% for individual or company borrowers, although it's 145% for higher tax rate payers buying in their individual name. This means that if your mortgage payment is £360 per month, then you need to achieve a rental income of at least £450–£522 per month.

- As an individual you often need to have a certain amount of non-property income. This can be anywhere in the range of £20,000–£30,000 as a minimum. Some lenders will take rental profits into account but not all. Outgoings may also be taken into consideration by some BTL lenders.

- You will often need to provide proof that you also own a residential property. This can sometimes be overlooked if the property you are buying is in a location far from where you live and work. Again, there are some mortgages available if you don't own your own home but less of them than if you do.

- Each mortgage applicant must usually be resident in the UK. If you are not a UK citizen you will need to provide evidence that you have the right to reside in the UK. There are some lenders that will lend to overseas nationals and/or residents but once again, fewer of them.

- The provider will require that you pass a credit check. Any CCJs, unpaid loans or a lot of recent searches associated with your credit file will no doubt put you at risk of non-approval. There are some lenders that will still lend to you with an impaired credit history, which is often referred to as 'sub-prime lending'.

- Stress testing the rental income to cover any increases in interest rates often at 5% per year. This is in addition to the 125%–145% rental coverage multiple mentioned earlier.

TPV TIP: If you don't meet all of these criteria, then a mortgage broker is likely to be an essential person to have on your team; they will know which lenders can be flexible or not. If you do meet all the main criteria, then there is an argument that you can save on broker fees by doing your own 'whole of market' search for a mortgage. So, use a broker to add value, save time or get you into a niche product that suits your situation.

Mortgage Types

There are three main types of BTL mortgages: interest only (higher risk by deferring the full mortgage balance until the end of the term but better cash-flow on the rental side of things), repayment (lower risk by paying down the mortgage but less cash is released from rental income) and part repayment (if you want to lower your risk/debt level but cannot afford full repayment).

With an **interest-only mortgage** you only pay the interest on what you have borrowed. Monthly payments are lower, which improves your cash flow – but this does not pay off the principal sum borrowed. From the example above, if you choose a £75,000 interest-only mortgage on a £100,000 property with a 25-year term, then at the end of the term you will still owe the lender £75,000. However, by the end of this term:

- Your property will hopefully be worth much more than the £100,000 you paid for it due to house price growth.

- Your increased cash flow may have enabled you to either take an income during ownership or purchase additional property at an earlier stage than otherwise possible, so multiplying your purchasing power and/or compounding your investment returns.

- Alternatively, you could set aside some of the surplus cash profits and repay some of the mortgage periodically to reduce your debt. This is known as 'overpayments' in the industry but make sure you check with the lender, as not all lenders allow overpayments and if they do they are usually capped at around 10% of the mortgage balance per year without an early repayment penalty being applied.

- The outstanding principal sum of £75,000, due to inflation, will seem a lot less in 25 years than it does today. In fact, this would be the equivalent of around £40,000 assuming a 2.5% annual inflation rate expressed in today's equivalent terms. That's where inflation can work in your favour! Inflation reduces the effective mortgage debt outstanding, whilst at the same time increasing the value of your property to create 'inflation equity' over time.

Depending on the property performance and your investment strategy you could:

- Sell the property, pay off the mortgage and pocket any profit.

- Refinance the property and continue as before.

- Refinance the property at a higher level (i.e. borrow more) and use the additional funds raised to buy another property.

- Refinance the property and pay yourself a tax-free lump sum from the additional funds if investing as an individual.

TPV TIP: Beware of two potential traps with constant refinancing. Too much refinancing can put you into a situation of becoming an unwitting hostage to the taxman and/or a mortgage prisoner with the lender! There needs to be enough equity in the property to cover any debt, even in times where house prices fall, which they do occasionally, and the taxman needs to be paid their slice regardless of whether there is enough equity available to cover the tax bill.

Using a **repayment mortgage**, you pay the interest due on the principal amount plus a portion of the capital itself. This option is lower risk because as time goes on you owe less and less on the property. At the end of the term you will own the property outright which can be attractive if your goal is to generate low risk income. The downside to this is that more of your own money is tied up in the property, which makes it more difficult to expand your property portfolio. The higher repayments will also mean lower net monthly cash flow for the duration of the mortgage. Also, keep in mind that the capital repayment element is not a tax-deductible expense, so you might find yourself in a situation where your tax bill is above your net cashflow.

A **part-repayment** mortgage effectively blends two products (loans) together under one mortgage. This would have part of the loan as interest-only and the rest as a repayment mortgage. There is limited benefit in attempting to set this option up, as your strategy would typically focus on either interest only or repayment, although it could be a hedge for those that want to reduce their LTV over time.

If you are unsure then you could select the interest-only option and, if you wish, set aside some of the rental income to overpay the monthly amount, which will bring down the principal sum owed. Overpayment is more flexible as you can vary the amount as much as you like as long as you make the minimum required payment and don't go over any overpayment cap (typically 10% of the mortgage per year). It is very important to understand what your overpayment options are and what, if any, penalties, charges and caps there are for making overpayments *before* you accept a mortgage offer.

TPV TIP: It's better to be in control of your own destiny rather than be at the mercy of someone else's. So, even if you set aside sums intended to pay down your mortgage, if you control this fund it allows more flexibility should your circumstances change. You can choose to overpay, spend or reinvest the surplus, or set it aside as a 'rainy day fund' instead.

Interest Rates and Types

Just as there are many different types of BTL mortgage there are also many different types of interest rate structures. The most common of those include:

Fixed

As the name suggests, a fixed-rate mortgage has an interest rate that is fixed for an initial term – 2, 3, 5 or even 10 years. This means that the mortgage repayments will remain the same over that initial period. Don't be confused between the fixed-rate period and the total mortgage term, as these are almost always different.

Tracker

A tracker mortgage mirrors (or tracks) by a certain margin above the base interest rate set by the Bank of England or sometimes another reference rate, such as the LIBOR rate (the rate at which banks lend to each other). These rates tend to be priced cheaper initially than fixed-rate deals as the mortgage provider is not guaranteeing that the interest rate won't rise over the term of the product. Beware of lenders setting a minimum rate, or 'floor', below which they won't go though! If they set a floor, then even if the reference rate that the mortgage is linked to falls, your mortgage payments would not.

Capped

A capped mortgage product is a combination of both fixed and tracker products. The interest rate is variable and changes in line with the base interest rate set by the Bank of England; however, there is a ceiling set to how limit how high the interest rate can go. A slight variation to this is a 'collar' where both the upper and/or lower rate is capped or limited in some way.

Standard Variable

This is often referred to as a standard variable rate (SVR) and is a variable interest rate that is determined by the mortgage lender. This rate does not track the Bank of England base rate, historically it typically tracks the LIBOR rate, and can be changed at any time. Although there is a plan in the industry to replace LIBOR with another reference point, the principle would remain the same. This is the interest rate that most mortgage products revert to after the initial term.

At the time of writing, interest rates are very low and typical BTL mortgages range between 1% and 4%. The base interest rate has been as high as 15% back in 1989, before BTL products existed. The Bank of England base rate has averaged 4% to 5%, incidentally, over the long-term. It is advisable to consult with your mortgage broker to find typical interest rates for products that suit your circumstances. You should always ensure you fully understand the interest structure, the rate and necessary payments before you make any commitments.

Discount Variable

A discounted product is linked to the standard variable rate of the lender offering the product. The interest rate of the product is at a level discounted from the standard variable rate. The ability of lenders to change their SVR at any time makes discounted mortgages less of a favourite than the tracker described above.

TPV TIP: It is very difficult to predict what interest rates will do over time, so some element of fixing or capping can be worthwhile and provide some additional peace of mind too. Work out how much difference a 1% to 3% change in interest rates would make to your cashflow to see how affordable some kind of variable rate would then become.

Repayment Terms

Most BTL mortgages are generally taken over a long term, typically up to 25 years, just like residential mortgages. The major difference from a residential mortgage is that many lenders are not so concerned about how close to retirement you are. As long as the lender is satisfied that the rental income will cover the mortgage payments you can typically apply for a BTL mortgage into your 70s. There are some providers, however, who still restrict the maximum age at the end of the term to 65.

The majority of fixed and tracker mortgages on the market today are structured with a short initial period where an attractive interest rate is on offer. This initial period can be 2, 3, 5 or even 10 years. After the initial period the interest rate will revert to the lender's rather less attractive SVR. Savvy investors will remortgage the property at this point onto another product that has an attractive rate for the initial period.

TPV TIP: Many lenders will offer you the option to renew your fixed rate between one and three months before your existing fixed rate is due to end. Whilst it is advisable to test the market, keep in mind that remortgaging with a new lender will carry additional costs, time and paperwork. So, this can be a useful 'middle ground' way to remain competitive with less fuss.

Fees and Costs

Buying property can be an expensive business, but like everything in this world nothing worth having comes for free. The purchase of a single property involves a team of professionals, all who want a little of your hard-earned cash. Below are some of the costs you can expect to pay.

Mortgage Fees

There are several different fees that are associated with BTL mortgages: a booking fee, valuation fee and an arrangement fee, among others. Depending on the lender some of these fees may be waived. It is common to have to pay between £1,000 and £2,000 or up to 2% of the loan amount in total for fees for a small to average sized loan. Often the largest fee, the arrangement fee, can be added to the mortgage – delaying its payment. This offers a cheaper way to purchase the property, but remember that you will pay interest on this and it also increases your debt.

Most fixed, tracker and discounted mortgages also come with an exit or early repayment fee, commonly known as Early Repayment Charges (ERCs). This fee is payable if the mortgage is paid off within the initial fixed term of the mortgage. Make sure you query these fees with your mortgage broker to understand any implications of repaying the mortgage early. You should also make sure that the initial term of the mortgage matches with your property strategy to avoid any unnecessary penalties, for example don't get a five-year fixed deal if you intend to sell the property in one to two years' time.

TPV TIP: Some lenders will allow you to 'port' or transfer your mortgage from one property to another one and so avoiding paying the ERCs. Whilst this is more common with your own home where you swap one property for another one, it could happen with an investment property too.

Broker Fees

If you decide to use a mortgage broker, they will probably charge you a fee for their services, as well as receiving a fee from the lender. The value of this fee will depend upon the individual broker and the value of the property being purchased. In some cases, you may find that a broker will forgo some of their fee and in lieu receive a commission from the mortgage lender, which they are legally obliged to disclose to you. Brokers' fees can range anywhere from £500–£1,500 typically.

Solicitor Fees

Once you have found a property and chosen a mortgage product you will need to use a solicitor to perform the legal conveyancing work for the purchase of the property. A solicitor will do all the necessary searches on your behalf, liaise with the mortgage provider to have funds transferred and register your ownership of the property and the legal charge with the land registry. Each solicitor will be able to provide you with an estimated cost for the legal work, as well as all the associated searches and document registration. You should expect to pay in the region of £600–£1,500 plus 'disbursements' (or costs) and VAT in total for all this conveyancing work. Watch out for mortgage lenders that insist that you use one of their 'panel solicitors' and/or ask you to cover the costs of their own separate solicitor. A panel solicitor is usually more expensive than you or I might find and if the lender asks you to pay their legal fees along with your own, this would effectively double the cost of the legal element.

Stamp Duty

The purchase of any BTL property will incur stamp duty land tax (SDLT) at 3% over the rate for residential purchases. There are different bands of tax due based on the purchase price of the property:

Purchase Price (£)	Rate of SDLT (percentage of total purchase price)*
0–40,000	0%

Purchase Price (£)	Rate of SDLT (percentage of total purchase price)*
0–125,000	3%
125,001–250,000	5%
250,001–925,000	8%
925,001–1.5m	13%
1.5m+	15%

* Rates correct as of March 2020 for England & Wales. Different rates and terminology apply in other parts of the UK. This table ignores the temporary reduction in Stamp Duty Land Tax introduced following the coronavirus pandemic in 2020.

TPV TIP: There are situations in which the SDLT liability can be legitimately reduced. Examples include buying mixed-use or commercial property, averaging the purchase price with several linked transactions bought at the same time or if the property is uninhabitable. Speak to your tax advisor or SDLT specialist if you think these reductions may apply to you, as solicitors rarely understand them!

Renovation Costs

If you are buying an existing property, especially a period property, you can expect to have to pay to have a couple of minor repairs or refurbishment done. This could include a coat of paint, new carpets or even a whole new kitchen or bathroom. The costs of this will depend on the extent of the work required and where the property is. Ensure that you have a reasonable assessment of the 'schedule of works' required and have the funds available before you get too carried away with calculating your profits.

Purchasing a new build house or flat does not escape having to pay for some minor works on completion. Often there is a snagging report to be performed, purchase of flooring and white goods (depending on the deal with the developer) and fittings for lights and windows. The specification of finish will dictate how much money you will need to put aside for this work. Equally, all new homes should come with either a new home warranty from a third party, such as NHBC or equivalent or what is known as a Professional Consultants Certificate (PCC). Keep in mind two things here though: first, most lenders won't lend without one of these and ideally the warranty; and second, these do not automatically mean that all problems arising will be covered under these policies.

Regulations

Unlike residential mortgages, most BTL mortgages are not regulated by the Financial Conduct Authority (FCA). The FCA is an independent watchdog set up by the Government to regulate the financial services industry in the UK and protect the rights of consumers.

The FCA does NOT regulate mortgages where either of the following conditions applies:

- The mortgage is a second charge on your home. 'Second charge' means you already have another loan secured against your home.

- Less than 40% of the property on which the loan is secured is used or will be used as a home by the borrower or a member of the borrower's immediate family.

It is this second condition that most often means that BTL mortgages are not covered by the FCA. Typically, investors purchase a property with the explicit intent of renting the property to tenants rather than as a home for themselves or for their immediate family.

What impact does the absence of this regulation mean? No longer does the mortgage product need to be sold by a suitably FCA qualified and supervised person. A full fact find of your personal circumstances and requirements is not necessary, as a BTL mortgage is seen more like commercial lending by a business. There is no also no requirement to prove that an offered product is the most appropriate available for you at the time.

Other Mortgage Types

There are even more types of mortgage than we have covered here, believe it or not. Light and Heavy Refurbishment, Further Advances and Commercial Mortgages can all be found in the Book Bonuses, freely available here: https://www.thepropertyvoice.net/bookbonus/. If you want the full and advanced view, then be sure to get these bonuses.

Advantages and Benefits

There are numerous advantages and benefits that come with using a BTL mortgage to buy investment property. Here are some of the major ones:

- Simple strategy to understand and execute.

- BTL mortgages generally offer cheaper solutions than other forms of lending.

- They are established and easily available products.

- They can give you access to an otherwise price-prohibitive property market.

- There are options for landlords and investors owning through a company and/or investing in properties for a non-residential usage.

- BTL mortgages can enable a higher return on your cash investment in the form of net rental income and/or capital growth based on reduced personal cash investment required, which is known as 'leveraging'.

- At the time of writing (2021) interest rates are at an all-time low with the Bank of England base rate at 0.1%. This helps to make a BTL mortgage a low-cost option.

Disadvantages and Risks

Efficient strategies using BTL mortgages and borrowing money at a low rate do not come without their disadvantages and risks. Here are but a few:

- Typically lenders will only offer up to 75% of the value of the property, leaving you with 25% to find by other means.

- Lenders will require assurances of the rental capability of the property, so properties in need of significant work may not meet the lenders criteria, being classed as 'unmortgageable'

- Interest rates may increase rapidly if the economy demands. The cost of borrowing will, in most cases, increase with this. The investor has little, or no, ability to influence this.

- Some BTL mortgage lenders have a limit on the total amount of borrowing that an individual, group or even a particular block or development can have. This is known as 'concentration risk' and may limit the growth of your portfolio.

- The ability to remortgage can be at risk in the event of property prices falling. Falling below the minimum LTV may mean that lenders do not allow you to refinance a property or require you to put in additional cash to reduce the LTV. This is often significant in times of a market crash or a 'credit crunch' for investors who have borrowed at high levels.

- Leveraging or taking a mortgage to part-fund property acquisition can be positive and magnify your gains with less personal cash required. However, it can also magnify your losses should your rental profits get squeezed and/or lead to a capital loss/mortgage coverage shortfall should house prices take a significant downturn.

Reality Check

Using a BTL mortgage to buy an investment property is probably the most widely used financial strategy in the property investment arena. There are very low barriers to entry and a wide range of products to suit most people's needs. Ask any property investor and they'll give you their opinion on the best types of products available and why you might use one product over another.

With the aid of a good mortgage broker, a first-time investor can easily use a BTL mortgage to buy a property, even with limited understanding of how mortgages work. It is advisable however to increase your knowledge on how BTL mortgages work to ensure that you are getting the right product for your own circumstances.

Before I go, this chapter could have been even longer than it already is. It's necessarily long because it contains many of the foundational elements to what follows, so subsequent chapters are shorter, I promise. However, I did have to trim the word count a little and so I moved the content about alternative types of mortgage into the free Book Bonus resources online. Make sure you check them out!

BTL Mortgage Case Study

Standard BTL Mortgage

Purchase of Victorian terraced property of standard construction with a traditional BTL lender.

Project Description & Actions Taken

Purchase of an investment grade, i.e. it can be rented out with minimal or zero work required, Victorian two-bed terraced property of standard brick walls and slate roof construction, that was ready to be tenanted. The project involved purchasing a family home from an owner occupier and renting out the property for a profit. Purchase price of the property was £105,000 with a proposed mortgage of 75% or £78,750.

A high street bank agreed to advance the 75% of the purchase price after their due diligence was carried out and a valuation surveyor confirmed the £105,000 purchase price was fair and reasonable. The mortgage taken out was a three-year fixed rate at 2.99% with all fees totalling £1,075. Legal fees also had to be covered amounting to £625.

Result

The property was purchased and between exchange and completion, the property was advertised 'to let' by a number of local agents. On the day of completion, a number of Open Day viewings were carried out and a tenant found for the property. The referencing of the tenants took approximately four working days and a move-in-date was selected that was two weeks after completion.

In that time the CP12 (Gas Safety Certificate) inspection was carried out and some minor alterations were made to the property to get it ready for let. This resulted in a total cost of £400. The property was then let out to a tenant on a 12-month Assured Shorthold Tenancy.

Main Risks

- Valuation surveyor of the mortgage company 'down-valuing' the property

- If a variable-rate mortgage taken out, figures no longer stacking up at a higher interest rate

- No tenant interest during the exchange period with an extended void period

- Initial rent projected not accurate and lower income received.

Financial Summary

PURCHASE		
Purchase Price	£105,000.00	
Deposit @ 25%		£26,250.00
Mortgage @ 75%		£78,750.00
	£105,000.00	£105,000.00

PURCHASE COSTS	
Deposit	£26,250.00
Legal costs	£625.00
Refurbishment works	£400.00
Valuation	£125.00
SDLT	£3,150.00
Arrangement fees	£950.00
Total Investment	**£31,500.00**

CASHFLOW	
Rental per year	£7,500.00
Mortgage costs @ 2.99%	£2,354.63
Gross Profit	**£5,145.38**
Management fees @ 10%	£750.00
Voids @ 6%	£450.00
Contingency @ 10%	£750.00
Total costs	**£1,950.00**
Net Profit	**£3,195.38**
Gross Yield	**7.1%**
Gross ROI	**18.1%**
Net ROI	**10.1%**

Investor Conclusion

This is an above-average BTL investment project, even outside of the south of the UK, and while the numbers may vary significantly dependant on the area in question, most landlords will be expecting gross yields of around the 6% mark, +/- 2%.

If a property is in an investment grade condition, then the process can be relatively straightforward and the time-frame quite quick. This particular project was six weeks from acceptance of offer to completion, with a further two weeks for a tenant to be found.

The benefit to deals such as this is the high Return on Investment (ROI) that can be enjoyed on the money tied up in the deal, along with the potential to accumulate capital appreciation.

Author's Insights & Observations

- Have a conservative deal evaluation (best, worst, average case) with respect to the valuation the mortgage provider will give, the interest rates you will pay, and the level of rent you will receive – if you can live with the worst, then go ahead as long as the due diligence checks out

- Mortgage lenders can take anywhere from 4–16 weeks from application through to transfer of funds. It is very dependent on your own personal circumstances, so be sure to establish as accurately as you can at the outset the time-frame, and communicate this with the vendor. If it is a mortgage provider you have already dealt with, it could be relatively fast and smooth, however some lenders will require more documentation than others, so plan for this with the project time-frame.

- Understand the realistic ongoing costs. The figures for Voids, Contingency and Management are only a guide. The location, size and age of the building will impact on these variables. If a property will be let for four years, but will then take four months to let out, then it is reasonable to account for one month void per year in your calculations to avoid cashflow issues in the future.

- Equally, prepare for any major expenses by saving up some of the money in advance of requiring it. A sinking fund can be used to save up for major works, such as roof replacement, to avoid the impact of a large bill in the future.

Now that you have seen the general structure and format of a Property Finance Case Study; why not see all of them? They are available as a book bonus; just go to the book bonuses page and download them all here: www.thepropertyvoice.net/property-finance-my-book-bonuses

Chapter Two

Consumer Finance: Personal Loans and Credit Cards

What You Need To Know

Consumer finance, such as personal loans and credit cards, is a convenient method to get access to quick unsecured lending. It offers a very simple and immediate solution to the "I've run out of cash" challenge and can be used effectively to pay for renovation works after a property is purchased.

At the time of writing, the APRs on personal loans from some lenders are close to mortgage lending rates. Equally, whilst raising cash and failing to repay credit card balances long-term can prove hellishly expensive, for a short-term cash bridge the actual interest costs compare favourably to bridging lending. Sometimes, 0% credit card interest rates can be utilised either with a balance transfer or coupled with a cash advance that usually carries something like a 2% to 3% arrangement up-front fee and no interest for 9–18 months.

Both forms of funding have been around for a long time, and most banks, building societies and supermarkets will offer personal loans and credit cards with relatively few checks. The decision process for both is very fast, from as little as a minute or two online for a small amount, to a few days for a more detailed or higher value application.

Most personal loans and credit cards are quite similar in nature. The sections below cover the main characteristics of personal loans and credit cards.

However, a word of caution before we go too far with this one.

Consumer finance, if not swiftly repaid, can get out of control very quickly, so it's definitely best to have a clear, short-term repayment strategy if you go down this route. An example would be property trading or a flip, where all debt is repaid out of the sale proceeds.

Equally, some have been tempted to use consumer finance to raise deposits. In fact, I used it myself for a home purchase back in the 1990s,when things were a bit different. However, things really are very different these days, and most lenders will automatically decline a mortgage or bridging finance application if they believe the deposit is coming from consumer finance. Also, keep in mind that all credit applications, whether taken up or not, remain on your credit file for six years, so are visible to any lenders on subsequent finance applications.

So, you have been warned. This is not a mainstream financing strategy and carries clear risks and limitations. I kind of feel like a separate financial disclaimer and warning should be inserted, into this chapter in particular: please act wisely and don't go around willy-nilly adding credit or consumer finance unnecessarily.

Lenders

Personal loans and credit cards are big business for lenders, so everyone's cashing in on them. You can now get personal loans and credit cards from a wide range of lender,; some quite surprisingly. Some of the top personal loan and credit card lenders in the UK are Barclaycard, Halifax, Lloyds, MBNA, Tesco, Santander, Fluid, Virgin, Nationwide and Sainsbury's. If you are already a customer, sometimes there is an even more attractive rate available, so sign up for those customer loyalty schemes, like Nectar and Clubcard, for example, before you apply!

Many of these lenders provide an online service so that you don't even have to go in-branch to apply. In addition to the traditional lenders there are other providers who operate online including M&S, The AA, Hitachi Personal Finance, Cahoot and the Post Office. There are even lenders for people who don't have a very good credit rating, but they tend to have very high interest rates and should only be considered in the event of an absolute emergency. And, if that isn't enough, there are also a growing number of peer-to-peer lenders who offer personal loans. These include Zopa, Lending Works and RateSetter to name just a few.

In order to compare personal loans and credit cards across lenders there are several comparison sites that do all the hard work for you. Such sites include moneysavingexpert.com, comparethemarket.com and gocompare.com.

TPV TIP: I would highly recommend paying a visit to the moneysavingexpert.com forum, as there are lots of 'how to' and best approach articles.

Lending Limits

Unsecured personal loans are normally available up to a value of £25,000, but it may be possible to borrow more if you have a good track record with the lender. In most cases the lender will restrict how long you have to repay the loan amount. For high-value loans this can be as long as 10 years but generally it will be 3–5 years for small amounts.

There is a very wide variation in the limit on credit cards, which is based on the credit history of the applicant. Lenders will normally grant new customers a low limit and then gradually increase this over time. If you have a good credit history it is common to be able to build up your credit card limit to between £10,000 and £15,000 per card.

TPV TIPS: Check on your credit rating BEFORE applying for consumer finance. A service called Credit Karma summarises the results of the top three credit reference agencies in a single free report. The Money Saving Expert Credit Club allows you to gain access to your credit file from Experian for free. There are also some credit builder type of services dotted around, such as the getbits app. Also, keep in mind that loan repayments are capital plus interest whilst credit card servicing is interest-only.

Lending Criteria

The lending criteria for credit cards, although tighter in recent years, are still often fairly low which is often why applications can be approved online within minutes using a credit scoring system or algorithm. If you know the criteria, then you can usually work out the likelihood of the computer saying yes, although some of the sites mentioned also offer insights into the most likely deals you might qualify for. Lenders will look at the following criteria:

- Resident in the UK

- Over 18 years of age

- Minimum income – this differs from lender to lender

- Repayments affordability check, taking into account monthly outgoings, including mortgage or rent, debt repayments and childcare

- Employment status

- Existing credit and credit history.

The lending criteria for personal loans are similar to those for credit cards. The criteria include the above as well as the following:

- Whether you own your home

- Ability to repay, including looking at your monthly outgoings

- Three years of accounts for those that are self-employed.

Interest Rates and Fees

The interest rates offered on a personal loan will vary depending on the amount being borrowed and the term over which the loan is being repaid. Typical interest rates range from around 3–8% at the time of writing.

Interest rates for credit cards average around 18% to 30% APR (in the UK in 2021). However, it is possible to get 0% interest rate deals for purchases or balance transfers which can last anywhere from 3 to 20 months.

These types of deals typically incur a transaction fee of up to 3% for each balance transfer.

Personal loans and credit cards typically incur no fees to set up or close down the line of credit. There are a couple of cards where an annual fee is charged, including those with associated perks, and these are sometimes termed 'charge cards'. American Express is an example of one such card, with an annual fee of up to £150.

Repayments and Renewal

Personal loans and credit cards both are repaid on a monthly basis. Personal loans will have a fixed repayment each month for the duration of the loan term. Credit cards, on the other hand, only require a minimum payment each month, normally 2–4% of the outstanding balance plus any interest and charges added to the account that month. It is possible, and advisable, to pay more than the minimum amount off the credit card to reduce the overall level of debt and interest incurred.

The term or length of a personal loan is set when the loan is being approved and cannot be changed. It is not possible to renew or refinance a personal loan without taking out further finance to pay off the debt or by settling it in cash.

Credit cards however have no set term and continue to be a line of credit until the account is closed. Introductory 0% interest rate deals do have set time periods and once this has passed the standard interest rate will apply. It is possible to balance transfer between cards with 0% introductory deals but lenders are very aware of this strategy and may choose to decline further credit if they see too much of this type of activity.

Risk as Use for a Deposit

The use of a credit card or a personal loan in a property purchase will almost certainly affect the mortgage offer and also the general credit rating. A lender will always ask the question: what is the source of the deposit funds? If the answer is a personal loan or credit card(s) this will impact their decision, either by declining because it does not meet their policy requirements to use unsecured borrowing for a deposit, or by looking at the extra borrowing alongside the borrowing of the property and the investor's personal circumstances. Either way, it is not guaranteed that the lender will approve of the situation, so it is probably safer to use these options as funding for renovation/refurbishment works rather than as a source for the deposit.

Risk to Your Credit Score

Frequent and continual use of both credit cards and personal loans can have an impact on your credit score. A lender will typically look at how many recent (and total) searches an investor has against them – high numbers of recent searches would negatively affect an automated credit scoring system and could lead to a declined application. It is due to this impact on personal credit scores that it is advisable to spread lending applications over an extended period of time. The exact period of time is open to debate but 6–12 months is typical. Keep in mind that your credit history, including credit accounts, is visible for a period of six years on your credit file in the UK and longer in the USA.

Advantages and Benefits

There are several advantages to using either a personal loan or credit card to fund renovation work:

- Allows you to undertake work on a property with very low cash inputs

- Readily available and flexible short-to-medium term financing

- Unsecured credit, so there is no asset at risk

- Lower credit checks, quick approval

- No need to use a broker

- Credit card minimum payment option allows flexible payback amounts in the short term (but extends the period and interest charges potentially).

Disadvantages and Risks

The risks associated with using a personal loan or credit card:

- Expensive interest rate levels

- Maximum credit limits are low and often insufficient to cover the entire purchase price on a property and using as deposit funds is likely to result in a declined mortgage application

- Can be difficult to be approved if you are self-employed or only have income from property

- Borrowing more than you can afford to repay

- May negatively impact future borrowing capability, most importantly buy-to-let mortgages

- Damaging your credit rating if you make too many applications or if payments aren't made on time.

Reality Check

Consumer finance, in the form of personal loans and credit cards, is familiar to most people. It is often used for short-term purchases like furniture, cars, clothes and holidays. It is unusual for these credit facilities to be used for long-term purchases like property, due to the high cost of the finance.

In times of tightening lending restrictions it may also prove to be difficult to justify the purpose of the finance to personal loan providers. Even if you do manage to get the finance, having this debt may impede your ability to get further finance for other properties.

Both credit cards and personal loans are best suited to low-value property prices or works costs, due to the restriction on the level of lending, or to short-term projects where a property will be sold on, ideally, or refinanced within a year.

Buying property such that there really is no money down makes it very difficult to calculate some of the typical investor metrics, like Return on Investment. It is best to look at the annual profit, or annual commitment, when in this type of situation.

There is one additional type of consumer finance that's worth a mention here: Trade Accounts. A trade account is where you receive credit terms from a trade supplier. Examples include builders merchants, such as Travis Perkins and Jewson. If you operate in a business-like manner, often these trade merchants will grant you credit terms. Such terms typically mean setting a credit limit on your spending and an extended time to pay. Time to pay is usually set as 'within 30 days of the invoice date' or 'at the end of the month following the month of invoice'. In the latter example, that could be anywhere between 30 and 60 days, depending on when you incurred the cost. So, aim to buy your materials at the start of the month rather than the end of the month to maximise your credit terms with merchants.

TPV TIP: In reality, not many property investors would use credit cards or personal loans as a consistent element of their strategy as it is unsustainable and has too many drawbacks. Therefore, whilst they can be considered by financially aware investors and developers, they are best only used on a very short-term basis and for expenditure not directly related to the purchase price of a property.

Consumer Finance Case Study

Using Credit Cards and Trade Accounts

Updating a mixed-use property with commercial on the ground floor and a mini-HMO replacing the flat above.

Project Description and Actions Taken

Purchase of a previously fire-damaged property for £90,000 with the intention to repair the damage and provide flexible office space on the ground floor with a three-bed HMO on the first floor. Whilst there was more to this project, we shall for simplicity here just focus on the use of trade accounts and credit cards.

Due to the extensive nature of the works involved with this project, the total came to around £130,000. Of that, £43,000 was acquired using either a trade account or a combination of a trade account and a credit card.

The trade accounts offered two clear advantages 1) access to trade discounts, in our case via our LNPG (Landlord's National Purchasing Group) membership and 2) deferred payment terms of 30 to 60 days from the point of invoice. Using the credit cards carefully also allowed an initial delay of 45 days to make the payment and by switching the balance to a different 0% credit card, the ability to defer payment for an additional 18 months, to align to the rental of the unit along with a nominal balance transfer fee of 3% becoming due.

Result

The property was converted and is currently awaiting tenanting and refinancing at the time of writing. The use of the trade accounts and the credit cards allowed the developer to defer their cashflow, take advantage of trade discounts and also enter into a DIY-payment plan by using the 0% balance transfer arrangement.

By avoiding overdraft and/or credit card interest costs, £42,800 of the cash required for the project was deferred at almost no cost, with £9,300 of that being aligned to rental income over an 18 month period at the cost of only £279.

Main Risks

- Any form of credit needs to be repaid at some point in time, so you need a clear repayment plan in place.

- There can be penalties for failing to make payments under any credit arrangement on time.

- Credit sits on your credit file, so consider how that will look to would-be lenders when it comes to your refinancing.

- Using trade accounts and credit cards is a form of cashflow management that, if done carefully, can work well; however, it can appear to an outside party, such as a bridging lender, that you don't have the required funds to undertake the project and lead them to question your plans.

Financial Summary

PROJECT COSTS (Excl. Interest)		
Purchase & Buying Costs	£93,000	
Development Works	£130,000	
Other Project Costs	£7,000	
Development Finance		£174,000
Totals	£230,000	£174,000 (76%)

TRADE ACCOUNT & CREDIT CARDS SPEND		
Electrical (materials & labour)	£21,000	90-day terms
Trade Merchants (Jewson & Travis Perkins)	£12,500	45-day terms
Kitchen (Magnet)	£4,000	18-mths @ 3%
Furniture (Fusion) & White Goods (AO)	£5,300	18-mths @ 3%
Trade & Card Total & Weighted Average Term/Total Cost	**£42,800**	**13 mths / £279**

EQUIVALENT FINANCING COST & TRADE DISCOUNT		
Interest £42,800 @ 10%	£4,280	
Materials Cost Trade Discount £28,800 @ 12% average	£3,456	
Effective Savings		**£7,736 (18%)**

Investor Conclusion

This is an example of how a self-managed project can generate access to greater purchasing power, cashflow management and savings on the cost of financing with some attention to commonplace credit terms.

Author's Insights and Observations

Using trade accounts and credit cards is not suitable for every project nor every investor, but it just goes to show what is possible with a little planning and shrewd selection of suppliers and payment mechanisms.

Chapter Three

Bridging Finance

What You Need To Know

A bridging loan is essentially a loan that is arranged over a very short time frame to an individual or company, secured against a residential, commercial or mixed-use property. The defining characteristic of this type of loan is that it 'bridges' the gap to a subsequent exit, which is usually a refinance or the sale of the property.

This type of finance is often used to buy an investment property using the temporary, short-term cash injection to cover ('bridge') part of, or the entire, purchase price. The finance is expected to be utilised for a shorter period of time than standard property finance options (generally no more than 18 months), and is also expected to be approved and released in a shorter period of time (generally 1–6 weeks).

Bridging finance allows an investor to take advantage of opportunities which require transactions to be completed quickly. The focus of most bridging finance is speed, but this speed does come at a cost.

Uses for Bridging Finance

Bridging loans can be used in a number of property purchase situations:

1. Auction purchases and other fast completions

2. Buy to develop and refinance / resell quickly

3.   Raise funds via a second charge

4.   Break a purchase chain

5.   Quasi-cash-buyer purchase

6.   'Unmortgageable' properties.

Here is a brief overview.

1.   Auction Purchases and Other Fast Completions

When purchasing at auction, there is often a requirement to exchange contracts on the day of the auction and complete within 21–45 days. Despite what people may claim, traditional finance, such as a Buy-to-Let mortgage or commercial loan, cannot usually complete in that time frame. It typically takes two to four months, including the legal searches to arrange traditional finance. Alternatively, the liquidation of other assets, including the sale of a property, to fund the purchase may not be possible within this time either. Most property transactions are slow and chains are prone to collapsing, with 30% of property transactions falling through, typically. In these cases, bridging finance can be used to ensure the sale goes through on time. There is an associated risk with auction property purchases in that the buyer can lose their 10% deposit if they do not complete in time; therefore, 'time is of the essence'.

Generally, bridging loans are used as an interim measure when purchasing at auction while more traditional financing is put in place, however it should be noted that due to the Council of Mortgage Lenders' (CML) '6-month guidance' there may be fewer lenders willing to refinance on properties within six months that are purchased in this way. A quick reminder from Chapter One: Buy-to-Let Mortgages, the CML offers policy guidance to its members, which are usually the 'high street lenders'. So, a non-CML member, such as a 'challenger bank', could potentially refinance sooner, albeit at a higher interest rate, typically.

TPV TIP: Using bridging for an auction purchase is all well and good BUT I would suggest getting an agreement in principle with your preferred lender that they will lend to you on auction purchases before you commit in the auction room. I would also speak to a specialist bridging finance broker to fully understand both the likely terms to be offered and also the process, in particular the timescales. As mentioned, it is unusual to rely on Traditional Finance being guaranteed to be available within the time required under auction condition.

2. Buy to Develop and Refinance/Resell

When a property is to be purchased for a quick turnaround, it may be beneficial to use bridging finance in order to reduce administration tasks and red tape, plus give the purchaser greater flexibility. The main reason that people use bridging finance in this situation is where there is an opportunity to quickly 'force the appreciation' or add value to the property. This is typically done by undertaking improvement works, splitting title, changing use and similar projects that can be undertaken in a matter of a few months. More traditional mortgages would not be suitable in this situation, as they are specifically designed to be kept in place for at least two years in the most part.

Some people in the industry do advocate using traditional mortgages for these types of projects as a way to 'hack the system' and get short-term bridging lending at long-term mortgage interest rates. I would strongly caution against this, however. The reason is that lenders disapprove of this and ultimately may choose not to lend to you in the future and could even 'black ball' you with other lenders if the 'abuse' of mortgage lending is pushed too far.

TPV TIP: Access to financing is literally the lifeblood of all property investors and developers and as such should be protected at all costs. We need lenders that will work with us time and time again. So, make sure you match the right type of finance to the right type of project. This will help to safeguard your access to lending over the long term rather than being tempted into a quick short-term gain.

3. Raise Funds Via a Second Charge

If an investor has an existing property that has a high level of equity or even no debt secured against it, it is possible to use bridging finance to raise deposit capital for an additional property by placing a second charge on the first property. If the new target property can be developed and sold quickly the bridging can be repaid removing any further risk of over-exposure of having more debt secured on the first property.

I interviewed Kevin Wright on *The Property Voice* podcast, who has a fascinating perspective on bridging finance, as a long-term landlord alongside a long career as an Independent Financial Advisor. Kevin mentioned the possibility of using bridging finance to shrink your deposit and leverage your purchasing power.

In simple terms, if you have £25,000, you may be able to use bridging finance to purchase properties worth £200,000 – £300,000. Contrast that with the properties around £100,000 usually open to you through a standard BTL mortgage with that kind of deposit. That's because some bridging lenders will lend on the value of the property, rather than the purchase price, which is what all mortgage lenders lend against. Knowing this can help to increase the value of the deals you can do and as a result, accelerate your property investment journey. However, it's important to seek specialist advice and guidance about using bridging finance, particularly in advanced strategies like this one.

TPV TIP: If you can secure a property at below its genuine open market value and use a bridging lender that will lend against its value, you can reduce your effective cash deposit as a result. Add to this a second charge as described above and you could reduce your personal cash funds still further! I have done this myself on occasion and managed to put a very low or even no cash deposit into a new property acquisition. This is great to reduce the cash required, although it comes at a cost in terms of fees, so do your sums before going too far.

4. Break a Purchase Chain

In some circumstances a deal must be completed quickly to meet the demands of the vendor. If a property transaction is dependent on the sale of another property, it is possible to use bridging finance to remove this dependency. Bridging finance can be used to meet the vendor's deadlines, with the intention to be repaid as soon as the other property is sold. This can be the difference between being able to complete the transaction or not. This solution terminates the 'chain' in the purchase process and puts the buying investor in a stronger position.

TPV TIP: There are two main property strategies where this could be used. One is where we are a buyer and the second is where we are the property owner. We can step into a broken chain to support the seller of a property who doesn't want to lose their onward purchase – clearly, if the numbers stack up. Equally, we could look to use bridging finance ourselves if our own sale collapses and we need the funds for other purposes in the short-term.

5. Quasi-Cash-Buyer Purchase

Similar to above, by utilising bridging finance you can make offers on the basis of a very quick turnaround (say 21 to 45 days completion). This speed can improve an investor's standing in the vendor's eyes and even allow negotiation of a lower price in return for a speedy transaction.

A good example of where this might be used is with repossession purchases. Often, the seller is a bank or asset management company, whose main interest is speed of the completion of the transaction. In fact, they often insist on a 'first past the post' system. This is where they leave a property on the market potentially accepting other buyers' offers, despite having accepted our offer. They usually say that the first to exchange secures the purchase, so it's a race in that sense.

TPV TIP: I am not a fan of repossession purchases in general, due to the risk of an 'abortive purchase' should someone else get to exchange before me. If following a bridging finance strategy in this sense, then be prepared to lose your costs and fees spent should you not get to exchange first. I'd recommend only using bridging as a 'quasi-cash buyer' on less risky situations than repossession purchases, where you can avoid this race to exchange risk, therefore.

---

6. Unmortgageable Properties

As property investors and developers, we get paid to fix problems. If we are confident that we can find a solution to a problem property, then we can create an opportunity to bag a discount and/or create a profit opportunity as a result. Equally, more traditional lenders don't like 'problem properties' very much. So, our opportunity is to bridge the gap between the current problem and the solution on the other side. This is a good way to view bridging finance as well; an opportunity to build a bridge between the current problem situation and a new problem-free situation down the track.

For example, it may be that the property is unsuitable for a mortgage due to not having a functioning kitchen or bathroom, or properties that have experienced fire damage or need considerable structural work to bring them to a habitable state, for example.

Often leasehold properties come onto the market where the lease has less than 80 years remaining. The majority of mortgage lenders won't lend on these types of properties and so bridging finance becomes a good option until you can extend the lease. Similarly, legal issues such as title disputes or retrospective planning permission can prevent standard mortgage lenders from agreeing to finance a property.

With bridging finance, lenders tend to look past these issues, as long as there is a clear exit plan that competently intends to fix the problem. So, bridging can be used as a short-term measure to apply solutions and improve the property over a short time period. Once the property is ready for conventional mortgaging, it is likely to have increased in value and can be sold on the open market or refinanced more traditionally at that time.

TPV TIP: Targeting so-called 'unmortgageable properties' is useful as it will remove most of the homeowner buyer segment of the market from our potential competition. Equally, plenty of *'Homes Under The Hammer'* style DIY investors would be put off by certain 'property problems'. However, if you know what you are doing and are certain you can fix the issue, these properties can offer up some of the best discounts and opportunities to make a profit. I have a saying 'the bigger the problem, the more we will get paid for fixing it'. Just make sure you can fix it, that's all!

Lending Criteria

The lending criteria for bridging finance varies from lender to lender, but the following are typically considered a normal set of conditions:

- Minimum loan of £50,000

- Minimum property value of £70,000 (£100,000 in London)

- No maximum loan or property value

- Maximum LTV of 75%

- Maximum LTP (Loan to Purchase Price) of 90% when lending against the value

- Security of first or second charge on the purchased property

- Clean credit history and a provable deposit

- Maximum term typically 12–18 months

- A clear exit strategy for repaying the loan.

Bridging finance, like buy-to-let mortgages, is not regulated by the FCA and as such doesn't have lending criteria as strict as those accompanying regulated finance, such as residential mortgages. Bridging lenders are not as much interested in you as an individual. That's because with a mortgage, the mortgage lender is looking at whether you and your investment property are able to make monthly payments into the long term.

A bridging lender is focussed mostly on the asset, because they know that they will be paid back within a few months. There are only two ways that the borrower can pay them back – either by selling the property or by refinancing it. If the bridging lender feels that you and they can get a return on investment in that property, then they should be happy to lend. In one sense, that's actually quite a good 'acid test' of the viability of your project: if a bridging lender is unhappy to lend, that's often a good indicator that you might want to revisit your plans!

Another difference between mortgage lending and bridging finance is how surveys are used. A mortgage lender may be very happy with you as an individual, but then they survey the property and if they find an issue that they consider makes the property unmortgageable, they will decline the application. That doesn't usually happen with bridging lenders. They will have checked out the property online at the very beginning of the under-writing process and decided whether they want to lend against it or not. A survey takes place to work out a value to lend against, but it's not a key part of the underwriting decision-making process as it is for mortgage lenders.

Costs

Bridging loans are generally more expensive on an annual interest rate or APR basis, compared to mortgages. However, as they are not usually intended to be held for a full 12 months, they should not really be compared on a like-for-like basis with a longer-term conventional mortgage.

Interest rates will vary anywhere from 0.65% up to 2% per month and loans up to around 75% LTV are common. There are of course variations to the interest rates and maximum LTV's available but this changes on a daily basis.

Arrangement fees are generally around 2%, while procuration fees (commissions to agents) are around 1–2%. Administration fees can be a further £500, and there are also legal fees on top. It is also common for the investor to have to pay the legal fees of the lender, in effect doubling the legal fees bill.

A fee is generally payable to the firm hired to survey the property, before funding is agreed. Some lenders also charge an exit fee equal to a month's interest, regardless of whether the loan has run to its full term or not. However, they usually don't charge an early repayment penalty on top of this. For this reason, it is usually best to arrange a longer financing term and repay early than vice versa.

As you can see, the costs of bridging finance are higher than with a typical buy to let mortgage. Therefore, bridging finance should be used in the right circumstances and of course if there is enough of a margin between the total cost of acquisition and the exit valuation. Sit tight as I will show you why this isn't as bad as it might sound at first.

Repayment Method

All bridging loans entered into will require an 'Exit Route' that defines the plan for repayment and usually the time frame. This time frame can be somewhat flexible, but changing the repayment from several months to several years is generally not acceptable to the lender. The exit needs to be solid and substantiated in some cases, especially with a subsequent refinancing of the property. Therefore, assessing the relative likely revaluation at the point of exit will be a key component of the risk assessment on the part of the lender – and the investor.

With regard to the interest costs, whilst it is possible to pay this monthly, known as 'debt servicing', in fact, this is surprisingly rare with bridging loans. There are two more commonly used repayment methods.

The first is 'rolled up interest' which effectively adds the monthly interest to the total loan balance and the borrower repays everything at the end. Second, and far more commonplace, is 'retained interest' meaning that the total interest for the agreed period of the loan is deducted from the initial loan advance.

For example, if you agreed to borrow £100,000 at 1% per month for one year, the total interest cost would be £12,000. Therefore, when you take out the loan, you would receive different levels of funds advanced at the beginning depending on what type of interest repayment structure is stipulated by the lender, as follows:

- Debt Servicing – £100,000 net advance with £1,000 in interest paid per month.

- Rolled-up Interest – £100,000 net advance with all interest added to the loan to make a £112,000 gross advance.

- Retained Interest – £88,000 net advance, with nothing further to pay until the end of the loan.

Many a property investor or developer will hope and expect to obtain bridging finance on a rolled-up interest basis, only to have their hopes dashed when they discover that their offer states that interest will be retained instead. Check *before* you apply, I would suggest.

Advantages and Benefits

There are a number of advantages associated with bridging finance:

- This type of finance has a very quick turnaround time, from initial enquiry to having funds transferred for the purchase. The loan could be completed from start to finish within just one week in some exceptional instances. Such speed can put you in a better negotiating position to secure a deal.

- It allows you to acquire property that is deemed inappropriate for a mortgage – such as those not having a working indoor bathroom or kitchen.

- The emphasis in this type of lending is generally more about the property than the borrower. This can often lead to an easier lending decision, especially for investors with less ability to obtain a standard buy to let mortgage due to employment circumstances or a poor credit rating.

- Very suitable for short-term projects, particularly refurbish/ renovate projects or as a stop-gap, rather than using our own cash reserves. The key is the speed to purchase and exit, the shorter the project the better.

- Sometimes offers flexible lending terms where finance is calculated on the open market value rather than a lower contractual purchase price.

- Bridging firms often accept non-standard forms of security including over other residential, semi-commercial or commercial properties. 'Cross-collateral borrowing', which is where secondary forms of security are provided, may also enable financing up to 100% of the price of the property if there is enough equity on another property.

Disadvantages and Risks

There are a number of disadvantages associated with bridging finance:

- Compared to conventional property financing, bridging finance can be extremely expensive. It is not suitable for longer-term financing and generally considered to be 'choice of last resort'.

- CML 'six-month guide' may impact on the ability to sell to a mortgage-backed buyer or to refinance within six months of initial purchase with some lenders. Note that this refinancing period could apply to a subsequent buyer within six months and not just the original investor/developer that acquires the property. As Michael Caine might say, "Not a lot of people know that!"

- Not very suitable for long-term projects where there is the risk of the property not reaching its estimated future value, if the market dips or the project over-runs. It becomes very expensive to hold property on bridging finance while waiting for the market to correct.

Reality Check

The biggest challenge or complexity when using bridging finance is often the project itself, rather than obtaining the financing for the project. Due to the additional cost of the borrowing, an investor needs to be sure that they can bring their project in on time and on budget. It's better to over-estimate the project length than to get it wrong, because most bridging lenders will not penalise you for repaying the loan early, but absolutely will for extending it, especially if the request is made close to the planned repayment date.

Bridging lenders are not very lenient when it comes to delays in receiving interest payments or worse, when there is a default on repaying the loan amount at the end of the borrowing period. Repossession in that situation is often swift, with the possibility of the investor recovering any of their invested funds being very low. So, it is essential that a realistic exit plan with an additional plan B and/or C is in place. I am reminded of the old adage that *it's easier to seek forgiveness than it is to get permission* ... only this does NOT usually apply to bridging lenders! If you envisage a problem with the timescales and/or payments, then flag it to them early; lenders do not like surprises, especially late in the process.

In many cases, attention to the costs of additional insurance and legal services is neglected or omitted from an investor or developer's project budget. Special and restricted insurance terms will be required during any period that a property is having works done and is unoccupied. This insurance costs more than standard buildings insurance and covers less.

Similarly, there will be three sets of legal costs and professional fees that the investor will need to cover: the legal/professional costs incurred purchasing the property, the lender's legal costs when bridging and the legal/professional costs incurred upon refinancing or resale. It is imperative that a project has a detailed, realistic budget drawn up before finance is obtained, to ensure that all relevant costs are included.

TPV TIP: With bridging finance, it is usually better to ask for a longer loan term than you need at the start, rather than asking to extend during the term. So, add in some breathing space to your financing requirements, as most lenders won't charge for unused time if funds are repaid early.

Bridging Finance Case Study

Bridging Finance Used Before Refinancing a Property

Purchase of ex-MOD property with concrete wall construction, making it unmortgageable with traditional lenders.

Project Description and Actions Taken

Purchase of a three-bed semi-detached property with concrete wall construction making it unsuitable for a mortgage with traditional lenders. The project involved converting the property to standard construction thus allowing greater financing options and improved value for future resale. Purchase price of the property was £75k with an estimated £25k of structural works.

A bridging lender agreed to advance 70% of the purchase price. An advance of £52.5k was provided by the lender over 12 months at a rate of 1.5% per month with monthly interest payments being made. In addition, set-up and exit fees were payable approximately equivalent to one month's interest in each case. Lender's solicitor fees also had to be covered. The remainder of the project funds were provided by the investor.

Result

The property was reconstructed and refurbished within an 18-month period that included a six-month approved extension of the bridging loan, due to a project over-run on site by the builder. The property was then revalued and refinanced with a mainstream lender on completion of the project and let out to a tenant.

Main Risks

- Potential for project timescales overruns

- Variables in project costs, end valuation/selling prices and rents

- Working with the lender if an extension to the agreed term is required

Financial Summary

PURCHASE		
Purchase Price	£75,000	
Deposit @ 30%		£22,500
Bridging Loan @ 70%		£52,500
Sub Total		**£75,000**

PURCHASE AND PROJECT COSTS		
Bridging Loan Deposit	£22,500	
Legal Costs and SDLT	£4,050	
Structural Works	£25,000	
Finance-related fees & interest	£18,575	
Total Cash Investment		**£70,125**

RE-VALUATION		
Property Value After Works	£145,000	
Bridging Loan Returned		£52,500

Purchase and Project Cash Costs	£70,125
Equity Uplift / Project Profit	£22,375
Project ROI on Cash	32%
New Mortgage @ 75% LTV	£108,750

RENTAL RETURNS AFTER REFINANCING	
Gross Rent p.a.	£8,400
Net Rent p.a. (after all costs)	£3,037
Investor Cash Left Invested	£13,875
Rental Income ROI	22%

Investor Conclusion

This was not an ideal project, especially for an inexperienced investor. However, provisions made for an overrun in the project timescale and lower-end property and rental valuations in the original deal analysis enabled the investor to absorb the 'pain' of the project over-run. That said, the overall returns are still very attractive with a project return on cash invested funds of 32% over 18 months (the situation had the property been resold at exit) and an ongoing residual income on cash left in of 22% per year (if the property was retained and rented, the chosen option here). In the latter case, the equity left in the property would also increase over time with capital appreciation.

Author's Insights and Observations

- Have a conservative deal evaluation (best, worst, average case) – if you can live with the worst, then go ahead as long as the due diligence checks out.

- Allow for project over-runs – estimate the time and then consider doubling it, allowing sufficient time in the bridging finance to cover the potential for over-run.

- Understand how costs of financing eat into margin – bridging is great for short-term projects but can be very expensive for longer-term projects – ensure there is enough profit in the deal to cover financing costs or look for alternative financing routes for longer-term projects. Paying cash is an option but, as well as tying up a large investment fund, is also not as effective for the ROI.

- The finance terms of the bridging finance in this example were quite expensive at 1.5% per month plus additional fees. This is likely down to the inexperience of the investor at the time, coupled with a higher risky project with the conversion work required.

Development Finance

What You Need To Know

Property development is considered to be where the developer is changing a property or a piece of land 'substantially'. This could be in the form of new build development, also known as 'ground-up development', or, as has become quite popular in recent times, conversion of an existing usage into something else, such as commercial to residential use, for example. A 'substantial' change might be described as spending at least 40% of the acquisition cost on the development activity, and very often significantly more than that.

'Development Finance' is the form of financing that specialises in funding the property development activity. If you consider the fact that the existing land or property has a value, then that could often be financed using one of the finance methods already discussed, i.e. cash, buy-to-let financing/commercial loan or bridging finance. It is often said that for every £1 in development cost that is spent on a development that it's value will increase by around £1.20 or hopefully much more. As development is a clear value-adding activity, this hopefully explains why certain lenders can get comfortable with financing this type of expenditure. This additional development expenditure goes on top of the acquisition cost and usually gets funded in one of the following ways:

1. **Cash/Equity** – the developer's own cash/equity or a suitable substitute, which could come from a number of different external sources, as will become apparent as we proceed through this book.

2. **Light/Heavy Refurbishment Finance** – So-called 'light or heavy refurbishment' financing products, which some of the institutional lenders have introduced into the market to cater for less intensive development activities, such as refurbishment, extensions and the like.

3. **Development Finance** – which is where a lender will agree to advance funds specifically to cover the build costs of a substantial development activity.

Whilst this particular chapter deals with the third point in the most detail, it is worth at least mentioning the first two here briefly.

1. Cash/Equity

Cash is a precious resource and that's why, as property investors and developers, we are often looking to raise finance to assist with our investment and development activities. If we can make a higher return on a third-party's funds than it costs us to take these on board, then why not use someone else's funds rather than our own? This is what is commonly known as using 'other people's money' or 'OPM'. Using our own cash does allow us to get moving more quickly, does not involve external parties and also is free … well, sort of free at least. There is always an 'opportunity cost' of using our own cash, as we could earn interest on it, for example. It does have a place and to some it means speed, control, discounts and incremental profit. We discussed cash earlier, so we can leave the recap there for now. Equally, there is a cost attached to using OPM too. There will be interest or profits expected on the part of the finance provider, along with security, development updates and so on.

TPV TIP: If you are a bit of a control freak, there's a lot to be said for using your cash in your development projects! It's a quicker process, has less external finance cost (dropping that saving on to your bottom line) and allows you far more flexibility too. You just need a lot of it to undertake multi-unit development projects, that's the main downside.

---

2. Light/Heavy Refurbishment Finance

The lending market has become increasingly diversified as time has gone by, with new lenders and new products coming to the market all the time. Sometimes, lenders have become creative in their product offerings, in order to meet market needs. One such need that many lenders spotted was the increase in smaller scale developers, very much in the mould of *Homes Under the Hammer*. Many investors and smaller developers were looking at refurbishment, light development, change of use, title split and similar property strategies as a way to add value to their property projects. In these situations, lenders agree to fund some or all of the additional works' costs involved in the 'small d' development works over a short-term development project.

This brings an added dimension to the funding options available to the aspiring property developer. Finance terms here are usually similar to bridging finance to help fund the property acquisition, along with an additional funding top-up to cover some or all of the works' cost, in a slightly different way.

The financing of most of these different forms of refurbishment finance typically splits down into separate sections, advances or 'tranches'.

The first tranche is to fund the initial property acquisition, very much like a bridging loan, which we covered in Chapter Three, so we won't repeat that here.

Then, the refurbishment works are funded on a 'pay and reclaim basis'. The work will be undertaken, then independently inspected, but if not, certainly evidenced against invoices and receipts. Then, the lender will approve and make a further advance or tranche of finance to the investor/developer.

This process is sometimes repeated a couple of times during the refurbishment works phase of the project.

Once the work is completed, this form of finance is exited, usually through a sale of the property or refinancing onto a more suitable long-term financing product.

To give some pointers to help distinguish, 'Light Refurbishment' would usually involve spending up to 15% of the purchase price of the property on the refurbishment activity. For 'Heavy Refurbishment' this is between 15% and 40%. Development finance, or where there was a substantial change to the land or property, would be in excess of 40%. Light refurbishment finance would be the easiest and most common to arrange, followed by heavy refurbishment finance and then development finance, which would be more complex and specialised.

The terms and costs of a refurbishment finance loan commonly look like this, at the time of writing:

Acquisition – up to 75% of the property purchase price, with lending rates at 0.6% to 1.5% per month and additional fees and costs on top.

Refurbishment – up to 100% of the works cost to a maximum loan to value of the property of around 70%. In addition, the funds will usually only be advanced in arrears, with interest paid from the point of usage or 'drawdown', often at higher annualised rates of interest than the acquisition financing component of, say, 0.8% to 1.5% per month. One point of note here is that the annualised interest rate might appear expensive. However, we should look at the actual interest cost in monetary terms and reflect this against the project profits more so than the underlying percentage rate, to make an effective judgement. Often, the monetary interest cost is lower than we might expect, as the funds only attract interest for the time these funds are drawn down.

TPV TIP: Refurbishment finance products such as this allow smaller investors and developers, that would usually need to use their own cash resources, to undertake a refurbishment project with less of their own cash and so increase their leverage OR it might allow them to run more than project at once to increase their 'deal velocity', or rate of recycling their cash.

---

3. Development Finance

Now we are getting to the meat of this chapter! It was perhaps helpful to run through the concept of a light/refurbishment finance loan above to help set the scene for development finance now, as there are some similarities.

There is usually an acquisition of some kind, followed by a development project where works are undertaken throughout. Both of these components can be financed, either separately or collectively. Some development finance lenders will also insist on funding the land or property on which the development work is undertaken, whilst others don't find that necessary. In either case, the lender will usually advance the funding in tranches, which are usually drawndown in arrears, as the work progresses and is evidenced as being completed. In the case of development finance proper, there will usually be a formal inspection of the work by the lender's appointed surveyor, usually a quantity surveyor. This will happen each time a drawdown is required and is paid for by the developer, as a courtesy to the lender. 😉

There are sometimes situations where the owner of the land or building that is being developed is owned by a different party to the developer. This starts to get complicated and is more like a 'Land Development Joint Venture' agreement, which we will cover in subsequent chapters. Needless to say, the development finance provider is most likely going to be looking to have some sort of security against the underlying land or property. This could be via a first or second charge in most cases.

The main differences between an 'all-inclusive' development finance loan and two distinct ones to fund the acquisition costs and development costs separately, is the type of security taken. There is usually only one party that can hold the first charge on a property asset as security. So, in the case of the development finance that is undertaken separately, a first charge is usually not possible. Here the lender might look to have a second charge or arrange other types of security instead. As you can probably tell, it can all get a little complicated, with different lenders operating with different terms, security and interest rates and with the funds being released in different ways too. Whilst property development is often seen as the profitable and glamorous niche for property investors to aspire to, it is not for the faint-hearted, which extends to development finance!

The costs and terms are likely to look something like this, subject to an awful lot of conditions and variations:

- **Acquisition Phase** – typically up to 75% of the property purchase price with lending rates at 0.6% to 1.5% per month. There will be additional fees and costs on top, such as arrangement fees, brokers' fees, surveys, two sets of solicitors' fees, etc. However, with development finance, we might also be looking to acquire land that requires planning permission to be able to undertake the development works. This adds both time and uncertainty to the project and so the lending terms on a property without planning permission are likely to be at a reduced loan to value of 50% in this case.

- **Development Phase** – most lenders start at the end and work back. They will assess the end value of the development, known as the Gross Development Value or 'GDV' and then cap their lending as a percentage against that. Then, they would work backwards, looking at the various cost components of the project or Gross Development Cost (GDC): acquisition cost, development works, surveys, professional and planning fees, utilities and services, warranties, etc. They will also add an assumption as to the minimum developer profit, which could be 20% of GDC or higher. Taking all of that into consideration, they would typically lend up to 100% of the development work itself, which may or may not extend to other costs and fees in the project GDC. The usual maximum loan to gross development value 'LTGDV' is around 60%–70%.

In addition, the funds will usually only be advanced in arrears in tranches, with interest paid from the point of usage or 'drawdown', often at higher annualised rates of interest than the acquisition finance component of 0.8% to 1.5% per month. If the funds are not utilised, then no interest is usually charged. However, you should carefully check the detailed terms of any development finance facility letter to confirm this is the case. I have seen some agreements that make a charge for 'funds being made available' in some way. This could be via a fee if not taken up or a trigger date for when funds will start attracting interest. There could also be a cancellation fee if funds are not utilised or needed any longer.

TPV TIP: It always pays to follow these timeless pieces of advice. I would suggest: a) Ask good questions – ask your broker and lender as much as you need to about the terms of the facility before you sign anything and ideally before money changes hands for fees and the like. b) Always read the small print, or have an expert do it for you, remembering that whilst you can delegate responsibility, you cannot delegate accountability!

This is at least similar in principle to the light/heavy refurbishment financing. The main differences are likely to be the number of tranches or drawdowns in what could be a build period of anything up to two years. Then there is the level of involvement and scrutiny on the part of the lender. They will usually insist on watertight contracts and collateral warranties with reputable builders that are monitored by a professional quantity surveyor appointed by them but paid for by the developer. In short, the level of involvement on the part of the lender, along with their costs, is considerably higher than in almost every other form of institutional finance discussed so far.

When it comes to the end of the development, as with bridging finance, an exit needs to take place. Typical exits are to sell the units and/or to rent and retain them. In either case, the development finance will need to be repaid. The repayment would come from the sale values and/or the refinancing of rental units. If the units are sold off individually, then the development finance facility often needs to be repaid before the developer, along with any other private finance partners or lenders, is repaid. There are always exceptions but some developers think they will be paid some part of the sale of the first unit, when often this is not the case.

TPV TIP: The costs of development finance, along with the extended length of time in a project, the planning and development risks mean that the level of profit also has to be higher for development activities than most other types of property projects. Ergo, make sure that you are only taking on board projects that afford high profits and can withstand changes in time, cost and end value. 20% profit on cost would be an absolute minimum for a build-to-sell (BTS) project. However, there is an argument that a build-to-rent (BTR) project can tolerate a lower 'project profit' given the fact that the BTR operator will receive both rental profits and capital gains over several years of ownership post-development. This could also mean a BTR developer could be more competitive on the acquisition side of things than a BTS developer.

Another consideration with development finance is the Catch-22 of developer experience or track record. Usually, a development finance lender will not lend to a developer that not only does not have a lot of development experience but also does not have the right *type* of development experience for the project at hand. You might have undertaken a refurbishment project or two, a house of multiple occupation or 'HMO' conversion and perhaps even a title split of a house into two flats. However, that will probably not allow you access to too many development finance lenders if you were to consider converting an office into 10 flats or a new build development of six houses. However, there are some exceptions, so make sure you speak to a good finance broker and make sure that they specialise in development finance to see if there are any that would consider working with you. I share mine with you in the Book Bonuses.

So, how do you get to undertake these projects to get the experience and track record under your belt, if you can't gain access to the funding you need to develop them in the first place? I'm glad you asked! Fortunately, there a few ways:

a.   Use your own cash. As long as you have enough cash, you don't strictly need to use development finance.

b.   Climb the 'development food chain'. Proceed in incremental steps perhaps starting with smaller projects using bridging finance. Then move on to slightly bigger projects using light/ heavy refurbishment finance. Finally, you could look to step up in terms of development types and sizes of project of multiple units, planning/change or use, conversions and so on. The main difference between these types of finance is usually scale and complexity of the underlying development project and it probably also makes a lot of sense to work your way up to earn your stripes in any case.

However, there is another way to gain access to development finance when you don't have it yourself – you can '*borrow*' it.

c.   We can borrow other people's experience and track record in several ways. The builder/main contractor and the professional team should all be very experienced with the type of development project you are working on, that's the first step. We could hire in the specialist knowledge and experience to work directly for our development company. We could also partner with other more experienced developers too.

TPV TIP: Borrowed experience is a great form of leveraging other people's experience and track record to be able to access development projects and finance that would otherwise be beyond our reach. I have worked with all three ways mentioned to 'borrow' the relevant experience. The one I really like is the 'senior developer/ junior developer partnership' as it allows an aspiring developer to genuinely de-risk themselves by working with and learning from someone more experienced who can also support them, as well as help them gain the necessary development finance required.

So far, I have illustrated development finance as being a loan or debt-based finance model. It can also be equity-based, or a mixture of debt and equity … just to confuse you even further – sorry for that!

If you cannot get a lender to advance you funds to undertake your development project, you might be able to get someone to put up the funds as an 'equity partner' instead. I mention it here, as it possibly lends itself well to the idea of borrowed experience and track record. As I mentioned, I quite like the 'junior developer-senior developer partnership arrangement'. This is where a less experienced or aspiring property developer will bring in a more experienced developer to work with them. The experienced developer is likely to be able to attract the development finance required, given their track record, which means less funding would be required from the junior developer. Equally, it will mean giving up a share of the profits and potentially a larger share in favour of the senior developer. However, there are some clear positives of this approach, including gaining some of that valuable track record ready for your next development project and development finance application. Therefore, it might pay off in the long term to give up a piece of the profit pie now in order to gain a bigger slice further down the track.

Do be careful here though. Make sure you review Chapter Nine on Private Finance before venturing too far down this path. You will need to find the right fit, do your due diligence and ensure everything is correctly documented using separate solicitors in order to protect yourself along with any partner you decide to work with. If someone baulks at proper documentation, then run and don't look back!

You could also look at partnerships on a purely financial basis with 'people with money' rather than being experienced developers. However, in this case, I would strongly suggest that you look to borrow the knowledge and track record of experienced professionals and contractors everywhere else in your project.

Stick around for some of the later Chapters on Alternative and Creative Finance, as these will open your eyes to a number of variations of the development finance theme…

Advantages and Benefits

Using development finance as a property finance strategy has the follow advantages:

- It allows us to use less of our own funds to expand the scale and reach into more profitable added-value development projects.

- Funds can be drawndown (released) in tranches (batches) so you don't have to pay interest unless and until you actually receive the money. This can reduce the actual monetary cost of finance below what looks like a high headline interest rate.

- The development finance company will ensure that there is a high level of scrutiny on your project and the team delivering it – this can actually be a good thing, as it brings in extra sets of experienced eyes to keep tabs on things.

- Property development can be a very profitable undertaking and the provision of development finance can mean more people can potentially have access to what is often a highly cash-intensive activity.

Disadvantages and Risks

Development finance, while being a great property finance model, can also present the following disadvantages:

- It can be very time-consuming to undertake all the paperwork and will open your project viability to a greater level of scrutinised examination and outside control.

- The associated costs of development finance can really rack up, with broker and lender application fees, detailed surveys of various kinds, professional inspection fees and so on.

- As with any property project, time and budget can sometimes run away from you. With development finance, as with bridging finance, there are usually very clear limits and also penalties in terms of a default rate of interest if you breach the terms of the facility; it could be problematic if you do and do not have adequate contingencies in place.

- Development in general is a completely different business model to other property strategies and the cost of learning could also be high.

Reality Check

I am a property investor, first and foremost. After around eight years, I ventured into property development projects. However, I quickly realised that property development and the associated area of development finance is a whole new world to discover. Progress steadily and diligently and it can be extremely rewarding. However, it can also give you a few unexpected surprises at times. Development projects rarely go 100% to plan and can involve many moving parts and different members on the project at various stages. So, keep that in mind and look at risk management and contingency planning as potential property development life-saving skills.

In addition, as with any form of property finance, the implications of burying your head in the sand should things start to go awry can be significant and painful. Therefore, open communication with your lender is one way in which this can be mitigated. That said, it is better to go with a solution than just a problem. So, consider some potential options and give comfort around what you can control and have at least considered, I suggest. Many lenders do not want to call in the loan, unless they believe their capital is severely at risk or if the borrower is being evasive or seems to be out of control. Most should work with you, in other words.

Equally, I mentioned the perplexing conundrum of no experience = no development finance = still no experience! However, I have pointed you towards a few alternative ways to go about accessing development financing, such as growing steadily or using 'borrowed experience', private financing and developer partnerships. I have had particular success with development finance provided by private individuals, before going to the institutional lenders for development finance. So, do make sure you stick around for some of the later chapters to look at these alternatives, won't you?

Overall, there are risks with development projects and hence with development finance as has been highlighted. However, there are significant potential upsides as well. Development can be one of the most financially and experientially rewarding activities in property. After all, we are creating something new from nothing in many respects. Equally, we are contributing to alleviating the national housing shortage by developing new homes for people to live in. Development finance allows us to finance a very significant chunk of the total development cost and so this also brings development activities into reach for more aspiring developers too.

Case Study

We have a great case study that has been provided by Alice Williams, Director of Pilot Fish. This is available as a Book Bonus and it contains some very interesting and advanced solutions too. Make sure you collect this, along with other great case studies and a few little extras too! Here's where you need to go: www.thepropertyvoice.net/property-finance-my-book-bonuses

Part Two

Alternative Financing

Chapter Five

Be Your Own Bank or Finance Broker

What You Need To Know

At some point in time, we will either think we don't have enough money to start or continue, or we may well run out of money before reaching our 'big hairy audacious goals' of financial freedom, lifestyle and choice.

Money's Too Tight To Mention was a song made famous in the 1980s by Simply Red. Investing in or developing property is one of the most capital-intensive activities we could aim to do as individuals, so no wonder money can become too tight to mention for us at times!

So, that's just that then is it? …

Well, this would be a short chapter if it was. So, what's the answer then?

Become Your Own Bank or Finance Broker!

I can't work miracles and conjure cash from thin air unlike the central banks! What I can suggest is some ways in which you might be able to raise that additional funding for your property plans and goals, under your own steam.

Here, then, are 12 ways to become your own bank or finance broker.

Self-Generating Savings and Bonuses Garage/Loft Clearance Alternative Income Streams	**Personal Equity Raise** Equity Release Second Charge/Further Advance Lending Alternative Asset Refinancing

Using a Company
Pensions
Intercompany Loans/Profit
   Extraction
Director's Loans
	Self-Broker Fund-Raising
	Friends & Family
	P2P & Crowdfunding
	Private Finance and Joint
	   Ventures (JVs)

Self-Generating

- **Savings and Bonuses** – This is the one everyone knows about. It's slow, boring, virtually risk-free and it also means you owe nothing to anyone to boot. You might need to become an 'extreme saver', much like members of the F.I.R.E (Financial Independence & Retire Early) community, to accelerate the process. However, saving along with good household budgeting is the cornerstone of all good personal financial management. Remember, delayed gratification is a success principle.

TPV TIP: Using tax-free wrappers, such as an ISA, can reduce the tax deductions that can eat into your savings growth. Also, watch out for asset or fund management fees taking a big bite out of your savings – aim for 1% or less.

- **Garage/Loft Clearance** – When I started investing in property, one of the ways in which I raised money was to get rid of all my old sh*t. I became an eBay and car boot legend, if only for a single summer. Nearly all of us have accumulated a seemingly unending pile of clutter over the years, so it's time for a clear out. In fact, I might have to have another go at this, having just spotted various unused electronic devices lurking in drawers and boxes around the house.

- **Alternative Income Streams** – If saving is a form of delayed gratification with your money, then a side hustle or second job is the equivalent with your time and/or know-how. When I was a student, I worked at KFC to help support my grant. However, that was already two sources of income at the tender age of 18. Fast forward a few years and I have operated side hustles, second jobs and multiple businesses/income streams to generate additional funds to invest. Equally, the Rent-A-Room Scheme currently allows you to earn up to £7,500 per year, tax-free, by taking in a lodger at home, so you can make money and make a start in property without setting foot outside your front door.

TPV TIP: 'Pay yourself first' as Robert Kiyosaki tells us in his book *Rich Dad, Poor Dad*. We often save or set money aside at the end of the month … if there's any money left! However, this idea turns the principle of saving on its head. Plan how much you will save at the start of the month and ideally automate this with a standing order or similar to get ahead of the crowd.

Personal Equity Raise

- **Equity Release** – Some people looking to get started in property start at home, literally! If you have equity in your home and can safely justify and afford the increased repayments, it can be the cheapest borrowing you can ever take on. Keep in mind that this is still borrowing – and being your home should mean taking extra care to make sure you don't overstretch yourself financially. Similarly, there is often treasure right in front of our noses, I have found. If you have an existing property portfolio, my guess is that it could be an untapped source of funding or income. I always undertake a portfolio review with my mentees, where we look at the current performance, asking the question: "Can we undertake one or more of 'The 3 Rs' here?". The 3 Rs are Repurpose to generate more income, Refinance to release equity for new investment or Redeploy the equity by selling and investing into better performing investments instead.

TPV TIP: You won't find them too easily but an offset mortgage would allow you to have a flexible financial drawdown facility that you can dip in and out of for project funding.

- **Second Charge/Further Advance Lending** – If you have enough equity in your home or an investment property, you could take a second charge or further advance on it to release additional funds. The further advance is usually permanent or long-term. With a second charge it can be used with bridging finance and so could be for a short period of time. This would allow a second-charge bridging loan to be repaid once you've completed your property project and sold/refinanced out.

TPV TIP: Did you know that you can use second-charge bridging finance for an investment property secured against your own home through 'regulated lenders'? This would allow you to potentially fund 100% of the acquisition and/or works cost on a project. Just make sure you can repay it on completion.

- **Alternative Asset Refinancing** – When you are clearing out the garage or loft, keep your eyes peeled for some fine art, vintage wine or the odd classic car! If you find something like this, then there are some specialist lenders that will offer borrowing secured against such assets, and I'm not talking about the pawnbroker for small ticket items either.

TPV TIP: Believe it or not, all of the following assets could be used as collateral or security for lending purposes: classic cars, works of art, fine wine, overseas holiday homes, cryptocurrency, certain pension funds, certain stocks and shares, investment funds and insurance policies. You might have more borrowing power available to you than you imagine but, at the same time, you should also be careful not to risk losing the family silver.

Using a Company

- Pensions – One of the best-kept secrets of the property community is the SSAS Pension. A SSAS (Small Self-Administered Scheme) is essentially a company pension for your own business, whether it's a property business or not. You could also transfer your own old pensions into your SSAS to make it a source of funding to your property business in the form of loan-backs or direct investment into qualifying investments. The sponsoring company of the SSAS needs to be established and have a 'trading activity'. Examples of trading activities for property businesses include commercial property rental (not residential), trading property (flips), development, serviced accommodation (grey area) and all kinds of services provision (lettings, project management, training, sourcing, etc.). If you have a trading business outside of property, as many do, then you can link your SSAS pension to this business. If you want to know more, then I suggest that you get a copy of the book *SSAS Pension Legacy* by Richard Parker.

TPV TIP: Personal contributions are topped up with the income tax you paid on them by HMRC and company contributions to any pension scheme are tax-deductible, so HMRC could become your bank too, start now and in ten years you might have enough to start that SSAS pension in a tax-efficient way. ☺

- **Intercompany Loan/Profit Extraction** – If you already have a business or contracting service company and have accumulated cash and profits, then one of the ways to utilise these in your property business in a tax-efficient way is by lending from your existing business into your property trading or investment company. Also, whilst not wanting to get too deep into taxation here, if you cease trading and have accumulated profits in your non-property investment company or if you sell some or all of your business, you can close the business down and extract those excess profits paying just 10% tax on them. This is what is known as Business Asset Disposal Relief (BADR), capped at £1 million in business sale consideration, which is correct at the time of writing but is also rumoured to be under review.

- **Director's Loans** – Similarly, withdrawing funds as a director or shareholder from a company you own can be another source of funding, particularly for short periods of time.

TPV TIP: Due to changes in the rules, taking out a director's loan is best done for only short period of time. Make sure that you repay any director's loan withdrawn from your company quickly to avoid the worst of the tax penalties and do also take professional advice before you do.

Self-Broker Fund-Raising

- Friends and Family – I have a saying: *the closer the source of funds is to our heart, the lower the interest rate!* OK, so that's not always true. Whether an interest-bearing loan, gifted deposit or even an early inheritance, the people closest to us usually want us to succeed in life and achieve our goals, so maybe it's worth a conversation at least.

TPV TIP: Treat any commercial arrangement with friends and family seriously, with a clear business/investment case, demonstrating taking great care of their money. Always put what is agreed in writing to save any misunderstanding or challenges with the relationship arising later.

- **P2P and Crowdfunding** – I have included this here as often you can go to these sites directly to raise funds without a middleman or broker. P2P or Peer-to-Peer is usually to raise debt and Crowdfunding usually for equity, where lots of everyday and not-so-everyday people are looking for a decent return on their money. See Chapter Seven: Crowdfunding and Peer-to-Peer Lending for a more in-depth explanation.

TPV TIP: Don't forget that you need to present yourself as being both 'bankable' and 'investible', so I suggest that you sign up as a lender/investor first to see how others do that and adopt the best of what you see in other people's propositions.

- **Private Financing and JVs** – Ah, the Holy Grail of the property investment community, coming in last! If I told you that it took me the first half of a decade of being in property to raise £250k and then the second half of that decade to raise over £5m, it probably tells you something. OK, so I didn't really know what I was doing in those first five years to be fair and it took some time to build my track record, credibility and not to mention self-belief. However, accessing private investment – and in particular as development finance or equity – was literally a game-changer. See Chapter Nine: Private Finance for a more in-depth explanation.

TPV TIP: If you chase the cash it will elude you … but if you relax and let the cash chase you, it will flow towards you. Consider that in a room of property investors, it's typically around 2% that have funds looking to invest, with the other 98% looking for funds for investment. So, to seriously improve your odds of raising private finance, go somewhere else to look for them.

There you go, a quick run through of how you could become your own bank or finance broker to raise funds for property investing and developing, taking you from *Money's Too Tight to Mention* to another 1980s classic *Money For Nothing* and out of Dire Straits, if you like!

Advantages and Benefits

Becoming your own bank or broker has the follow advantages:

- It frees and enables us to be self-sufficient and in control of our property financing activities, which is one of the core competencies of being a successful property investor or developer.

- By thinking laterally and creatively, we can spot a whole raft of possibilities beyond the vanilla offerings presented to us by institutions. I have mentioned 12 different ways to go about this. There are, in fact, more!

- Many of the people that I mentor had no idea that they had access to such untapped sources of financing for their property journey, and when they did, it made the world of difference and became a game-changer for growth.

- You don't need anyone's permission to be your own bank or broker so, don't delay, start today.

Disadvantages and Risks

Becoming your own bank, while being a great creative financing strategy, can also present the following disadvantages:

- We might not be professional bankers or finance brokers, so we could end up taking longer or making a mistake in how we go about things. I've made lots of mistakes here, but I've gotten better as I've practised and achieved better results.

- You may be in heaps of debt and still have plenty of month left after the end of the money! OK, I hear you – when I started, I was in debt and had a negative monthly budget. Start where you can, even if that's by saving £1 per week. Change your thinking and you change your destiny.

- You might not be that financially-minded or savvy and this might sound like a whole new world. If so, I suggest two things: get yourself educated and/or get someone alongside you that is a little more financially-minded.

Reality Check

Many of the people that I speak to and mentor often mention aiming to become financially independent and using property as the means to achieve this objective. This could involve giving up the day job at some point in time. However, one word of caution …

In property, we need *three pots of money*.

1. We need cash for deposits to buy properties.

2. We need cash to undertake improvement works on property projects, assuming we are following a 'value-adding strategy'.

3.   We need cash to cover the costs of voids, repairs and maintenance and also updates, refurbishment and replacement too.

Many people aim to quit working as soon as their net property income matches their day-job income but overlook the idea of the 'three pots of money'. That would be a mistake in my mind. We need to generate additional funds to fill up the second or at least the third pot, even after achieving financial independence. However, the good news is that armed with this knowledge we can become our own bank or broker; along with all of the other alternative and creative ways of raising money described in this book, we are well-placed to stay ahead of the herd as we head out to those rich pastures and the reach the oasis of 'financial independence'.

Make sure you get hold of the Book Bonuses. The case studies for this chapter include the stories of Darren and Dominick. Darren is living his 'van life' dream after raising over £235,000 by being his own bank. Then, Dominick is well on his way to financial freedom having personally brokered joint ventures and raised additional funding of £500,000 from his own business and existing property portfolio.

Chapter Six

Friends and Family Finance

Introduction

*The closer the person is to us, the higher the
likelihood and lower the cost of finance for our
property projects it could be.*

Richard W J Brown

Raising additional funds through friends and family allows us several potential opportunities: faster growth, greater purchasing power and shared resources. One of the most obvious ways to raise additional finance is through friends and family. We should at least tick a few of the 'know, like and trust' stages to securing a commitment with people that know us well. Funding through friends and family can look a lot like many of the other forms of property financing outlined in this book. The difference being the relationship, along with the odd twist as we shall see.

Whilst I believe that any financial partnership needs to be properly documented and taken seriously, the consequences of things going wrong in the case of family and friends could go well beyond a bad property project. Therefore, there should be careful advance thought and discussion, consideration of the wider implications beyond funding arrangements, and avoiding a potential misunderstanding by committing our agreement to writing.

What You Need to Know

There are numerous reasons why a property investor or developer might wish to buy property with financing help from their friends and family. The most common reasons include:

- Combining the skills/network/resources of each individual to gain a more valuable partnership

- Spreading the risk/workload of the investment

- Sharing in the financing objectives of the investment.

Acquiring a property or undertaking a property project with funding from friends and family can be seen as a slight variation of many of the property financing strategies outlined in this book. The major difference is that the personal relationships are often strong and susceptible to more emotional responses and behaviours, which should be treated with care. There are numerous ways in which these types of friends and family financial arrangements can be structured:

1. Acquiring property in joint names, with equal or even non-equal investment.

2. Silent investment from one partner in return for a fixed fee, return on investment, equity share or a combination of these.

3. Gifted financial investment.

Each of these different structures comes with their own set of legal implications and it is important to have the necessary documents drawn up.

Acquiring Property in Joint Names

Property acquired in joint names is a fairly common strategy between family members, particularly between spouses, parents and children or siblings. A married couple may choose to purchase a property together for tax reasons, i.e. one partner is in the low tax band while the other is in the high tax band or to share the involvement in the investment or simply so that asset ownership is clearly documented. It is also common for siblings, or even parent-child relationships to jointly own property. In the latter case particularly to assist in first-time purchases; you have no doubt heard of the phrase the 'Bank of Mum and Dad'.

Even though a property is owned in joint names, the financial investment in the property is not necessarily required to be equal and does not have to match the return from the investment. The ownership and/or income of the property could be divided into non-equal shares, should that be agreed and beneficial to all. Where a property is held in joint names there must be a decision made as to how the legal title will be held, either *joint tenants* or *tenants in common*. It is this legal title that dictates the legal ownership interest of each party in the property.

In the case of joint tenants, each co-owner owns all of the property from a legal standpoint – the co-owners are entitled to an equal share of the property no matter the amount of financial investment. If one co-owner dies, their interest also dies with them and since the surviving co-owner already owns all of the property, nothing passes or is transferred under any will.

Owning the property under a tenants-in-common arrangement, the law requires each co-owner to have a separate and distinct share of the property. This does not necessarily need to be an equal share. On the death of a co-owner their share will not automatically pass to the survivor but will pass according to the wishes expressed in the deceased's will.

The simplest way of recording whether the parties intend to own the property in equal or unequal shares is to make an express declaration to that effect using a Land Registry form or a separate declaration of trust, or both.

It is therefore very important that each of the parties seeks independent legal and tax advice in order to fully understand the implications to their respective positions, during lifetime or even upon death. Sorry to be so morbid but it needs to be flagged up to avoid any nasty shocks at a particularly difficult time for people.

From a property financing point of view, the parties will need to consider how any property lending deposit and lending obligations are undertaken. Whilst the funding of the deposit can be unequal, it is inevitable that any lending around the property would need to be in joint names, almost regardless of the actual ownership splits. This will also mean that ALL the parties would automatically become 'jointly and severally liable' for the lending and therefore also its repayment. Jointly and severally is a legal term that means each party is seen as responsible for the entire debt, much like joint tenants ownership. The implication of this is that, should one party renege on their responsibilities, the other one remains fully liable for the entire debt.

A jointly owned investment property and any debt associated with that also forms what is known as a 'financial link' between the parties. Put simply, this link would usually be shown on both parties' credit reports and so could join together some of the credit of the parties, which could have wider ramifications beyond the property investment at hand. It does not automatically follow that one party's credit will affect the other one's but it could do under certain circumstances – so consider this option very carefully.

TPV TIP: Having spent the past few paragraphs outlining the potential merits and pitfalls of joint ownership, I would like to mention how avoiding joint ownership could also be a potential advantage. Many lenders have some kind of lending limit on the number or amount of lending that they will provide to an individual. Joint ownership means these lending limits are applied equally to the joint parties. However, if a property is owned in a sole party's name, then that lending cap can be spread across the parties individually and so more widely. This will allow for greater access to lending, which would be useful in the case of people looking to scale up on the most favourable of terms. In this case, the parties might choose that one party would become a silent partner or that they might operate a 'one for you, one for me' type of arrangement.

Silent Investment

With a silent investment structure, one party invests financially either in the form of debt (a loan) or equity (an asset value/income split) in a property in return for one or more of the following:

- A fixed or variable rate of interest return on the sum invested, with an agreement made as to the length of the capital repayment

- A fixed fee over a fixed period of time

- A share of the annual rental profits

- A profit share upon sale of the property or repayment of the finance.

A silent investment would normally involve one party taking ownership of the property and full responsibility for the day-to-day expenses and involvement in all property related activities. The property ownership might be for a short-term project period, such as a refurbishment and resell (flip) and/ or for a longer-term ownership basis, such as with Buy-to-Let. A variation of the silent investment could be where the friend or family member wants to support the property investor or developer with their financing needs but does not necessarily wish to gain financially in doing so. Unlike a gift, which we will discuss next, in this case the original investment would need to be repaid, although not necessarily with 'market rate' interest, profit or other gains on top.

TPV TIP: Silent investment can be particularly useful when one or more of the parties prefers to keep their financial affairs private. Whilst lending and ownership records at the Land Registry are public documents, some of the documentation relating to silent investment remains private between the parties.

It is imperative that a legal document be drawn up that covers the terms of ownership, responsibilities and financial involvement of the two (or more) parties. However, unlike acquiring a property jointly, the parties are not automatically drawn into a financial link, joint lending and such like. Again, legal and tax advice is very important in order to ensure that the outcome of the arrangement works for the parties.

Gifted Investment

A gifted investment is when one party literally gifts or donates to the other party the money required to purchase or fund a property investment/development. Often this is to help with the full purchase price of the property or a deposit to go towards other lending. It could in some cases also be used for funding refurbishment or development costs. Finally, it could also be the gift or, I suppose, loan of an actual property instead; check out the Assisted Sale and Rent-to-Rent chapters to see how this could work in practice. As the name implies, a gift is not expected to be repaid.

This gift can be for an investment property, although it is probably more commonly heard of in respect of home ownership with the recipient of the gift, say an adult child, for help to buy their first home. This situation also arises when elderly relatives are moving into the later stages of their life and want to gift money to their family as part of a larger inheritance planning exercise. You could say this might be an early inheritance or, as my friend Sue calls it, 'warm-body giving' rather than 'cold-body giving'.

TPV TIP: A twist on the gifted deposit idea is the alternative provision of a guarantee. There are some quite clever residential mortgages in particular that allow a relative to either guarantee the loan of the borrower and/or place a sum of money on deposit or into escrow to be used only in the event that the borrower defaults. Perhaps another way to look at this could be that a reduced deposit on a home purchase frees up more funds for alternative investment property purposes, which is a form of 'arbitrage'.

There are specific inheritance tax guidelines that must be followed to ensure that this money is deemed to be a gift and not subject to inheritance tax somewhere down the line. At the time of writing in May 2021, the first provision for gifting is an annual allowance of £3,000 on an inheritance tax-free basis to anyone the donor chooses. If the previous year's allowance was not used then an additional £3,000 can also be gifted inheritance tax-free. The second inheritance tax provision exempts any transfers or gifts above the annual gift allowance that were made more than seven years before death. All such transfers after seven years have elapsed are considered exempt from inheritance tax. Gifts made in the three years prior to death are taxed at the highest rate. However, gifts made between three and seven years previously are taxed on a reduced, sliding scale, known as 'taper relief'. The same applies if an asset is given away, as long as the person making the gift had no continuing interest in the asset, such as rent, a profit share or they reside in the property. As with all matters of tax, the rules keep changing and so it is extremely advisable to seek professional advice for all the parties to fully understand their tax position.

It is equally advisable with respect to all monetary gifts that adequate documentation is kept to ensure that proof of the gift and/or asset values at the time they are made can be produced later, if and when necessary. Not all lenders like gifted deposits, although a good mortgage broker will be able to help find a suitable product in this situation.

TPV TIP: Whilst nobody really wants to contemplate their ultimate demise, let alone talk about it, careful estate planning can also lead to a better tax position to a deceased person's estate AND also to the beneficiaries of that estate. Not the best discussion for a sixtieth birthday party no doubt, but a sensitive and well-timed conversation might be worth broaching at some stage, as most aging people would want to leave as much of a financial legacy as possible upon their passing, and tax deductions can potentially reduce the value of that legacy.

Documentation to Consider in Any of These Situations

In addition to the normal conveyancing and legal documentation there is additional paperwork that must be completed to ensure a smooth transaction. These include but are not limited to:

- **Declaration/Deed of Trust**

  This is a legal document that sets out who the beneficial owner(s) of an asset is and describes the entitlement of each party. It can be used to define the contribution each person made towards the purchase costs, the distribution of benefits from the asset and the entitlement of each party upon sale of the asset. It is important to distinguish legal ownership, which is identified on the recorded title deeds, from beneficial owners, which essentially varies the legal ownership through a trust arrangement. The deeds are public documents, whereas a declaration of trust is usually not.

- **Land Registry restriction**

  Every property and its title is registered with the Land Registry noting the details of ownership, dates and fixed-charge or mortgage lender (if applicable). It is also possible to put a restriction on the title, with the written permission of the legal owner, such that all parties who own the property must consent before it can be sold or refinanced. An alternative is not a restriction but a notification placed on the title instead. In this latter case, a named person gets notified in the event of a change in the title in terms of ownership, such as a sale or any legal charges applied against the property title, such as for a mortgage. A notification is more to alert to any changes made after the fact, whereas a restriction can prevent them from taking place without consent.

- **Joint bank account**

  Depending on the relationship of the investor and their friend or family member a joint bank account may not be required, particularly in the case of a silent investment. In the event of joint ownership and management of the property it is recommended so that both parties have access to funds and can view the day-to-day financial details of the investment. As with a legal ownership on the deeds and/or a joint loan, a joint bank account creates another financial linkage between the parties and so would be shown up on any credit reports for up to six years after the arrangement has ended.

- **Joint accounting**

  Similar to the point above, if the two (or more) parties purchasing the property are going to be involved in the day-to-day running of the property then it is important that all record-keeping is shared. It is advisable to set up some type of shared storage for all paperwork and an accountant is retained once a year to generate the required submissions for HMRC. Even if the day-to-day arrangements are not shared, any case of joint ownership, lending, interest, profits, etc. should be recorded and updated regularly between the parties.

- **Gifted deposit declaration**

  In the event that the funds for the deposit were provided as a gift, the lender will almost certainly require that a formal letter be drafted declaring where the funds have come from and will want assurance that there are no conditions attached to the gift, such as repayment. Most lenders will provide a template for such a declaration and your solicitor and/or mortgage broker will be able to provide advice on how to complete the form.

Advantages and Benefits

There are several advantages that come with joining forces with friends and family to finance investment property:

- Reduced financial investment in the purchase

- Greater combined purchasing power or 'deal velocity' (speed of recycling projects and finance)

- Combined skillsets and experience of the parties

- Reduced on-going expenses (in shared responsibility arrangements)

- Reduced risk and exposure, such as if an investment/tenant goes bad

- A sounding board to help with difficult decisions

- Exempt from the Financial Conduct Authority regulations allowing profit share promotions and arrangements without restriction.

Disadvantages and Risks

There are also several disadvantages of financing property with friends and family:

- Additional legal documentation and advice

- Each decision must be jointly made (in shared responsibility arrangements)

- Risk of one party defaulting on expense payments (e.g. mortgage) falling onto the other party to resolve

- Conflict over different exit strategies (e.g. when to sell the property) or tax positions

- Pressure or strain from or on to existing personal relationships

- All parties become financially linked with regard to credit checking where a joint mortgage has been taken out. A CCJ of one person may have implications for the other person.

Reality Check

On the surface, this could be one of the easiest ways to raise funds if you have family and friends that trust each other and are willing to work together.

However, it is not uncommon to hear of friends and family members falling out, damaging and even severing their relationship should things not go as planned. Therefore, it is very important to discuss and then document your expectations and requirements of each other to ensure that there are no misconceptions regarding how the business/investment relationship will work.

Raising finance from friends and family appears on the surface to be an obvious thing to consider. After all, your friends and family are more likely to be supportive, cheerleaders of your goals, plans and aims. As I alluded to at the very start of this chapter, those that know, like (or love) and trust you the most could be more receptive to supporting you financially.

However, there are some clear issues to consider and work through, as identified. Some friends and family members may not want to mix personal relationships with financial arrangements. So, be mindful and respectful of that. Equally, some of these structures – joint, silent or gifted investment – carry with them a range of financial, legal and tax implications for each of the parties too.

That all said, if you have good relationships and a genuine desire on both sides, raising investment through friends and family could be an excellent way to finance your property investing and development activities. Just be sure to take extra care to avoid potential strain or tension on these relationships.

Chapter Seven

Crowdfunding and Peer-To-Peer Lending

What You Need To Know

After the 2008 Global Financial Crisis, as lenders tightened their lending criteria and traditional finance products became harder to obtain, Crowdfunding (CF) and Peer-to-Peer lending (P2P) enjoyed increasing popularity. They made fund-raising simpler and took away the barriers to entry for many, so it's no surprise that they thrived in the void left by the banks.

CF and P2P providers are essentially intermediaries that arrange finance between two types of party: the finance provider and the finance recipient. Finance is usually in the form of debt (loans) or equity (shares), although sometimes these distinctions can become a little blurred.

The finance providers could be in the form of 'the crowd', meaning many different people essentially clubbing together to provide the finance, which I often refer to as 'one-to-many finance'. Alternatively, it could come from 'peers', which could be as few as one party, 'one-to-one finance' on the one hand, or several parties on the other; 'one-to-many finance' once more.

The one-to-one versus one-to-many part of the equation, along with sometimes blurry distinctions between debt and equity finance, is partly why people can get a little mixed up. However, if you keep in mind that CF is usually all about raising equity or shares and P2P is usually about raising debt or loans, and that the providers of the finance could be either an individual, a small group or a larger number of people collectively, it should help.

What CF and P2P have in common is often an online platform and streamlined, tech-enabled access to services for both the providers and recipients of finance. However, the principle is that either the crowd or our peers are the ones actually providing the finance, rather than the platform itself, a bank or another financial institution. So, any intermediary that arranges this type of financing could fall under the description of being a CF or P2P intermediary.

As CF and P2P became mainstream, new specialist platforms sprang up, including those that provide funding for businesses and property investment. Keep in mind that we could view CF and P2P as two sides of the same coin. We could be the recipient of the finance provided or we could be the provider of the finance instead. Whilst this book is aimed at finding ways to be a recipient of finance for our property investment, development and business activities, it may also be appropriate for some to consider being involved in property as a provider of finance.

It is also important to recognise the way in which the sector is regulated and protected. CF and P2P providers do need to be approved and regulated by the Financial Conduct Authority (FCA) in the UK and often the equivalent in other countries. This is good news to some extent, in that there is some regulation and control over the sector. However, do keep in mind that, unlike with a bank for example, funds held in a CF and P2P platform are not protected by the Financial Services Compensation Scheme (FSCS). Remember that there are actually at least three parties involved here: the provider(s) and the recipient of the finance but also the platform or intermediary itself. The FCA ensures that all three parties' interests are covered when it comes to regulation.

Equally, in order to be a provider of funds through either a CF or P2P platform, the provider cannot be what is known as a Retail Investor and instead needs to be classed as either a Sophisticated Investor 'SI', High-Net-Worth Investor 'HNWI' or a Business Investor 'BI'.

I mention these terms elsewhere in the book but for completeness they are repeated here, as follows:

Sophisticated Investor – to class and self-certify as a sophisticated investor you must:

- Have made at least one investment in an unlisted security in the previous two years; or

- Have been a member of a business angels network for at least six months; or

- Have worked in a professional capacity in the provision of finance to SMEs in the last two years or in the provision of private equity; or

- Be or have been within the last two years a director of a company with a turnover of at least £1m.

- Alternatively, you can be a Certified Sophisticated Investor having passed the appropriate tests – you'd know it if you did that!

High-Net-Worth Investor – to class and self-certify as a high-net-worth investor you must:

- Earn at least £100,000 a year; or

- Have net assets excluding your home and pensions of at least £250,000.

Business Investor – to be classed as a business investor you must be investing funds through a 'corporate body', such as a limited company/partnership, trust, pension fund, etc.

Retail Investor – at the simplest level, if you don't fit into one of the categories mentioned above, then you would likely be classed as a retail investor and would not be permitted to provide funds through one of these platforms. Note that the rules and regulations preventing retail investors from investing in regulated investments exclude friends and family in the most part, so check the chapter on Friends and Family Finance for more information on that.

Note that these descriptive terms (SI/HNWI/BI) relate to the provider of the funds and not necessarily to the recipient of the funds. This means you can benefit from using these platforms without meeting some of these criteria yourself. However, in order to use the platforms, whether as a provider or the recipient of finance, it is a requirement that identification and anti-money laundering checks are undertaken. This usually means uploading copies of your passport/driving licence, proof of address and often a 'soft search' on your credit file to verify that you are who you say you are.

Before we get too far into things, I want you to know that I'm not recommending any of the platforms mentioned in this chapter, they're just here for illustrative purposes. There are several CF and P2P platforms that have folded or changed significantly over the years, so I will only mention those that have been around for a while and seem to have a solid history. Things can and do change in this emerging sector.

Let's Dig In A Little Deeper Then ...

Crowd-funding

Either reward-based or equity-based. Reward-based platforms like Kickstarter give people the opportunity to support a project that resonates with them, perhaps a proposed book about property finance, say. Like-minded folk can make a contribution, starting at a few pounds, and get a special mention in the book. Or they can invest more and get a signed copy of the book or a one-hour video tutorial from the author. As you can see, investors are rewarded for their cash, with unique experiences that no-one else can get.

In some cases, with a property-related project, it is possible to get benefits other than a pure return on the investment made. For example, learning or shadowing an investor or developer, which I refer to as 'earn and learn'. This idea of learning or having another type of 'experience' through investing is not exclusive to CF and P2P but it seems fitting to mention it here. If that type of 'experiential investing' appeals, either as a provider or recipient of finance, then see what options are available both within the context of CF and P2P and in other ways.

TPV TIP: As a recipient of funds, consider that many investors want more than purely a transactional return on their investment, where they can go to the next guy and perhaps get an extra half a percentage point. Consider what value you can offer to potential investors and lenders over and beyond the financial return. This could be learning, participation of some kind or even being part of a community where a relationship can form, for example. Just as with any form of commercial exchange, people like to deal with people and value is often expressed and received differently too.

Equity-based crowdfunding is more like an investment in shares or the profits of a project. It gives investors a chance to acquire a stake in the business, which is often a start-up or at an early stage. For investors, if the business does well, they could make a great return. But if not, they could potentially lose their entire investment. CrowdCube and SEEDRS are a well-known examples of equity-based crowd-funding platforms for businesses. In fact, I personally invest through several of these platforms myself as a form of diversification with my own investments. There are also some platforms that specialise in the property sector. However, I have decided not to mention any specifically by name, as they have changed a fair amount over a fairly short period of time, so I suggest you make your own inquiries as to the current providers open for business when you need them.

Peer-to-Peer

With peer-to-peer or P2P, investors' money is usually matched, via an online platform, to loans for people or businesses. Investors don't get a stake in the business, they act as a lender to allow someone else to purchase or develop something. It's a specific amount of money, repaid over a defined repayment term, and investors earn a return via interest payable on the loan. Often, but certainly not always, P2P finance is subject to there being tangible security supporting the loan. This is usually in the form of a first charge or a debenture, or a fixed or floating charge over assets in the case of a company loan.

TPV TIP: Sometimes there can be an additional bonus that is paid on top of the basic interest return. This has the tendency to make a loan seem a little more like an equity or profit-sharing arrangement. So, look out for how that could be used to bring investors into the potential upside of a project without extending their risk position as much as with an equity-based arrangement. I often refer to this type of mix and match between fixed and variable returns as a 'mixed-return investment'. Once again, this concept is not restricted to CF and P2P, so keep that in mind.

In general, both the risks and the rewards for the provider of funds are lower with peer-to-peer lending than for crowdfunding investments, where the potential upside and risk of partial or even total loss of capital can be higher. As the recipient of finance, consider carefully what it is you want out of the finance arrangement and what you are prepared to give up in return. Consider P2P for the bottom part of the Funding Stack and CF for the top half of the Funding Stack if you like.

Before we proceed, a quick word on tax. One of the characteristics of CF and P2P is that sometimes the platforms offer tax benefits to their investors. In the case of CF, this could be in the form of tax relief in the Enterprise Investment Scheme 'EIS' or the Seed Enterprise Investment Scheme 'SEIS'. At the time of writing, qualifying EIS investments allow investors to reclaim 30%, and qualifying SEIS investments allow investors to reclaim 50%, of their investment against their income tax bill. This tax offset essentially helps to reduce the risk on their investment.

Equally, there are now some P2P platforms that offer what is known as an Innovative Finance ISA 'IFISA'. A qualifying IFISA means that all capital and interest returns within this wrapper are tax-free, which has the effect of increasing the net returns to an investor.

Tax benefits don't make an investment safe but they do help!

> **TPV TIP:** As a recipient of finance, consider what might be important to your finance providers. Net return after tax is one of several key elements, along with security and risk-mitigation, that can often be appealing benefits to an investor or provider of finance. Think about what the investor will retain after tax and keep in mind that any gain shared with an investor or provider of finance is tax-deductible to the recipient as a legitimate business expense.

It may have become apparent by now that there is a key characteristic of both CF and P2P that needs to be explored further. It is that both usually operate via a technology platform. From the perspective of the recipient of finance, this platform with its access and reach to many individual providers of finance can be quite compelling. However, it does also bring another responsibility to keep in mind, which I will broadly describe as 'Investor Relations'.

Whenever we engage with a provider of finance, there is usually a level of interaction that is required, regardless of the type of finance received. Often with a straightforward loan arrangement, including P2P, the level of engagement is mostly front-loaded. In essence, this means at the time of application there is a lot of information shared but once the funds are provided that should really be that – assuming all goes well. However, with a large crowd or peer network and especially so with CF, there can be more engagement required along the journey. Therefore, be prepared to share regular updates on the progress of the project in these cases. Keep in mind that someone investing £1,000 is likely to be as interested in what is going on as someone who investing £1,000,000.

> **TPV TIP:** Consider how you will have an investor relations engagement strategy for any form of investment and in particular when accessing the crowd. Keep this in mind: someone in the crowd that provided a small sum through a platform might just have additional funds to provide, potentially outside the platform. So, view

your Investor Relations Engagement in the context of it being a potential door-opener to additional direct finance provision further down the line.

So, now you know what the difference is, how are crowdfunding and peer-to-peer relevant to property investors?

The Platforms

In addition to evaluating the provider and recipient, there is also the platform itself to consider. When I first drafted this chapter some years ago, there was a list of platform providers, many of which either no longer exist or have changed the way in which they operate. So, we also need to consider what is known as 'platform risk' when deciding where to go to either provide or receive finance. It's still a sector very much in its infancy and so it might be a highly changeable one.

Both CF and P2P operate through intermediaries using technology platforms, where the platform provides the interface between the provider and recipient of finance. Some platforms are specifically utilising Blockchain Technology, which is taking the sector into what is known as the Financial Technology sector 'FinTech' or even into Property Technology or 'PropTech'.

As with all young growth industries, platform providers have adapted and grown over time too. For example, some P2P platforms that originally received all of their funds from individuals or peers now have access to finance from institutions such as banks, funds, family offices. Others have wholly switched away from their P2P roots and now match funds from a suite of different sources that may not include the crowd or peer network at all.

TPV TIP: When considering using either a CF or a P2P platform, consider what it is you are really expecting that is different to other forms of finance-raising. To me, this boils down to three key elements in addition to reach: speed, a simplified process and better terms. One of the reasons that CF and P2P started to emerge was that they offered something a little different in one or more of these elements. However, if you don't see a difference in at least one of these elements, then perhaps they are what I like to call 'a bank in disguise', in which case they might or might not be able to offer us something different at all. Reach is important in itself of course, but I for one would want to see something else in terms of speed, process and terms to offset the additional work of engaging with the crowd.

There are some specialist intermediaries, or brokers, that can provide P2P access to individual peers or investors by way of a direct introduction, or by having a 'whole of market' view of all the different CF and P2P platform providers. I would suggest that in a constantly changing landscape, enlisting the support of a specialist broker in this sector is possibly a very good idea. That said, an emerging trend is what is known as 'disintermediation' where the middle man is being cut out by a technology platform. See Chapter Five: Be Your Own Bank to assess whether going direct to one of these platforms could suit you.

Disintermediation is essentially what is happening in the CF and P2P sector. If the area of FinTech or PropTech interests you, then be sure to check out one of my other books #PropTech, which addresses these concepts more widely.

Property Crowdfunding Platforms

There are a few property strategies out there that require little money to get started, like Rent-to-Rent, for example. However, it's fair to say that for a traditional Buy-to-Let investment you generally need a lump sum of at least £20k to get started – even at the bottom end of the market.

Crowdfunding platforms allow people to invest in property with as little as between £100-£1000. There are now over 40 property crowdfunding platforms servicing the UK market. Most of these are for Buy-to-Let crowdfunding, which aims to give you a long-term rental income, with a share in any capital gain if and when the property is sold in future. They include Property Partner, which also offers a secondary market where investors can trade their share in a BTL-owning company if they wish to liquidate their investment within a few days, on average. There's a lot to be said for enjoying some of the return of property investment without any of the hassle of direct ownership, particularly in an increasingly regulated environment like we've seen in the UK Private Rented Sector or PRS in the last few years. In addition, this kind of property crowdfunding platform can appeal to aspiring investors who don't have quite enough money for a deposit on a BTL of their own but would like to dip a toe in the water.

There are also a number of platforms that cater to people looking to invest in the rather riskier but potentially more rewarding development finance market. If you do this through a crowdfunding site, you'll be advancing money for between six months and two years and then you'll make a return – or not – when the development is sold.

When it comes to returns – from both the BTL and development crowdfunding sites, there are no guarantees. Rather, they will give you projections of an expected return. There are plenty of examples of projects that did not go to plan where investors lost money, in some cases significant amounts. The same rules apply to innovative finance as they do to any form of investment. Make sure you do your own due diligence and don't simply rely on the platform provider.

There are a few specialist platforms that can provide 100% of the funds required for a project, usually a development project. Due to the changing nature of this area, I won't mention any by name, however I can describe how they tend to operate in outline, which could be extremely compelling to some of us.

These platforms often offer a combination of debt and equity and often secure these funds from both institutions and the crowd or peer-to-peer network. In addition, they often take both a fee and a profit share on the project at hand. This makes them a completely different animal: a cross between a CF and P2P platform, a finance broker and a joint venture partner in many ways. I have seen examples where a developer can secure 100% of the total funds required for their project and retain 40% of the profit, with the remaining 60% split between the platform and the crowd/P2P network. There could be variations to this commercial model.

This is an exciting and to some extent revolutionary area of raising finance, in particular for those with a strong track record, a good project and the appetite or capacity to take on more projects than their current investment funds would allow.

As a potential recipient of finance, keep in mind that these 40+ platforms offer a wide net to capture investment. However, also keep in mind that we are still making an investment proposal and so we need to ensure that we come over as professional, knowledgeable and therefore, 'investible'.

Property Peer-to-Peer (P2P) Lenders

LendInvest was launched in 2013 and offers P2P investments for high-net-worth individuals and businesses, plus short-term finance for landlords and developers. In the new world of post-global financial crisis lending for property investors, LendInvest was able to step in, gradually adding loans from High-Net-Worth Investors, dedicated funds, smaller banking lines and a retail bond to access funding from a wider capital base. This can be a defence in times of tight bank credit, that can help us as investors to find funding when traditional lending is unavailable.

Founded in 2014, CrowdProperty is another well-known site that matches lenders (on average ca. 1500 lenders per project) with property professionals who are looking for finance. At the time of writing, it has a 100% record of paying back capital and interest to investors and permits investment through a variety of vehicles including SSAS and SIPP pensions and their own Innovative Finance ISA. Here is an example where the terminology can become blurred – despite being called CrowdProperty they are in fact a P2P lender.

Non-Property Peer-To-Peer Platforms

When I say these platforms are non-property, I mean they are not specifically geared towards funding property investment directly. However, they could potentially be used for that purpose, depending on the circumstances. Zopa,

Funding Circle and Assetz Capital are a few of the more established players in the market, although it's by no means an exhaustive list!

Advantages and Benefits

The advantages of using crowdfunding or peer-to-peer lending are:

- Finance provision criteria can sometimes be more relaxed than banks

- Decision times are usually quicker than traditional lenders

- Tech-enabled platforms mean less bureaucracy, faster speed and a better process than traditional funding methods

- By definition, the reach of investors can be further by accessing a crowd or peer-to-peer network and some could go on to invest directly.

Disadvantages and Risks

The disadvantages of using crowdfunding or peer-to-peer lending are:

- Typically higher overall costs of financing through interest cost, equity shared and the platform fees involved

- P2P loans are typically on a repayment basis, not interest only (though not always!)

- The responsibility for investor relations with dozens, hundreds or in some cases, thousands of investors collectively

- There has been a significant amount of churn in the P2P/ Crowdfunding marketplaces.

Reality Check

Many of the options described in this chapter still involve having to invest some of your own money, often referred to as having 'some skin in the game'. One way around this would be to get debt finance from P2P or other lenders and then equity finance from a crowdfunding provider. However, keep in mind that most lenders will want to know what the source of the deposit funds, and may decline the application if it was another source of debt or if they felt that the amount of external funding meant that the investor or developer had little to lose should things start to go wrong and so could simply walk away.

With P2P in particular, many providers and platforms are indeed operating as 'banks in disguise' and are hardly indistinguishable from mainstream lenders it seems. However, if you shop around and do your research, some of them offer niche products that are appealing to us as investors and developers. Also keep in mind the three elements that I mentioned; speed, process and terms. Look for providers that offer something different and compelling in at least one of these areas, I suggest.

Do keep in mind that one of the big plus points for CF and P2P is their wide reach and access to hundreds or even thousands of potential providers of funds. Whilst that can bring some headaches, such as the investor relations discussed earlier, it can also provide some opportunities too, such as being a sprat to catch a mackerel as the saying goes.

At the time of writing, loan interest rates on larger amounts through mainstream lenders are at historically low levels, making P2P solutions much less appealing than at times of high interest rates or in a Credit Crunch. The emergence of crowdfunding and in particular the new breed of hybrid provider combining crowdfunding, P2P, broker, and JV partner all in one that I mentioned might just offer a significant step-change in access to finance in this area going forward, so watch this space!

Chapter Eight

Private Financing – Debt and Equity

What You Need To Know

Private Financing is a form of property financing that is provided by an individual or partnership or an entity owned and controlled by them. Examples include private lenders and joint venture partners, along with small companies/partnerships, SIPP/SSAS pension funds, family offices and similar.

Private financing breaks down into two main categories: debt and equity. Debt-based private financing is typically in the form of loans with returns on a fixed-rate of interest basis. Equity-based private financing is typically some kind of profit-share arrangement with variable returns based on the success or otherwise of the venture. The level of security and return provided usually varies in line with the arrangement, which is covered in more detail within this chapter.

As you can see, there are several different alternatives available, which can allow a variety of different types of security to be discussed between the parties to arrive at something suitable. It is also worth mentioning that security can be layered to offer different types of security to different parties. This might allow you to offer a first charge to a traditional lender along with a second charge or debenture to a development finance lender and then shares to an equity partner for example.

TPV TIP: Security is in the eye of the beholder! Security is often a sticking point when it comes to property finance. Let's face it, everyone will want a first charge as it is top of the tree when it comes to security. However, not everyone can have this type of security if there are several parties providing debt and equity to a property investor or developer. Both parties should carefully consider what they actually 'need' rather than what they 'want' and remember, there is usually a trade-off with greater security attracting lower rates of return due to the lower level of risk of capital loss, and vice-versa. The following graphic illustrates the point that security, reward and risk are trade-offs.

One of the main benefits of private finance is that the exact terms of the arrangement can vary, with no hard and fast rules, as it's negotiated and structured to suit the parties concerned. The roles of the parties can also vary to be purely a 'money-in, money-out' financial arrangement. For example, in some cases, there could be a more involved engagement of the parties relating to the property or development project. Examples might include a finance provider also lending their experience and contacts, or a skilled tradesman (e.g. builder) or professional (e.g. architect) offering advice or even a working contribution to a project.

However, there are some very clear rules and compliance procedures that need to be followed, particularly with regard to equity-based or profit-sharing arrangements to protect the provider of the financing. The property investor or developer needs to be aware of the rules – and adhere to them. For example, the Financial Conduct Authority (FCA) has published its Policy Statement PS13/3 which prohibits the promotion of variable return/profit-sharing financial structures on an unsolicited basis to so-called 'retail investors'. Exceptions, include High-Net-Worth Investors (HNWI), Sophisticated Investors (SI) and Business Investors (BI), provided these have been identified and qualified as such BEFORE offering any investment in this area. In other words, we need to ask if people are so-called 'non-retail investors' before pitching them with certain financial arrangements. If they do not qualify, then we cannot pitch to them under the law. A further exception is with friends and family, however. This is an area that is regulated by the FCA in the U.K. and has equivalents in other countries, such as the Securities and Exchange Commission (SEC) in the U.S.A.

Besides these, there are also additional compliance requirements, such as Know Your Client 'KYC' and Anti-Money Laundering 'AML' checks that need to be undertaken. These are legal requirements placed on anyone dealing in property, investment and financing designed to protect and alert the authorities to illegal, terrorist and otherwise criminal activity.

TPV TIP: Make sure you understand the compliance, rules and regulations relating to private financing and property to avoid falling foul of these, or worse, becoming embroiled in criminal activity, whether by accident or design. Trust but verify is the key phrase here. Some suggested places to visit to find out more are the FCA website and look up AML/KYC requirements via the HMRC website.

Why Use or Provide Private Finance?

One of the most precious commodities a property investor or developer has is finance. Sooner or later, EVERYONE will run out of their own capital resources if they have plans to grow or scale. So why not consider using private finance as a part of the financial plans of the business?

From a private finance provider's point of view, returns on capital can be very low, such as in banks and deposit accounts. Alternatively, they can come with risk, uncertainty and lack of engagement or control in some cases, such as with the stock market. Equally, providing private finance offers an opportunity for either active or passive investing, as you prefer. Crucially, private finance in property enables people to deal with real people, rather than with faceless institutions. So, why not?

Partnerships of various descriptions exist in most businesses and can be a very useful way of expanding a business, and this includes a property investment/development business. In a partnership, the parties usually bring with them complementary or incremental skills and resources for the wider benefit of the partnership. Examples of different aspects each party can bring to the project include: time, money, know-how, contacts. Private finance usually brings money to the table, although in certain situations the provider can bring additional resources to the table too.

Where to Find Private Finance?

We can find potential providers of private finance in some of the following places:

- Friends and family

- Property meetings and online property forums

- Business networking and investor events

- Where wealthy people go, such as gyms, golf clubs, flying clubs

- Personal contacts and professional/business/social media connections

- Social media content subscribers and followers

- Pension trustees or family offices

- Brokers, agents and other intermediary introducers.

In terms of qualification, in order to discuss equity or profit-sharing arrangements, aside from friends and family who we can identify pretty well, we may need to check if the person we are speaking to is either HNWI, SI or BI. It would not be advisable to walk up to people and ask them if they are 'loaded' as a conversation opener and so starting a conversation and getting to know people naturally is better. Slowly does it here, to avoid scaring people off. If you focus on getting to know people and having a conversation, rather than how much money people have, you are less likely to convey a 'needy' approach with them. Equally, if you are a potential provider of finance, then it is probably not a great idea to wear a sandwich board-like advertisement that you have a bag of cash ready to splash around.

Be careful not to jump straight into the 'have I got a deal for you' pitch either. When the time is right, we can elaborate, depending on the status of the person we are speaking to. It is always better to let the conversation flow and see if curiosity is aroused. Later on, we will need to formally document that we qualified the investor in writing, in the case of equity investment. Equally, it is perhaps not appropriate at a first meeting to whip out a self-certified statement of high net worth and ask them to sign it!

When it comes to Private Financing, there are six key areas that need to be considered, regardless of whether the financing is debt or equity:

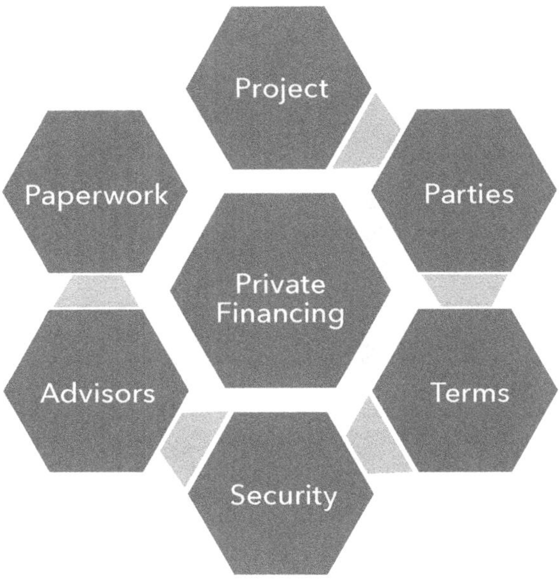

Project

This is the property project at hand and forms the foundation of the private financing arrangement – it answers the question 'so, what's the deal here?'. The project could be a single property, multiple properties, a block or portfolio. It could be a short-term arrangement or a longer time period. It could involve some kind of development or improvement activity, or not. However, the main thing is to be very clear as what the project is, to be able to describe it and, importantly, what the private financing exit looks like.

When it comes to property projects, there are essentially two main objectives: sell at a profit or rent at a profit. There could be a third, which is capital growth, which is more relevant for longer-term arrangements. Often, a property investor or developer will want to attract private finance in order to help fund their activities in support of their own and/or more traditional types of financing. This allows the investor or developer greater purchasing power or 'leverage' or to do more with less, in other words. It can also allow them to do bigger projects or more projects at the same time and so scale. For the provider of private finance, it offers them the opportunity to achieve a good return on investment, with an asset class that is familiar and tangible. With this in mind, here are some typical examples of a project that might use private finance.

Flip – This is a short-term project, typically taking three to 12 months, where a property is bought with the intention of being sold at a profit. It is also known as property trading. A flip project involves adding value to the property and/or capitalising on a significant discount achieved on the purchase price. The private finance provided is usually repaid from the sale proceeds.

BRR – Similar to the flip project, except the project is not sold and rented out after the 'project phase' is complete. Property investors and developers usually like to realise and release some of the value added through the project phase and so often refinance at the end of the project phase. This would then be what is known as a Buy-Refurbish-Refinance 'BRR' project. Some people refer to this as 'BRRR' or Buy-Refurbish-Rent-Refinance to explain the full sequence of events. In this case, the private finance exit would be repayment out of the proceeds of the refinancing upon project completion. Care should be taken to ensure that there is enough money released on refinancing to repay any private finance provider.

TPV TIP: Some people can get a little hung up on the Holy Grail of pulling all of their cash and that of private investors out of a deal upon refinancing. However, there is another way: the 'staggered arrangement' as I like to refer to it. Here, the investor and/or the private finance provider leaves some, but not usually all, of their funds in the project for a secondary phase. This secondary phase can be anything, but a good time-frame might be 2–5 years. This would then allow for a 'secondary exit event' to take place, such as a deferred sale or another refinancing. It would also allow a second bite at the cherry of sharing in the rental and/or revaluation profits during this phase. This helps to take some of the stress, pressure and risk away from that cliff-edge moment of absolutely needing to find a certain figure on refinancing after the project phase. Let's face it, a future revaluation is down to some matters outside of our control, including market conditions, lender policy and the dreaded 'valuer's opinion', which can lead to a bit of head-scratching at times!

BTS – Build-To-Sell is typically a flip project for a multi-unit, or at least more involved, conversion or development project. There is usually greater complexity, time and, arguably, greater risk and reward too. Here the property or site is transformed into something new or different, often by converting or changing its use with planning permission or under 'permitted development rights' or by building something from scratch with new-build development. The exit with traditional development is to sell the units upon completion to repay the private financing.

B2R – Build-To-Rent is an alternative to BTS in that it relates to a multi-unit project, where the exit is to refinance and retain the units to rent similar to the BRR strategy for single unit projects, as mentioned earlier.

The key with the project is to be clear about what will happen to the property or site, what work is involved and what the timescales, risk factors and exit to the private financing will look like. This is what I call the 'investment case'. The investment case sets out the plan and strategy for the project and so is open to scrutiny and test by all parties. Scrutiny should not really be feared, after all, another set of eyes on your plans and numbers can act as an additional check and balance as to the project's feasibility. It is important for both parties to do their own research on the project in order to satisfy themselves that it is realistic, viable and, therefore, likely to achieve the outcome predicted.

TPV TIP: There is also a hybrid exit to a multi-unit project that allows greater flexibility. Here, some units are sold and some are retained, which can be a great way for a property developer and/or private financier to have a 'no-money left in deal' and/or ensure the Build-to-Rent developer gets paid for their work through some of the sale proceeds during the project phase. This dovetails into what

I mentioned earlier about a staggered arrangement. So, if you have a private finance partner that is comfortable to leave some funds in the project, you can probably mix and match a little by selling some units and retaining others. I'd say that's a win-win type of arrangement, wouldn't you?

Parties

It is important to not only identify the parties to the private finance arrangement but also what their roles will be in order to set clear expectations, roles, responsibilities, contributions and returns. This will avoid confusion and potential for dispute later on. At the simplest level, one party provides the financing and the other receives that financing and undertakes the project. However, it's not always that simple in practice!

The parties to debt finance are lender and borrower or with equity financing, they are equity provider and equity recipient, which is simple enough. However, there are cases where the parties' roles may extend beyond this.

The borrower may also put funds into the project themselves, whether that's in the form of debt or equity. This is often referred to having some 'skin in the game'.

Equally, a private finance partner could also play a role in the project themselves, such as by seeking planning permission, undertaking project management and so on.

Some of these variations do start to take us into more into an equity joint venture type of structure, which is an alternative and variation to a straightforward debt-finance arrangement.

The parties to equity financing could have several different labels to describe them, depending on the legal structure involved. The developer or property investor could receive the equity personally, or into their investment/development company or into a specially created company 'SPC' for the project at hand ... also known as an 'SPV' (special purpose vehicle).

Therefore, an equity provider could be described as a joint venture partner or a shareholder. For ease, I shall use the terms of 'developer' as the recipient of the equity finance and 'partner' for provider of these funds.

As mentioned above, the key is to clearly identify who the parties will be, including what sort of legal entity is involved, along with the roles, contributions and rewards that are expected. It is also relevant here to mention the experience, financial and credit standing, track record and reputation of the parties and their suitability for the project and financing at hand. Finally, I believe that the objectives, character and especially the values of the parties should be aligned. Going into a full-on joint venture with someone you just met at a networking meeting is not always a recipe for a happy partnership.

TPV TIP: There can be multiple parties involved in the financing arrangements, which can also extend to institutions. To illustrate, I have undertaken projects with financing provided by an institutional lender, a private debt financier and also a private equity partner. However, it is usually best to keep a single party in each category for simplicity's sake at least.

Terms

Terms relate to the financing from a commercial point of view. These are the how much, what form, how long and what return questions that everyone will have. These points are important to understand and document to ensure clarity and avoid potential for dispute later down the line. It's worth having the conversation up front, as it helps to flush out any hidden expectations.

How much – an important consideration here is how much of the finance is being put forward as a proportion of the property value. This is often known as 'loan-to-value' or LTV with debt financing or 'equity-to-value' ETV with equity financing. Value is an interesting point to dwell on. It could relate to the value as is today, such as the purchase price or current resale value of the property or site. Alternatively, it could relate to some future value, such as with the benefit of planning permission known as 'planning uplifted value' or after completion of a development project, usually known as the gross development value or 'GDV'.

For clarity's sake, it's crucial to understand what the value being discussed relates to and more importantly, what risk factors or dependencies need to be addressed in order for that value to be achieved. For example, the GDV may only be realised if planning permission is awarded or if the work to develop the site is undertaken – the risk factor here is the likelihood of planning permission being granted and/or the work being completed on time and within budget. Generally speaking, the higher the LTV or lower the ETV is, the greater the risk there is to the provider of the private finance, so that needs to be weighed up.

What form – usually this finance is in the form of debt or equity. However, it could also be land/property in lieu of cash funds or, in the case of equity, potential contacts, know-how, track record or even 'sweat equity' in providing time and services. All of these things have a value and could come into the discussion between the parties.

TPV TIP: Many times someone providing private finance will believe that they are making the biggest contribution and also taking on the most risk. However, consider the time, know-how, experience/track record, contacts, site finding, site management, risk of payment/return, costs on abortive projects, etc. on the part of the developer. With this in mind, perhaps the private finance provider can then see that there is a balance or 'value exchange' and 'risk-sharing' position that takes place, which goes beyond the pure financial inputs and outputs. It's really important to have that conversation, so that all contributions, be they financial or non-financial, can be understood, valued and recognised by all. One of the main benefits of private finance in property is the potential to have a relationship between individuals, which you can't get with many other types of investment. It's not for everyone but for those it is for, this can be highly appreciated and rewarding.

How long – as the term suggest, this could relate to how long the funds will be out for. However, it could also be extended to include:

- Exactly how they are intended to be repaid, such as via a sale, refinancing or a combination, known as the exit or alternative exits

- Exactly when and how the funds will be advanced, whether all up-front or in separate batches or drawdowns sometimes called 'tranches' linked to certain timescales, development milestones or works progression.

What return – this is the quantification of how much you expect to give/get back on top of what has been put in. Returns can take several shapes and forms such as:

- Fixed or variable rate of interest return (% or £)

- Fixed fee

- Profit / equity share

- Share of rental income

- Retention of a property

- Or even a combination of more than one the above.

The return is what you expect to get back on top of what you put in, which we will call your original capital. However, this highlights the point about risk of return but also risk of loss of original capital too, which is different. The return could be linked to the performance of the project in general, especially if it is variable rather than fixed. The return of capital is also linked to the success of the project in many ways, however, it is also linked to the type of security that underpins that capital. Therefore, two important considerations when looking at return are the balance between reward and security, which cues us up to the next point nicely.

TPV TIP: I have a saying: 'the closer you are to the source of finance's heart, the lower the cost of finance'. That's not always true, of course. However, it is a general rule as the people closest to us would usually like to support us in our goals. The opposite is also one to watch out for – beware of people offering apparently stellar returns that have no real vested interest in doing so, especially if you have only just met them. It could cost you a lot more in the long run, including your identity!

Security

Reward (or return) and security are sometimes diametrically opposed. Often, with more security comes lower returns and vice versa.

We outlined the main types of security earlier. Security is valuable and helps to protect the capital position from a private finance provider's point of view. However, from a developer or property investor's point of view, security is both precious and in scarce supply. For these reasons, there is often a tug of war taking place over security among the parties.

Equally, keep in mind that finance can come in several layers and so there is a hierarchy as we move up the 'Funding Stack'. Higher levels of security, usually accompanied by a lower return/cost of finance, are found at the bottom of the funding stack. Which means there is less security and often higher rates of return/cost of financing as we move up the funding stack.

Equity financing may have limited or even no tangible security, whereas debt financing is often accompanied by some form of tangible security.

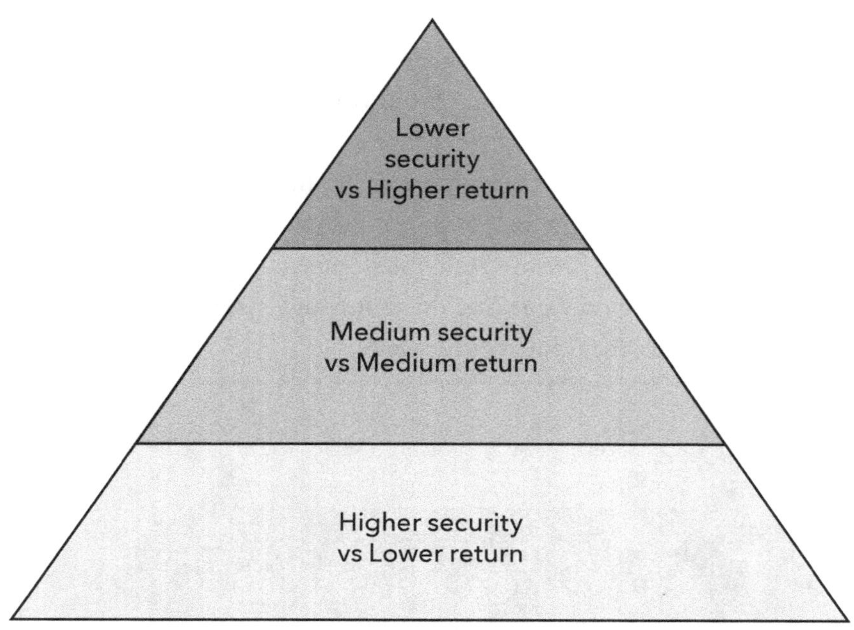

Here is a table that sets out the main types of security that you could consider.

Type of Security	Description
Charge over specific property	This is a legal charge, similar to what a mortgage lender would adopt. Usually it's a 'first charge' but can also be a second or third charge in order of priority ranking. The charge holder controls when a property is sold or refinanced and they take priority over all other lenders, equity partners, creditors, etc. This means they usually get paid back first or can repossess the property should the borrower default.
Debenture over a company assets (fixed or floating)	A debenture is similar in construct to a charge in many ways. A fixed charge debenture fixes the security over a specific asset, which could be property but could also be other assets of a business. A floating charge attaches to all the assets excluding those subject to a fixed charge, so ranks behind any fixed charge/debenture holders in terms of security priority. There could also be a fixed and floating charge which, as the name suggests, secures against all assets of a business.

Type of Security	Description
Declaration/Deed of Trust (DoT)	A deed of trust that sets out the 'beneficial owner-ship' of an asset which can be different to the registered 'legal ownership' documented at the Land Registry. A DoT is not always made public and so can offer some privacy between parties.
Shares in a company	These could be preference shares (first-ranking), which usually carry a fixed dividend or ordinary shares (second-ranking), which carry a variable dividend. These provide ownership rights in a company and therefore ultimately ownership of all the company's assets. Shares could also be issued in different classes of share: A, B, C, etc. These are known as 'alphabet shares' with each class poten-tially issued with different terms, such as different voting and/or dividend rights. Some share classes could be convertible from one type to another under certain pre-set conditions, such as preference shares converting to ordinary shares after planning approval is obtained, for example.
Guarantees and personal loans	There are several forms of guarantee: personal (by an individual), director/shareholder (by owner-operators of a company), cross-company (by related or connected parties). A guarantee is a legal promise that the guarantor will step into an agree-ment to assume the liability on behalf of the party they are guaranteeing, should that party default on a financial or other arrangement. A personal loan is essentially a personal guarantee, as it allows the lender recourse to all of the borrower's personal assets.
Title security	There are two main forms of title security, where the Land Registry is informed that certain actions need to take place under certain conditions. The most common is a 'restriction on title' or RX1 Form, which prevents something happening (e.g. sale or refi-nance) without the formal consent of a certain party, such as a lender. Another is a 'notification on title', where a named party is informed of some change on that title (e.g. sale or refinance) after the change has been made. Title restrictions can be used on their own or alongside other forms of security.

Type of Security	Description
Others	Two other types of security worth mentioning here are cross-collateralisation and options. Cross-collateralisation is a term that means providing additional or alternative forms of security to support a loan, such as another property, another type of asset, etc. An option agreement is the right but not the obligation to buy an asset under pre-set conditions at or within a set period of time.

Advisors

Whilst each party has a responsibility to research and undertake their own due diligence, they can and often should also have specialised advisors to offer support in evaluating the financing at hand. The three principal types of advisor that you might want to consider are financial, legal and tax advisors.

Financial – whilst this could be an Independent Financial Advisor or 'IFA', it need not necessarily be so. An accountant, wealth advisor or trusted, independent connection that is a Sophisticated Investor, 'SI', or a High-Net-Worth Individual, 'HNWI', could also be a valuable source of advice and an independent sanity check.

Legal – if you have ever bought and sold property, then you will have used a conveyancing solicitor. However, a legal advisor will go way beyond standard conveyancing searches and opinion in the case of private financing. The most relevant distinction being the drafting or review of the legal and security documentation, which is often undertaken by a commercial solicitor. They don't come cheap, however, expect to pay between £1,000 and £5,000 for engaging a decent commercial solicitor.

Tax – returns as a private financier are usually paid 'pre-tax' and so any taxation becomes their responsibility to take care of. When you consider that there are different rates of taxes and allowances, such as Income Tax, Corporation Tax, Capital Gains Tax and so on, it can have a significant impact on your retained or 'post-tax' returns. Whilst an accountant can often play the tax advisory role, not all accountants are actually tax specialists. So, a chartered tax advisor or specialist tax accountant could be a useful member of your advisory team.

Others – you may want or need to engage other specialists under your instruction to assist in certain advisory situations, such as pensions advisors, surveyors/valuers, architects, planning consultants and so on.

All of these advisors come at a cost, of course. So, there is another trade-off to be made here. The cost of specialist advice against your returns. You can choose not to have some or all of these advisors but that also has a cost or potential cost attached to it: namely risk. Your 'risk tolerance' or 'risk appetite', along with your professional investing experience are factors that you should take into consideration when deciding on which type of advisors you have on your team.

TPV TIP: Free advice is said to be worth every penny! Unless you are yourself an experienced, specialist advisor or a 'sophisticated investor', then you would be wise to engage the services of an independent professional or have your own professional team to safeguard your interests.

Paperwork

I have another saying: 'unless it is written down, it didn't happen!'. OK, so you might say that a conversation that has either audio or video recording could prove what's been agreed but that is usually not admissible in a court of law without the express consent of both parties.

There, I said it – a court of law. Nobody wants to end up in court and nobody expects they will do so either, especially in the honeymoon period of a shiny new property project. However, things can and do go wrong from time to time. Even if they don't go wrong, memories fade and people can see, hear or experience the same thing and still have a different interpretation or reach a different conclusion. Just as we take out insurance policies to protect against certain remote risks, having the correct paperwork in place is a form of insurance in property finance – for all parties.

Having the right paperwork in place ties into many of the other elements of these considerations, which by now you will observe are interrelated and interdependent. Your advisors will play a key role in helping to ensure things are properly documented and recorded, such as charges registered at HM Land Registry, for example.

I would recommend outlining the main terms of an agreement to enter into a private financing arrangement in what is called a 'Heads of Terms' or HoT. An HoT is not usually legally binding, with the exception of confidentiality and exclusivity undertakings. So, it's good to draft and sign these for clarity's sake. The HoT should then be converted into a full legal agreement format that *is* legally binding in order to protect the parties.

A full legal agreement might contain quite a few provisions, as you might expect from reviewing this chapter. It could and ideally should include certain additional provisions for added clarity. In the standard joint venture agreement that I use, I have included the following additional provisions, among others:

- Ownership/income rights and split

- Roles and responsibilities of the parties

- What each party will put in and get out of the JV

- Definition of the project(s)

- The proposed project strategy

- The security (if any)

- The exit and contingency plans

- The time period the agreement will exist for.

- Dispute resolution

- Overcoming 'deadlock'.

Within the Book Bonuses, I include a summary of the full provisions of the debt and equity agreements that I tend to include in the agreements that I personally use, for your benefit.

TPV TIP: Always, always, always commit what's been agreed to writing, in the proper form and signed by all parties. Couples and families split, friends come and go and in a 'wealth or investment industry', such as property, there are chameleons, charlatans and cobras lurking and waiting to pounce. Consider this a wealth warning, therefore.

Advantages and Benefits

Using Private Financing as a property financing strategy has the following advantages:

- There are many ways of structuring an agreement, which can offer flexible, creative and rewarding solutions to suit all parties.

- An alternative to mainstream lender financing, potentially accessing an almost unlimited supply of private finance and often at a lower level of capital input on the part of the investor/developer.

- Dealing with another human being, instead of 'computer says no.' Suitable even if you have poor credit or cannot get a mortgage for some reason.

- Allows more rapid portfolio expansion, brings added inputs and insights into the business from new sources.

Disadvantages and Risks

Using Private Financing as a property financing strategy has the following disadvantages:

- It is not always easy to find a private investor on mutually agreeable terms.

- There are some strict legal and compliance issues that need to be carefully navigated.

- The cost of financing or equity/profit dilution can put some investors/developers off.

- Potential for dispute or dissatisfaction should things go wrong and therefore a compromised relationship between the parties.

Reality Check

Private financing is something of a 'Holy Grail' to property investors and developers and can be somewhat elusive to find. To illustrate, I managed to raise around £250,000 in private financing in my first five years of being fully committed to property. However, in my second five years, I raised over £5,000,000. It's fair to say that experience and track record played some part in this 20 x improvement.

However, I simply wasn't as effective in raising private investment as I could have been at the start. It is a skill or in some ways a bit of an art form, as we are dealing with the human psyche … on both sides! I often speak to my mentees, apprentices and Mastermind group about the intricacies of raising private financing, along with overcoming our own limiting beliefs. It can seem like a struggle at the beginning, especially if you go fishing in the same small pond as many other property investors. They often say that it's not what you know but who you know. I'd say that with raising personal financing that it's most definitely both.

Nowadays, I have raised significant investor funds; most of these have come from just three or four individuals. I can honestly say that these investors have not only played a role in the expansion of my property business but they have become trusted and valued friends in the process. I take care of my investment partners and their funds, perhaps even more than I take care of myself and my own money. They are my lifeblood for effective expansion and are the reason that I have been able to scale so rapidly over recent years. I have significant growth plans that will mean raising higher levels of private financing to underpin these, all in the pursuit of my legacy foundation goal. So, I have more to do myself, although I feel ready to make another step change and break through yet another glass ceiling, as I did in the past. The same could apply to you and perhaps having read this book, you will achieve more in less time as a result – I sincerely hope you do.

Chapter Nine

Bonds, Shares and Mezzanine Finance

Context

Alternative finance can also get a bit more complicated as we get more advanced. So, I will do my best at simplifying things here as much as possible, starting with setting the context to this chapter and its contents in advance. There are several types of financial structures:

Debt – in the form of loans and bonds. They tend to offer a fixed rate of return by amount or percentage.

Equity – in the form of an equity share or profit share. They tend to offer a variable or risk-based rate of return depending on the success of the project.

Mezzanine – which is a hybrid or blend of debt and equity and could change or convert from one form to another as well. This, by definition, could get a little complex!

Before we proceed, this is an advanced property finance topic, which may or may not be appropriate for you today. However, if you have plans to grow, scale or enter into more advanced property strategies, such as property development, blocks/portfolio acquisition or even property business mergers and acquisitions, then read on. If you are scraping together the funds for your first buy-to-let, please feel free to read on to see what could be on the horizon for you later! However, I will also give you the option to mark this chapter as one to return to in future, if you feel it might be beyond your current needs. Personally, I hope you stick around, as I think it is quite eye-opening and also helps us to see the full spectrum of the property finance landscape.

Traditional property finance in the form of buy-to-let mortgages, bridging finance and development finance, could also be described as 'Senior Debt' within finance circles. The seniority referred to is that the debt is secured on an asset, usually a specific property in this case, and ranks ahead of other creditors in terms of priority, including other lenders, should the worst happen and the borrower fail to repay, become insolvent, etc. Here, a First Charge (fixed charge or mortgage) is taken over the property, which places the lender at the front of the queue to get repaid in advance of all other lenders or creditors in these worst-case situations. Therefore, this is seen as the most secure and least risky form of finance to most lenders. As a result, it is usually also the least costly form of financing due to the 'risk-reward ratio' that we referred to earlier in this book playing out. The downside is that the maximum amount of lending available here is usually capped at 50% to 75% of the total value of the assets available as security.

So far, these types of loans could apply equally to borrowers using their own name, either as an individual or as a common partnership and a so-called 'corporate body', such as a limited company or a limited liability partnership (LLP), although I will use the term 'company' going forward. However, there are some forms of finance that are mostly only available to companies, which opens up the finance options available to property developers but also to other forms of property company, such as with the acquisition of larger blocks and portfolios or mergers and acquisitions (M&A), for example.

Besides there being first-charge loans on a specific property, there could also be second-charge lending secured on that same property. This second-charge lending is also known as a 'Subordinated Loan' because it ranks below the first-charge holders, but still above other creditors or lenders.

A loan could also be secured on the general assets of a company instead of on a specific property. This loan could also be called a 'Debenture' and is often accompanied by a 'Fixed Charge' over a company's specified assets in the U.K. at least (a debenture in the U.S.A. is often unsecured). This fixed charge is typically secured against a specific property when it comes to property finance, although in general business finance this could also extend to other assets, like stock, customer debts and fixed assets. Then, we could have a 'Floating Charge', which, as the name suggests, could be secured against all the company's assets, and which could change over time, such as stock, cash and debtors, but also any and all other assets of the business, such as fixed assets, including property.

TPV TIP: If you are asked to sign a floating charge for any form of finance to a company, make sure that you understand this could mean you are then unable to secure any other lending for any other property or asset without the express written consent of the floating charge holder or lender. A floating charge can be a very powerful tool with certain types of business financing as we shall see later, but for a regular property investor operating through a general property investment company, it could be a seriously limiting factor in obtaining finance in the future.

Now that we have set the scene with debt finance, we can discuss bonds in more detail, as they are a form of debt finance. Bonds could either be secured against specific property or the assets of a company and could be classified as senior debt (first-ranking) or subordinated debt (second or third-ranking). We will cover the details of bond finance later.

After debt finance, we have equity finance, which, as mentioned, comes in the form of shares or stock in a company or alternatively as a share of profit in a project or investment, such as under a joint venture or partnership agreement. Equity in the form of shares breaks down into 'Ordinary Shares' or common stock and 'Preference Shares' or preferred (higher-ranking) stock. Much like with senior debt and subordinated debt, ordinary shares and preference shares also have a ranking, with preference shares requiring their dividends or capital to be repaid before that of the ordinary shareholders.

Equity in the form of a joint venture or partnership agreement is often specified in certain legal documents, such as a joint venture, partnership, collaboration agreement or alternatively under a Declaration or Deed of Trust. Again, we will cover the details of equity finance below.

If you are still with me, then Mezzanine Finance is a form of finance that sits in between debt and equity and might be constructed in a variety of ways that take components of either and/or debt and equity finance options. As a result, the structure and documentation of mezzanine finance can be varied and let's face it, a little bit more complicated too! More on this below, however.

It should be apparent from this context section that we are into more advanced forms of finance here. As a result, both the property investor/developer seeking finance and the people offering finance using these types of finance structure should seek their own independent financial and legal advice before proceeding too deeply into this highly-regulated area of finance. It's not for the faint-hearted in other words. For the bold and the brave, however … read on!

Bonds

What You Need To Know

There are essentially two types of bond that we will discuss here: 'Property Bonds' and 'General Bonds'. A property bond, sometimes also known as a 'Property Investment Bond' or 'Loan Note', is a loan that is usually secured against a specific property or piece of land. A general bond is a loan that is not secured against a specific property, but is secured against the assets of a company.

In essence, a property bond is a secured loan and behaves like a commercial loan for the most part, with a fixed rate of interest being paid. There can sometimes be a twist with a property bond, where in addition to a fixed rate of interest being paid to the bond-holder, that an additional bonus could be payable on top. This bonus could be to reward the bond-holder for leaving their money in for a longer period of time, for deferring repayment of interest and/or should the success of the project or development that the bond relates to exceed a certain milestone or threshold, such as a minimum profit level.

The key difference with a bond is usually who the bond-holder is. With traditional lending, the lender is typically a bank, commercial lender or similar types of institution. With a bond-holder, it is often a private/pension fund, family office, non-institutional lender (such as a venture capitalist or another company) or even an individual or collection of individuals.

As bonds are a regulated form of finance, they can only be marketed or offered to certain types of qualified investors. These would be so-called 'non-retail investors', such as funds or business investors and certain types of individual investor that are classed as either 'Sophisticated Investors' (SI) or 'High-Net-Worth Investors' (HNWI).

Some definitions…

Sophisticated Investor – To class and self-certify as a sophisticated investor you must:

- Have made at least one investment in an unlisted security in the previous two years; or

- Have been a member of a business angels network for at least six months; or

- Have worked in a professional capacity in the provision of finance to SMEs in the last two years or in the provision of private equity; or

- Be or have been within the last two years a director of a company with a turnover of at least £1m.

- Alternatively, you can be a Certified Sophisticated Investor having passed the appropriate tests – you'd know it if you did!

High-Net-Worth Investor – To class and self-certify as a high-net-worth investor you must:

- Earn at least £100,000 a year; or

- Have net assets excluding your home and pensions of at least £250,000.

A note on security…

I mentioned that a property bond is usually secured against land or property. However, as you will notice from the funding stack, security or charges over land or property can be layered and ranked.

Usually, the lender that provides the more traditional acquisition finance, such as a commercial loan mortgage or bridging finance, will require the first-charge security on the property. The same goes for a lender that provides acquisition and development finance together, usually. Some development finance providers do not provide the funding for the acquisition of the land and property. In this case they will usually take a second charge, which ranks behind the first charge holders in terms of priority. As a result of the higher risk to the lender, the interest cost is usually higher.

In the case of a property bond, it most likely won't be used to fund the acquisition of the land and property – and in some cases not all of the development cost either. However, it could still be secured on the land or property by way of a second or third charge and thus will rank in this order or priority as well.

In the case of a general bond, it too could be secured. It could be secured by way of a debenture or charge over some or all of the assets of the company. It could also be secured by way of a floating charge, which automatically takes a charge over all of the assets specified as they come and go. The key point with a floating charge, as I mentioned previously, is that the charge holder will forbid anyone else to take security over the assets they hold a charge over without their express, written permission … which they will mostly deny merely to protect their own interests. Some fixed-charge holders do manage to 'get ahead' of the floating charge holders, so make sure you understand the levels and ranking of security that are being made available.

So, why am I labouring the point around security you may be wondering? That would be a fair question! The reason is that you can effectively slice and dice or layer different types of finance and attach different types of security along with them.

Imagine taking bridging finance or a commercial loan to acquire a property or piece of land. Then add development finance to fund the development costs up to say 65% of the gross development value or 85% of the gross development cost. This would not be untypical with a property development project. However, add in a property bond on top and this could potentially take the available lending all the way up to 100% of the gross development cost, in theory. In this case, the property bond holders could be secured by way of a third charge or a fixed or floating charge over the company's assets. In either case, the specific first and second-charge holders that provide the acquisition and development finance would rank ahead of the property bond holders.

Clearly, this layering and ranking is potentially good news for the property developer, as it means they could leverage or borrow more highly by using a property bond and this will also mean they need less of their own equity. It would also mean the profit is funded by a lower level of equity, which will significantly boost the return on cash investment for the developer. That's a very efficient way to fund your development activities!

On the other hand, whilst leverage magnifies the return on cash investment profits, it also magnifies any potential losses. With higher levels of external debt, it also means greater dilution of the 'margin of safety' for the debt providers in terms of asset security coverage. In other words, in the case of a loss and despite the security they have, some of them might not get all their money back, to put it plainly.

TPV TIP: When layering different types of debt finance to a high overall level of loan to value or loan to development cost/value, keep in mind that small changes in the performance of the project, such as the project duration and/or the development cost and/or the end-value, could lead to significant swings in the net profit and return on equity. So, have contingencies built into your development plans that cater for these swings and model a best, mid and worst-case scenario to see how it could turn out. As attractive as it is to layer up the debt, be cautious not to over-extend the lending-to-asset security level to the point that a small negative change in the project could lead to the whole house of cards tumbling down.

When looking to arrange and set up a property bond – because it is a specialist area and often requires the assistance of a professional administrator and trustee – it can be complex, time-consuming and potentially expensive, depending on how it is done. The following costs are illustrative for a one-year bond when using experienced professionals to assist you:

- Professional advisor fees could be 1% to 3% of funds raised.

- Bond administrator and trustee set up fees could be 0.5% to 2% of funds raised.

- Annual 'assets under management fees' could be 0.5% to 1.5% of funds raised.

- Bond funding sourcing fees could be 1% to 5% of funds raised.

- Interest returns to bond holders could be 4% to 10% of funds raised (rising to 15% of funds raised, for longer durations with additional bonuses on top).

As you can see, it is not a low-cost form of financing at 7% at the lower end and as much as 21.5% at the upper end. Do keep in mind that a property bond is usually the final layer of debt finance that a developer will take on before using their own equity or raising equity externally. A bond can partially or even fully replace some of this equity. As equity is usually the most expensive and scarcest form of finance you will come across, perhaps you can see why these costs arise.

Advantages and Benefits

Using property bonds as a property finance strategy has the following advantages:

- It allows us to use less of our own equity funds to expand the scale and reach of our development projects.

- It is another layer of debt financing that could sit on top of other more traditional and/or readily accessible forms of finance.

- There are professionals and specialists that can assist in all aspects of the bond set-up and fund-raising process.

- Property bonds allow a greater level of leverage or borrowing, which has the effect of magnifying the returns of cash investment or equity for the developer.

Disadvantages and Risks

Using property bonds as a property finance strategy has the following disadvantages:

- It can be complex, time-consuming and relatively expensive to set up and administer a property bond, so it its not optimal for a smaller, one-time development project.

- The higher levels of leverage or loan to cost, whilst compelling, can mean that small fluctuations in the development time or cost get magnified negatively in terms of the return on equity.

- Over-extending the debt levels in a project is not only potentially risky to us as the developer but also to the property bond holders; so leave a reasonable 'margin of safety' of equity in there.

- Fundraising via property bonds is a regulated activity, which requires clear understanding and adherence to the rules and regulations in order to avoid falling foul of penalties, bans or even criminal action for failing to do so.

Reality Check

If your eyes were glazing over when reading this section, then you can see that whilst a property bond sounds appealing as an additional layer of debt finance, it is complicated. And it can also be a bit of a minefield if you're not too careful.

Property bonds are often used by established developers and marketed through professional and accredited fund-raising specialists. They are best suited to larger, repeating developers, therefore.

Shares

What You Need To Know

There are essentially two types of equity that we will discuss here: issued shares in a company and a profit share in a joint venture arrangement.

As previously mentioned, the creation and issuance of shares in a company creates an equity stake in that company. This allows the owners of these shares to participate in all of the profits of that company, be it through dividends and/or the sale proceeds of the shares or assets of the company. This means that there is a 'legal ownership' through the share certificate, along with a 'beneficial ownership' of the profits and gains that the company realises.

In contrast, a joint venture arrangement, whilst allowing a similar division of profits and therefore a beneficial ownership, would not automatically involve legal ownership of the underlying company or property.

TPV TIP: Regardless of whether issuing shares or agreeing a profit-sharing joint venture, always put down what is agreed into a formal written agreement. In the case of shares, it is usually in the form of a shareholders' agreement. In the case of a joint venture, it is usually in the form of a joint venture or collaboration agreement, but it could also be in the form of a Declaration or Deed of Trust.

In the case of issued shares in a company, this could get a little complicated, so bear with me here.

Issued shares fall broadly into two categories: ordinary shares and preference shares. Ordinary shares are the most common form of shares issued in a company. They usually carry voting and dividend rights in line with the percentage of the issued shares held. There are cases where the voting and/or dividend rights can be restricted or removed, which would be disclosed in the company documentation – so always read the company documentation! Equally, ordinary shares can be issued in different share classes: Class A, Class B, Class C, etc., which is sometimes referred to as 'Alphabet Shares'. Again, the different share classes could carry differing rights and benefits, which would be set out in the company documentation.

The other main share type is 'Preference Shares'. Preference shares, as their name implies, rank higher than ordinary shares in the case of a break up and distribution of dividends and the capital of the company. They need to be repaid before the ordinary shareholders, in other words. Preference shares might carry a fixed dividend and are usually non-voting but, you guessed it, it will all be set out in the company documentation!

To add to the complexity, preference shares could also be convertible to ordinary shares under certain circumstances. This might be where the holder of preference shares wants to ensure they rank higher than say the founders or ordinary shareholders in terms of dividend and capital repayment during an initial period, such as pre-planning or pre-completion of a development for example. Then, they may be happy to convert to ordinary shares and rank alongside the other ordinary shareholders later on when the profits and risks are more predictable, such as when a property or development enters the sales and/or rental phase, for example.

The main thing to be aware of with shares or equity is that the shareholders/equity holders are always the last in line, with the preference shareholders standing one place above dead last being the ordinary shareholders. In the event that a company is sold, broken up or, dare I say it, liquidated, there is a very clear sequence in which everyone gets paid off under the law. It looks a little like this:

- Secured lenders – first to be repaid in order of their ranking (first charge, second charge, fixed charge holders, etc.).

- Liquidators' fees and expenses – are next to be paid, if applicable obviously.

- Preferential creditors – these are things like rent, salaries and the taxman.

- Floating charge holders – these will feast on whatever assets are left by this stage (such as cash, stock, debtors, other fixed assets, etc.).

- Unsecured creditors – people like trade creditors and suppliers.

- Interest on unsecured debts arising after liquidation – self-explanatory.

- Shareholders – with preference shareholders ranking above ordinary shareholders.

So, you can now clearly see why equity shareholders are seen as the most risk-taking and also therefore probably fully deserving of making the highest level of return as well.

As the business owner, we would prefer to retain as much equity as possible to fully retain what we hope are high levels of profit that our diligent hard work deserves. However, as I like to say, 50% of something is better than 100% of nothing. So, there are clear cases when we might need or want to give up an equity stake.

The most obvious ways in which we might want to consider giving up an equity stake are these:

- To access larger projects and developments.

- To undertake more projects simultaneously.

- To bring in additional co-owners with different experience, contacts, resources, etc.

- To reduce our personal capital and leverage other people's capital instead.

- To share some of our risk with others.

- To grow our business vertically, horizontally or through mergers and acquisition (M&A).

In the case of a joint venture arrangement, some or all of these same factors could apply. However, unlike an issued shareholding in a company, the terms of how profits, gains, losses and risks are split will depend on the documented joint venture agreement and might also be limited to a specific project or development, rather than an entire business.

A quick note around 'special purpose vehicles' or SPVs

An SPV is an entity, usually a company but not necessarily so. The term special purpose company is sometimes also used. An SPV, as its name suggests, is something that is created for a specific purpose. Examples could include undertaking a development project, owning a specific property for rental purposes, formalising a joint venture, undertaking an acquisition and so on. An SPV will usually differ from a property investment company, a property trading company, a property management company or a property services company by limiting either its scope or duration around its specific purpose. The other property company types I've just mentioned are formed with the intention of ongoing activity, rather than a one-off.

TPV TIP: An SPV is often a cleaner, ring-fenced way of undertaking a property development, especially when it involves different equity shareholders to the general property business. There is also a range of tax benefits that could arise, depending on how things are structured, owned and concluded once the specific purpose has come to an end. Equally, an SPV also has the effect of ring-fencing the entity outside of other parts of the owner's business so it can, in theory at least, stand or fall on its own. As with all things in this book, however, always seek your own professional advice.

When looking to arrange and set up either an equity shareholding or joint venture arrangement, it can be undertaken in a couple of different ways. There is the relatively informal way, where the parties discuss and agree things between themselves, shake hands on the arrangement and then issue the shares and the correct documentation: namely the shareholders agreement or joint venture agreement/declaration of trust. Technically, this could mostly be done between the parties without any outside intervention. Much would depend on the relative commercial awareness or level of financial sophistication of each party as to how much outside professional support they would need. However, it is always advisable to have some kind of professional advice and support.

Beyond this, there are also ways in which an equity shareholding can follow a similar path to the issuance of property bonds, which we discussed earlier. There are ways to raise equity through external providers. Many are beyond the scope of this section, such as a stock market listing or Initial Public Offering 'IPO' or are discussed elsewhere, such as crowdfunding.

However, here are the illustrative costs for an equity share raise when using experienced professionals to assist you:

- Professional advisor fees could be 1% to 3% of funds raised.

- Share administrator and trustee set up fees could be 0.5% to 2% of funds raised.

- Annual 'assets under management fees' could be 0.5% to 1.5% of funds raised.

- Equity funding sourcing fees could be 2% to 7% of funds raised.

- Expected variable returns to shareholders could be 10% to 25%+ of funds raised.

Again, it is definitely not a low-cost form of finance at 14% at the lower end to as much as 42.5% or perhaps more at the upper end. However, equity is the final piece in the property finance puzzle, you could say. As identified, it could make the difference of 'deal or no deal' without external equity coming on board. It will also mean carving up the profit-and-return-on-equity pie into smaller pieces. Though it could also mean that the overall size of that pie is now much, much bigger than we could handle on our own!

Advantages and Benefits

Using external equity as a property finance strategy has the following advantages:

- It allows us to use less of our own equity funds to expand the scale and reach of our development projects.

- It is another layer of finance that could sit on top of other more traditional and/or readily accessible forms of finance.

- There are professionals and specialists that can assist in all aspects of the equity set up and fund-raising process.

- External equity allows a greater level of leverage, which has the effect of magnifying the returns of cash investment or equity for the developer.

Disadvantages and Risks

Using external equity as a property finance strategy has the following disadvantages:

- It can be complex, time-consuming and relatively expensive to set up and administer, so it's not the best fit for a smaller, one-time development project.

- The higher levels of leverage or finance-to-cost ratio, whilst compelling, can mean that small fluctuations in the development time or cost get magnified in terms of the return on equity.

- Over-extending the finance levels in a project is not only potentially risky to us as the developer but also to the equity and debt holders; so leave a reasonable 'margin of safety' of equity in there.

- Fund-raising via equity is a regulated activity, which requires clear understanding and adherence to the rules and regulations in order to avoid falling foul of penalties, bans or even criminal action for failing to do so.

Reality Check

Although equity finance can appear to be an attractive way to source an extra layer of debt finance, again, like bonds, it is complex and there are plenty of pitfalls for newbies to fall into!

Equity finance is often used by established developers and marketed through professional and accredited fund-raising specialists. It is best suited to larger, repeating developers, therefore. However, I would say that external equity is used to 'fund the last mile of finance' when it comes to property projects and that could be the most important and valuable mile of all!

I have used equity finance myself, so it need not be undertaken on the basis of appointing external professionals. However, make sure that you are aware of the rules and regulations and get some professional support if you decide to go down this route.

Mezzanine

What You Need To Know

Mezzanine finance is a hybrid between debt (loans) and equity (shares), as we explained at the start of this chapter. As such it usually sits in the middle between more traditional debt finance, also called 'senior debt', and the developer's own equity. It could even morph between the two, just to spice things up a bit more!

At its heart, mezzanine finance usually comes in the form of secured loans (with security over property, equity and personal guarantees) and/or preference shares and/or ordinary shares and sometimes all of these. It might also be the case that some forms of finance could also be termed as 'convertible'. Here, they start out as one form of finance, such as debt or preference shares, and then convert to another form of finance, such as ordinary shares, later on. This conversion could be triggered by a specific event, such as securing other debt finance, obtaining planning permission, completing a development and/or after a set period of time.

The convertible option could be either a 'put option' or a 'call option'. A put option is where the finance provider asks for the conversion to take place, such as converting debt to equity. Alternatively, with a call option, it would be the recipient of the finance that asks for the conversion to take place instead. The merits of conversion depend on the circumstances, costs and interests of the parties.

Due to the nature of mezzanine finance, it is often accessed and arranged through specialist finance agents, brokers or so-called 'boutique providers', who are most likely to have contacts with equity, venture and pension funds, family offices, high-net-worth and sophisticated investors, peer-to-peer, crowdfunding or the other specialist lenders and finance providers required to sew it all together.

However, it could also be accessed directly from any one of these potential finance providers – if you have the right connections or can get past the gatekeepers!

It is possible to raise 100% of the funds required for a property development project under certain conditions. With a combination of debt, mezzanine and equity, the whole of the development cost could be funded, potentially. This is usually only available for larger developments, with experienced developers with a solid track record and where the profit potential is also high … but it can be done. In some ways, the mezzanine and equity portion of the funding is like a joint venture arrangement.

There are a few specialist funders that do provide the whole funding stack in return for an equity stake and fee. For example, I know of one that will provide 100% of the funds for a development project with 40% of the profit going to the external equity providers, 20% for themselves and leaving 40% for the developer. That's 40% of something for none of your own cash – as I said before, a smaller percentage of something is better than 100% of nothing.

Due to the variety and potential complexity of how mezzanine finance could be structured, I won't elaborate too much in this section. Terms can vary a lot, with interest being fixed or part-fixed and part-variable, at a return expectation range of anywhere between 10% and 25%+. Suffice to say that it could be really handy, but can be harder to access and comes at a cost that is consistent with a hybrid of the property bond and equity financing costs outlined earlier.

Equally, the advantages, disadvantages, challenges, complexity and reality are also broadly similar to those outlined for property bonds and shares, in combination.

Reality Check

This chapter was one of a couple that I was weighing up whether to include in this book or not. As you can see, it can be complex, detailed, costly, specialised and hard to access bonds, shares and mezzanine finance. It could be argued that this is beyond the scope of the average property investor and developer and possibly sits in the realm of a follow-up book on deeper or more complex financial structures. Who knows, perhaps I will write that one as well some day!

However, I decided to share this chapter as I myself am operating in this realm now. So, I figured that if I am swimming in these waters, then many others will be or want to be as well. If you have aspirations to grow and scale your property business and goals, then it would be well worth becoming acquainted with the potential funding structures that are outlined in this chapter. Particularly so if you are considering property development, large-scale blocks and portfolio acquisition or even business mergers and acquisitions.

Therefore, I hope that on balance you feel better to have read this chapter than not to have done so. If you are not reading this line, then there's no problem, as you probably already decided to skip it with a promise that you might return to it another day.

Chapter Ten

Grants and 'Soft' Loans – Free Money!

Grants and Soft Loans

There is plenty of financial aid and assistance available to us in property; we just need to know where to look for it. This chapter will give signpost you towards some of the common ones to follow up. But first, a word of caution. Even during the time that I was writing this chapter, things changed and in some cases, pretty abruptly too. One example was the Green Homes Grant, which formed a key part of the type of subsidy that was available to landlords. It was due to be end in March 2022, although the government decided to end it immediately after the March 2021 Budget instead. That's also a prompt to remind you how frequently the rules around grants can change, so make sure that you check in with the latest info from the government, local authorities or a grant and government-backed loans specialist before progressing too far with this one.

What You Need To Know

Below is a table summarising some of the main grants and what I like to call 'soft loans', along with the type of property business they might best relate to. A soft loan is one that has reduced lending criteria or is otherwise favourable due to it being supported by the government or a local authority in some way.

Property Business Type	Grants	Soft Loans
Homeowner	Energy Company Obligation (ECO) Empty Homes Grant Domestic Renewable Heat Incentive (D-RHI)	Help to Buy Right to Buy Green Deal Finance Plan
Private Landlord	Energy Company Obligation (ECO) Empty Homes Grant Domestic Renewable Heat Incentive (D-RHI)	Green Deal Finance Plan Tenant Rent Arrears Loans (Scot & Wales) Recovery Loan Scheme
Property Trader	Employment Grants	Start Up Loan Scheme Recovery Loan Scheme
Property Developer	Employment Grants Domestic Renewable Heat Incentive (D-RHI)	Start Up Loan Scheme Recovery Loan Scheme Building Fund Loans
Property Services Businesses	Employment Grants	Start Up Loan Scheme Recovery Loan Scheme

The Headlines

Here we will summarise the key types of grant and soft loan available. Later, we will cover the details should you want to dig a bit deeper.

Grants

There are literally hundreds of different grants available right now. Some are managed at a national level, many at a regional level and most at a local level. So, yes, it's bloomin' complicated I grant you that! 😉 However, if you know where to look, how to hit the right notes and have the patience to push through the red tape, there's money to be had to help support your property business.

1. **Energy-Related Grants** – the Energy Company Obligation (ECO) is an obligation on energy suppliers to fund the cost of certain energy-improvement works for people on benefits (including tenants). Then, the Domestic Renewable Heat Incentive (D-RHI) reimburses some of the cost of installation of renewable heat equipment with incoming payments over seven years.

2. **Empty Homes Grant** – this grant is operated locally by each local authority and as such varies from authority to authority. Most local authorities will prioritise bringing empty homes back into the housing stock and could provide some financial aid in that regard. A typical grant award can be between £5,000 or £15,000 and up to 50% of the total cost of the renovation work, depending on subsequent occupation and who is applying. I have just received one of these grants myself, as it happens.

3. **Business Grants** – the government wants to incentivise the employment of young people, with their Kickstart Scheme and Apprenticeships. In a nutshell, employ a young person and you can be awarded up to £5,000 in government grants for doing so. Under the Kickstart Scheme, the young person also has national minimum wage covered for 25 hours per week for 6 months. The Apprenticeship Scheme has a one-off cash grant payment and then 90% of the cost of training paid for by the government.

Soft Loans

There are a number of government-backed or 'soft loans' available right now that can benefit the property sector.

1. **Help to Buy (HTB)** – is something of an umbrella term that includes Help to Buy Equity Loan and Help to Buy Shared Ownership, which can help home buyers get on the housing ladder. In addition, developers can make their new-build developments more appealing to buyers with low deposits. This has been supplemented by the Mortgage Guarantee Scheme announced in the March 2021 Budget, enabling

more 95% LTV mortgages to come to the market. There is also Right to Buy in three guises that enables social housing tenants to buy their homes at a discount for a 'curveball play'.

2. **Business Loans** – there are a number of government-backed loans, which allow lenders to offer financing to businesses in the property sector that might not otherwise qualify. For example, some of the loans might not require additional security in the form of guarantees or charges against the home of the business owner, making the lending less risky to both the borrower and lender alike. There is the Building Fund Loan, available to developers, which can offer up to 80% loan-to-cost on a development project. There is the Recovery Loan Scheme, which replaces the Bounce Back and Coronavirus Business Interruption Loan Schemes, again on favourable terms. There is also the Start Up Loan Scheme, which provides lending for businesses starting out to help them with their business planning, start-up mentoring and other related costs of up to £25,000.

3. **Landlord-Friendly Loans** – there is a loan scheme available under the Green Deal. The loan allows a landlord to significantly or even fully fund energy improvement works with payments spread out over time. Whilst most of the schemes that I refer to relate to England due to space limitations, it is worth checking what the equivalent is with other devolved UK nations. One area where England lags behind is with tenant arrears. However, if your rental property is in Scotland or Wales, then there are tenant arrears loan schemes to assist tenants that have fallen into arrears due to Coronavirus. Come on England, let's catch up!

The Details

In their different ways, national government, local government, landlords and developers all share an interest in improving the quality and quantity of the country's housing stock. Although grants are available to landlords, investors and developers, the picture may be confusing at times because of the different policies at national and at local level, along with the regular tinkering that seems to take place – including during the writing of this book!

Section 1 – Grants

1. Energy-Related Grants

There are currently two main types of grant relevant to the property sector: Domestic Renewable Heat Incentive (D-RHI) and Energy Company Obligation (ECO).

Domestic Renewable Heat Incentive (RHI)

The Domestic Renewable Heat Incentive (D-RHI) is a government financial incentive to promote the use of renewable heat. Switching to heating systems that use eligible energy sources can help the UK reduce its carbon emissions and meet its renewable energy targets.

People who join the scheme and stick to its rules receive quarterly payments for seven years for the amount of clean, green renewable heat it's estimated their system produces. The four eligible renewable technologies that qualify are biomass boilers and stoves, ground source and air source heat pumps, and solar thermal panels

The scheme is open to anyone who can meet the joining requirements. It's for households both off and on the gas grid and is administered by OFGEM.

ECO – Energy Company Obligation

If you want to make energy improvements to your property or its heating system, then the main source of help is a scheme called the Energy Company Obligation (ECO). This is a nationwide scheme that obliges energy companies to install energy efficiency measures in the homes of those who need them most.

If someone in the occupant's household receives a pension or is on benefits, then more support schemes are available. However, some financial support, grants and loans are available to everyone. Different grants are available in England, Scotland, Wales and Northern Ireland.

The ECO scheme means that medium and large gas and electricity suppliers are obliged to help households with energy efficiency measures. Energy efficiency measures available through ECO include loft insulation, cavity wall insulation, solid wall insulation and boiler replacement or repair. They're all designed to help save people money on their energy bills, keep homes warmer and help to reduce carbon emissions.

The current scheme, called ECO3, was launched in December 2018. It runs until 31 March 2022 and is focused exclusively on those customers with lower incomes who are considered to be in vulnerable situations or living in fuel poverty.

It's quite complicated to work out if you're eligible for ECO funding. It depends on what improvements your home needs, where you live, the level of carbon or cost savings made, and if you or your tenants receive any benefits. If the occupant receives the Warm Home Discount, or certain types of benefits, you're likely to be eligible. The ECO3 scheme, unlike previous schemes, includes those receiving Child Benefit and disability benefits. Your energy supplier should advise you if you're eligible for an ECO grant, also known as Affordable Warmth. You may also be eligible for help with insulation or installing a gas boiler or heating system if you're a social housing tenant and in a home with an energy efficiency rating of E, F or G. You can also contact the Energy Saving Trust for more details or Home Energy Scotland. To benefit from ECO, you must either own your home or have the landlord's permission. Even if you are eligible, an energy supplier doesn't have to install an energy efficient measure in your home.

TPV TIP: There can sometimes be a financial reward for doing good! Energy efficiency supports the environmental agenda and helping tenants that are in danger of 'fuel poverty' to reduce their energy-related cost of living is good for society at large. You might not need incentivising to consider these sorts of issues, but a little bit of financial support can be a welcome upside for doing so.

---

2. Empty Homes Grants

There are a range of grants and loans for landlords and property investors to incentivise bringing empty homes back into the housing stock. However, what is available varies from council to council.

There are grants available for improving energy efficiency, HMO conversions and the renovation of empty properties for use by tenants. This form of funding is very complicated and each council has different criteria for awarding these types of grants to landlords. For example, some means-test landlords to assess whether they are eligible for the grant and others specifically target landlords that already have tenants in place.

According to the Homes and Communities Agency, empty housing accounts for 700,000 or more dwellings. The amount of funding is allocated on a regional basis, so it could be something of a 'postcode lottery' you might say.

If you own a property and it has been empty for more than one year, you also have the option of being able to let it to council-nominated tenants on a long-term lease – usually between five and ten years. If you do this, you could be eligible for an Empty Property grant.

This form of funding covers 50% of the cost of renovation work, including any heating or insulation improvement works. The grant can also be used for properties that are in a substantial state of disrepair or to convert a property from being a single household to a multi household.

Depending on where you intend to buy to let, you might also apply for different types of improvement grants offered by a number of local authorities.

Most of the local authorities that make grants available also impose conditions on use. For example, some local authorities will attach conditions that grants are used to bring properties up to the Decent Homes Standard.

TPV TIP: Targeting empty homes to acquire and renovate and applying for a grant to subsidise the work is great potential property strategy. It combines the creative approach of looking for empty properties, both on and off the open market, with a grant subsidy that can improve our overall return on investment.

These grants are provided at the discretion of your local authority and are means-tested. This basically means that the amount you will receive is dependent on your income, so the more you earn the less the grant will be. Besides this, here are some of the common criteria:

- £20,000 maximum award for homeowners/tenants. It cannot be a second or holiday home.

- £5,000 to £15,000 awarded for landlords.

- The property must have been built more than 10 years ago.

- In the case of homeowner applications, it must have been unoccupied for at least three years before the grant request (one year for landlords).

- There are also conditions to be met for 10 years by homeowner and five years for landlords. If the conditions are not met or the property is sold, then the grant must be repaid.

Renovations that qualify for this grant are those needed to improve the property up to the Decent Homes Standard. This can include improvements such as damp-proofing, roofing, double-glazed window and doors replacement, insulation and heating system improvement works. Energy efficiency improvement helps to increase the property's value, can save on fuel bills and also reduces the property's carbon footprint.

3. Houses in Multiple Occupation (HMO) Conversion Grant

The HMO conversion grant can be anything up to £30,000 and is used to bring the property in line with the minimum HMO standards. This type of work includes fitting the appropriate fire precaution and safety measures for tenants and meeting the minimum standards required for fixed amenities, such as kitchens and bathrooms. There are many conditions to meet in order to be eligible for the HMO Conversion grant and these vary depending on your local council.

TPV TIP: HMO supply varies across the country. In some locations, they have mushroomed and led to Article 4 Directives being put in place to limit their supply. However, in other areas, there is still a need for this type of housing and a number of local authorities earmark particular grants for bringing HMOs in their area up to government standards.

---

4. Business Grants

The most relevant areas where property-related businesses can make grant claims surrounds employment. In addition, there may be certain tax breaks open to businesses, which you will find more information on in Chapter 11: Tax Reliefs and Credits.

There are two main employment grant schemes: Apprenticeships and the Kickstart Scheme, which are both targeted at reducing young people's unemployment.

Apprenticeships

Here are the key criteria:

- Apprentices are aged 16 or over and combine working with studying to gain skills and knowledge in a specific job.

- Apprentices can be new or current employees.

- They must be paid at least the minimum wage.

- The apprentice must: work with experienced staff, learn job-specific skills and get at least 20% of their normal working hours off for training or study.

You can hire your apprentice yourself or use a training provider to help. You can claim £3,000 for apprentices who start between 1 April 2021 and 30 September 2021. The government will cover 95% of the cost of their training. Apprenticeships must last for at least a year. They can last up to five years depending on the level the apprentice is studying.

Clearly, this scheme will end soon after the publication of this book. However, keep checking the gov.uk website, as schemes could be revised, extended or replaced to meet the government's unemployment targets.

Kickstart Scheme Grant

If you're an employer looking to create job placements for young people, you can apply for funding as part of the Kickstart Scheme. The Kickstart Scheme provides funding to create new job placements for people aged 16 to 24 claiming Universal Credit, who are at risk of long-term unemployment.

Employers can spread the start date of the job placements up until the end of December 2021. Further funding is available to provide support so that young people on the scheme can get a job in the future.

The funding:
- You'll get £1,500 funding per job placement. This should be spent on set-up costs and supporting the young person to develop their employability skills.

- 100% of the National Minimum/Living Wage (depending on the age of the participant) for 25 hours per week for a total of six months.

- Associated employer National Insurance contributions and employer minimum automatic enrolment contributions.

Employers can pay a higher wage and for more hours but the funding will not cover this.

The job placements created with the Kickstart Scheme funding must be for 'net new jobs' and are best suited for jobs needing only basic training. You must help the young person become more employable in the future. It is fair to say that many of the candidates for this scheme could be considered as vulnerable to long-term unemployment without this support.

TPV TIP: As an employer, we need to take a view on what type of role is best suited and also the contribution towards the job seeker's future employment prospects, regardless of which of these schemes catches our eye. Just as we should not let the tax tail wag the property business dog, the same can be said about grants – they are notoriously tricky processes to navigate. Free money is not necessarily easy money!

Section 2 – Soft Loans (Government-Backed)

1. Help-to-Buy (HTB)

The government has created the Help to Buy schemes including Help to Buy: Shared Ownership and Help to Buy: Equity Loan to help people buy their own home. These schemes help developers to sell their new-build developments too.

HTB Equity Loan

If you're a first-time buyer in England, you can apply for a Help to Buy: Equity Loan. This is a loan from the government that you put towards the cost of buying a newly built home. You can borrow a minimum of 5% and up to a maximum of 20% (40% in London) of the full purchase price of a new-build home. The homebuilder must be registered for Help to Buy: Equity Loan.

The amount you pay for a home using the scheme is capped and depends on where in England you buy it. The price caps until 2023 range from approximately £186,000 in the north-east to £600,000 in London.

The equity loan, the deposit saved, and the repayment mortgage cover the total cost of buying the newly built home. The percentage borrowed is based on the market value of your home when you buy it. You do not pay interest on the equity loan for the first five years. You start to pay interest in year six, on the equity loan amount you borrowed.

When deciding if an equity loan is right for you, it's important to consider the full cost of your borrowing. For the first five years, the equity loan is interest-free. From year six, you pay monthly interest at 1.75% of the equity loan, which will rise each year in April by the Consumer Price Index (CPI), plus 2% until you repay your loan in full.

You must repay your equity loan in full at the end of the equity loan term, when you pay off the repayment mortgage, when you sell your home or if you are in breach of the loan terms. The amount you pay back is worked out as a percentage of the market value at the time you choose to repay. If the market value of your home rises, so does the amount you owe on your equity loan. And if the value of your home falls, the amount you owe on your equity loan falls too.

This makes the government your joint venture partner in case you hadn't realised!

HTB Shared Ownership

If you can't quite afford the mortgage on 100% of the purchase price of a new home, Help to Buy: Shared Ownership offers you the chance to buy a share of your home (between 25% and 75% of the home's value) and pay rent on the remaining share. Later on, you could buy bigger shares when you can afford to.

You could buy a home through Help to Buy: Shared Ownership in England if your household earns £80,000 a year or less (£90,000 in London) and you are a first-time buyer, you used to own a home but can't afford to buy one now or are an existing shared owner looking to move.

With Help to Buy: Shared Ownership you can buy a newly built home or an existing one through resale programmes from housing associations. You'll need to take out a mortgage to pay for your share of the home's purchase price, or fund this through your savings. Shared Ownership properties are always leasehold.

In addition to military personnel, councils with their own shared ownership home-building programmes may have some priority groups, based on local housing needs. Specialist support could be available for people with disabilities or the elderly.

Right to Buy/Acquire

A quick word about Right to Buy or Acquire, which allows qualified tenants to purchase their home at an attractive discount. It's very niche but if it does apply to you, or someone close to you, there's money to be claimed.

- Right to Buy – if you're a council tenant in England the Right to Buy scheme could help you buy the home you rent with a discount of up to £78,600 (£104,900 in London).

- Right to Acquire – if you're a housing association tenant in England you could be eligible to buy the home you rent with a discount of between £9,000 and £16,000.

- Preserved Right to Buy – if you're a housing association tenant in England you could be eligible to buy the home you rent with a discount of up to £78,600 (£104,900 in London).

Mortgage Guarantee Scheme

In the March 2021 Budget, Chancellor Rishi Sunak confirmed that the government was launching a mortgage guarantee scheme aimed to make it easier for those with a 5% deposit to buy a home.

The mortgage guarantee scheme will see the government guaranteeing 95% mortgages for buyers with 5% deposits. The scheme has been designed to encourage banks to start offering 95% mortgages again, after nearly every single one was withdrawn during the pandemic. Under the terms of the scheme, the government will guarantee the portion of the mortgage over 80% (so, with a 95% mortgage, the excess of 15% is guaranteed). This might sound complicated, but in practice it just means the government will partially compensate the lender if a homeowner fails to pay their mortgage.

Some of the eligibility criteria:

- Buyers with a 5% deposit will be able to apply for a 95% loan-to-value (LTV) mortgage deal with participating lenders.

- Available on properties costing a maximum of £600,000.

- The Government will act as a guarantor to the lender.

- Available to both first-time buyers and those who have already owned a property.

- Similar affordability and eligibility requirements would be needed for a standard mortgage.

TPV TIP: You might be wondering why I have chosen to include a section on Help to Buy, Right to Buy/Acquire and the Mortgage Guarantee Scheme in this book. The short explanation is this: leverage. These schemes offer favourable terms to homeowner buyers, with some strings attached. However, by carefully adopting one or more of these subsidy schemes, we could acquire either our own home with a lower deposit or even a discount for ourselves or a family member with Right to Buy/Acquire. In addition, if we are able to put down a lower deposit on buying our own home, then we might have additional funds available to consider for a subsequent investment property as well. Every little helps…

2. Business Loans

Start Up Loans

The Start Up Loans initiative offered via the British Business Bank provides government-backed unsecured personal loans for UK entrepreneurs to start a business. These government-funded loans are designed for new businesses, either in the planning stage or in the first 12 months of trading. A Start Up Loan can help you achieve your business goals with a loan of up to £25,000, at 6% interest p.a., repayment term of one to five years, no application or set up fees and free mentoring for 12 months.

Enterprise Finance Guarantee (EFG)

If you're looking to grow your business, an Enterprise Finance Guarantee (EFG) government loan could be a good option. The EFG scheme encourages lending to viable UK businesses that lack sufficient security but otherwise qualify for a loan. The scheme covers new term loans for working capital or investment purposes, asset finance, debt consolidation and refinancing.

This government loan guarantee scheme provides accredited lenders with a government-backed guarantee for 75% of the loan value. Loans of £1,000 to £1.2 million are available, with a minimum term of three months and a maximum of ten years for loans under £600,000, and five years for larger loans.

Start-ups and small businesses with few or no assets to borrow against often find that open market borrowing is out of their reach and government loans can bridge this gap with a focus on the longer-term benefits. These can often be in the form of low-cost government loans with the potential for discounted rates and in some cases no or limited security.

3. Support for Developers

Home Building Fund

In England, small builders can access finance via the Home Building Fund. Secured loans of between £250,000 and £250 million are available with smaller sums for innovative housing projects. Similar schemes are available in other parts of the UK. Government redevelopment loans may be available for projects in designated redevelopment areas with loan terms of typically five years.

The revitalised fund will continue to be available nationally, although there will be an increased focus on investment in areas with the highest affordability pressures.

The other major programmes open to private developers for the purposes of this book are:

- The £150m **Custom Build Serviced Plots Loan Fund** supports projects that create five or more serviced building plots for private homebuilders.

- The £525m **Builders Finance Fund** supports projects of five to 250 homes undertaken by smaller developers.

- Grant funding and technical support is available via the £22.5m **Neighbourhood Planning programme** and the £3.5m **Community Buildings Fund**.

- The **Housing Growth Partnership** has been established by the Government in partnership with Lloyds Banking Group to make £100m available to small and medium-sized builders to support projects of between five and 75 homes.

Homes England/Invest & Fund 7-year lending partnership

Homes England and Invest & Fund, a P2P lender, recently announced a seven-year partnership to increase the amount of finance available to SME developers to help them grow and deliver more homes at pace.

The collaboration will create a £25m revolving fund to allow Invest & Fund to support small builders with construction loans of between £400k and £2.5m, funding schemes of two homes and upwards, at up to 80% Loan-To-Cost or 65% LTGDV.

TPV TIP: Many developers struggle to raise finance on decent terms, which is something of a Catch-22 situation. These government-backed schemes are designed to overcome this conundrum. They are even more likely to be accepted where the scheme has a wider level of environmental, historical or societal impact.

---

4. Coronavirus Business Support Loans

Bounce Back Loan Scheme (BBLS)

BBLS was introduced during the coronavirus pandemic during 2020. BBLS offered lending on favourable terms to small and medium-sized businesses in the UK. The BBLS has closed to new applications, so by now you will either have one or not. The reason that this is mentioned here is that if you do have an existing BBLS in place, then there is a so-called Pay As You Grow 'PAYG' range of additional support measures that may be of interest to support you.

PAYG Additional Measures

- request an extension of their loan term to 10 years from six years, at the same fixed interest rate of 2.5%

- reduce monthly repayments for six months by paying interest only. This option is available up to three times during the term of their Bounce Back Loan

- take a repayment holiday for up to six months. This option is available once during the term of their Bounce Back Loan.

Borrowers can use these options individually or in combination with each other.

Recovery Loan Scheme

The Recovery Loan Scheme provides businesses of any size access to loans and other kinds of finance up to £10 million per business once the previous COVID-19 loan schemes, i.e. Bounce Back Loans Scheme or BBLS and Coronavirus Business Interruption Loans Scheme or CBILS), close. This will provide support as businesses recover and grow following the disruption of the pandemic and the end of the transition period.

Once received, the finance can be used for any legitimate business purpose, including growth and investment. The government guarantees 80% of the finance to the lender to ensure they continue to have the confidence to lend to businesses. The scheme launches in April 2021 and is open until December 2021, subject to review. Loans will be available through a network of accredited lenders.

The type of finance available:

- Term loans and overdrafts will be available between £25,001 and £10 million per business.

- Invoice finance and asset finance will be available between £1,000 and £10 million per business.

Finance terms are up to six years for term loans and asset finance facilities. For overdrafts and invoice finance facilities, terms will be up to three years. No personal guarantees will be taken on facilities up to £250,000, and a borrower's principal private residence cannot be taken as security.

You will be able to apply for a loan if your business is trading in the UK, is viable or would be viable were it not for the pandemic, has been impacted by the coronavirus pandemic and is not in collective insolvency proceedings. Businesses that have received support under the existing COVID-19 guaranteed loan schemes will still be eligible to access finance under this scheme.

TPV TIP: There has not been as much peacetime financial aid to businesses as there has been throughout and following the global pandemic. Every business should carefully examine its financial needs and if it genuinely qualifies for these sorts of supported lending schemes, they can offer very attractive terms with potentially lower levels of security than would otherwise be the case.

---

5. Landlord-Friendly Loans

Green Deal Finance Plan

The Green Deal Finance Plan is available to support the government's Green Deal scheme for owners of any residential property (owner-occupiers and landlords) for home improvements that lead to energy saving in areas such as heating, insulation, double glazing, draught exclusion measures or renewable energy installations.

Provided the property has an electricity meter (including pre-paid meters), you may apply for a Green Deal assessment, which recommends any qualifying energy saving improvements that may be made and the amount you are likely to save on your energy bills each year. The Green Deal Finance Plan links the repayment of the improvements to the energy bill for the property. The cost of the work is financed, usually with interest from a finance company, over an extended period of time. The repayment term usually reflects in how long the energy savings will take to be repaid, to offset the subsequent costs of the finance. Thus, repayments are directly linked to the energy savings predicted.

Tenant Arrears Loans (Scotland & Wales Only)

In Scotland only, a £10 million fund which offers interest-free loans to tenants who are struggling with rent arrears during the pandemic opened for applications. The Tenant Hardship Loan Fund is designed to help tenants who have had their finances or employment impacted by the coronavirus pandemic.

By giving tenants access to loans to cover a maximum of nine months worth of rent arrears and five-year repayment terms, it provides another option for people who can't claim support from other means, such as welfare benefits.

A similar scheme called Tenant Saver Loan is open in Wales until September 2021, having been extended from March 2021. It remains to be seen if it will be continued after this date.

From a landlord's point of view, these schemes enable a tenant to take a loan to repay their rental arrears and so avoids financial pressure being transferred on to the landlord or a threat of eviction to the tenant. It's a pity that they are only available in Scotland and Wales…

TPV TIP: These are novel and niche ways to support us in our property endeavours. Taking the Green Deal Finance Plan as an example, even though the finance might carry interest, it can still be paid for out of future energy savings. This makes it a viable business case to consider undertaking energy-improvement investment in our existing portfolio without an up-front cash outlay.

Advantages and Benefits

There are several advantages to seeking out grants and soft loans:

- Grants are essentially 'free money' that can subsidise our property investing, developing or business activities. The funds drop straight onto the bottom line to convert a poor investment proposition into a good one or make a good one even better.

- Soft loans are a little like the Star Trek Enterprise – they allow us to go where no man (and woman) has gone before! Or to translate – funding options are available to us where the mainstream lenders would simply say no.

- Many of these forms of finance have environmental or societal benefits attached to them. As a result, they encourage and financially incentivise action for the greater good.

Disadvantages and Risks

There are, naturally, also several disadvantages to seeking out grants and soft loans:

- Grants might be 'free money' but they are rarely 'easy money'. This is taxpayers' money and so quite rightly, there needs to be a high level of scrutiny, red tape and hoops to jump through before you get it. Everything comes at a price, including free money!

- Soft loans sound appealing on the surface, although at times the criteria can be quite restrictive and so not as readily available as you might have expected. Equally, the process is often more drawn out with 'work' at the start, middle and end in a lot of cases.

- There are literally hundreds of grants and soft loans available at any given time. In addition, the rules are constantly changing, so its difficult to stay up to date with everything that's going on. In some cases, grants need to be paid during a certain financial year to become a 'use it or lose it' kind of game.

Reality Check

I'm often in two minds when it comes to the topic of applying for state aid, be that in the form of grants or soft loans. On the one hand, it can literally be 'free money' or 'money with strings attached' anyway. This can significantly and positively impact our financial returns. It can often turn a no-project into a maybe and a maybe-project into a yes. In fact, I have first-hand experience of claiming grants and soft loans in several of my own businesses over the years. There is always that warm, fuzzy feeling that you get when you see the funds drop into your bank account.

On the other hand, it can also be a torturous or tiresome process to go through. Government funding has to be carefully controlled, for obvious reasons. This can mean a much higher level of time input, administrative compliance and wading through the sheer volume of options and eligibility criteria – sometimes with an ultimately disappointing outcome. As I like to say, there's always a trade-off or a price to pay for everything that we do. So, we just need to assess whether we are prepared to pay that price or not really.

On balance, I would say that it is worth the time to explore the idea of using grants and soft loans in your property business. One final recommendation would be to not be too greedy and look to give up approximately 10% to 15% of the grant award to hire in a specialist to support you with the search and application process. It will save you time and hassle worth far more than it costs financially. That's probably a fair compromise to get a decent outcome, I would suggest.

Finally, as with all matters relating to government policy, things can and do change – often! I mentioned that certain grants and loan options changed as I was writing this book and sometimes abruptly. So, please keep this in mind and remember that it is the principle of accessing and utilising grants and soft loans that is more important, rather than the specifics that are outlined within this book. Some of what I mentioned will expire, change shape or be replaced in the shelf life of this book. This is fair warning in case some grants and loans mentioned are no longer available when you go to look.

Chapter Eleven

Tax Breaks, Reliefs and Credits

What You Need To Know

The first point to make about tax is this: it's another area that's bloomin' complicated! There are literally dozens of different taxes and reliefs that we could encounter as property business operators. Equally, the legal entity/ entities we choose to operate through, along with the specific activities that we undertake (investment, trading, development, services, etc.) also have an impact on how we are taxed.

This is not a book on property taxation. It is a book that includes some suggestions on how we can utilise taxation to help finance our property businesses. For this reason, there is a double disclaimer for this section. This is for information purposes only; I am not giving financial and/or tax advice. I am also specifically advising that you consult the appropriate professional advisors before implementing anything outlined here, just to be sure.

Everyone's situation is different and often there is a trade-off to be made. With the potential cost of a tax investigation, non-compliance or contravention of the rules being potentially high, the risk of getting it wrong should also be taken into consideration. So, taking personalised, professional advice is the only way to go in my opinion.

That all being said, here are some of the juicy ways in which you could consider legitimate tax strategies as a part of your overall property finance strategy.

Landlord Tax Reliefs

As a landlord you can claim various deductions from your rental profits to reduce the tax due and payable on your rental income.

TPV TIP: If you own property in individual names and jointly with another person, such as your spouse, partner or even a business/investment partner, you can agree to an uneven split of income between the parties. This could then allow a person with a more favourable income tax position to assume most of the tax burden and so potentially reduce the overall tax deductions on the property.

These are the main deductions and/or reliefs allowed as a landlord, assuming you own a property in individual name(s):

Allowable expense deductions – these include letting agent fees, council tax and utility bills (when you are responsible to pay these), insurances, licenses and service charges, professional fees (except those directly relating to arranging property finance, which is subject to different rules) and finally, repairs and maintenance (subject to conditions as outlined below).

Replacement of 'Domestic Items' – in the past, there was the 'fair wear and tear allowance', which no longer applies. Instead, as a landlord we are allowed to deduct the cost of replacing an item on a 'like-for-like basis' but NOT claim for the original investment or an upgraded replacement against our Income Tax. Costs to repair and/or replace an item on a like-for-like basis are allowable deductions from our Income Tax bill. Initial capital expenditure can, however, usually only be offset against any capital gain on disposal of an asset.

Finance-related costs – this has changed a LOT in recent times, with the so-called Section 24 mortgage interest relief being introduced in April 2017.

It can be complex to work it out. Essentially, we are allowed a relief rather than a tax deduction (the distinction is relevant) from our rental profits equivalent to the basic rate of tax on both finance interest payments and the professional fees (broker, lender, legal, etc.) associated with arranging that finance. If you are a higher-rate taxpayer, then you can only receive the relief up to the basic rate level. Equally, as the relief is applied AFTER establishing the rental profits, this also means that these finance-related expenses are INCLUDED in the profit calculation, which could additionally change which tax band you are taxed in. Yes, if you read that carefully it could mean you are penalised twice should this push you into a higher tax bracket!

TPV TIP: Whilst tax rates and bands change, an individual earning up to around £50,000 per year or a couple earning up to around £100,000 per year may not be unduly affected by these S24 tax limitations to interest deductions. For the accidental or amateur landlord that is a basic rate taxpayer, owning rental property in individual names might well be the best bet. However, for more professional landlords – those in it for the long-term and those seeking to acquire significant property interests or higher-rate taxpayers – looking at company ownership or furnished holiday lets might well be worth exploring as a tax mitigation strategy. There are also several non-tax reasons to consider alternatives, including estate planning, limited liability and so on.

Other allowable expenses – there are some other deductions and reliefs available to a landlord as a legitimate tax deduction. These include, the costs of travel and other costs relating to managing your portfolio, upgrading your existing knowledge through training, mentoring, etc. (sadly not learning something new), using your home as an office and a tax-free allowance on certain interest received from lending to the property business.

Different rules apply to property investment companies and owners of qualifying Furnished Holiday Lets (FHL). In particular, the costs of financing are fully deductible in these situations and the corporation tax rate is lower than the personal Income Tax rate, currently.

Tax is such a complex area that is forever changing, so my best advice is to retain the services of a decent tax accountant who clearly understands the property sector – they should be worth the fee once you get to a reasonable level of investment.

TPV TIP: I use the 80/20 Rule when it comes to tax, I have a working knowledge of the main areas of taxation by subscribing to tax briefing services such as *Tax Insider* or *Tax Café* to get an 80% view. I then speak to my tax accountant a couple of times a year or when I have a significant 'tax event' to discuss with them the remaining 20% for more specialist or current knowledge. It's worth being generally tax-aware but best to pay for specialist tax advice when it's required to be safe.

Other Tax Breaks

Capital Gains Tax

When you sell an asset, such as a property, at a profit, the profit or gain will be subject to Capital Gains Tax (CGT). There are some offsets against CGT that can help to reduce the tax charge, including:

Qualifying capital expenditure – these are costs associated with improving the capital value of the property, which have not been claimed against income tax. These might include structural alterations, initial furnishing costs and other capital improvements, such as an upgraded kitchen, solar panels and so on.

Buying and selling costs – these are the costs associated with buying and selling the property, including estate agent fees, legal conveyancing fees, original purchase financing fees and surveys.

Allowances – in addition to the actual costs which can be deducted, we are also permitted to make a deduction for Primary Residence Relief (time when we lived in the property as our main home), our personal annual CGT allowance (£12,300 per owner at the time of writing in May 2021) and also capital losses and reliefs from the current or previous tax years.

TPV TIP: Buying and selling a property for profit without renting it is classed as a trading activity and therefore is subject to Income Tax for an individual. However, selling a property that has been rented for a reasonable period of time is subject to CGT and not Income Tax. Due to the reliefs and allowances available in the case of CGT, it could make more sense to hold property and rent it for a time before selling it on. Care must be taken not to use this as a deliberate and repeating strategy to avoid attempting to game the system and still be classed as a property trader, however. It's just a way to recognise that the tax treatment on rental property gains is more favourable to that on straightforward property trading that's all.

Reduced Rate VAT

VAT is an additional cost to most investors and developers. It not only adds to the cost of the work on a property but also drags on the cashflow as well. The most straightforward way to reclaim VAT is to become VAT registered – this can be done on a voluntary basis and you don't need to turnover more than the annual VAT threshold that's required to formerly register and charge VAT. This means that all 'input VAT' can be reclaimed back from HMRC on all expenses that attract VAT.

The downside, besides the additional administration and accounting work, is that 'output VAT' would then also need to be applied to any qualifying turnover as well. This could make such turnover more expensive to people and businesses that are not themselves VAT registered. Fortunately, rent on residential and letting property is VAT exempt. Equally, on commercial property, unless the owner has 'opted to tax', VAT would not be an additional cost. However, some charges made by property investors, developers or service providers would attract output VAT, including commercial rent and the sale of a commercial building (if opted to tax) and serviced accommodation/short-term letting charges. Other charges – such as services, training, sourcing fees and the like, with other activities in the property sector – could also be subject to VAT, if you elect to be VAT registered or when your VAT-able supplies exceed the annual VAT threshold (£85,000 in May 2021.

For property developers, there are some VAT savings in two key areas: new-build developments and conversion projects. New-build development work is zero-rated for VAT purposes, which means that you should be able to get your contractors to charge VAT at 0% for ground-up development work. Be careful here though, as not all work would qualify to be zero-rated, such as professional fees, general site or general project costs being examples. Equally, you might need to enlist a specialist to ensure that you have the correct certification BEFORE starting work to avoid potential challenges and painful reclaims later on.

In the case of property conversions, a reduced rate of 5% VAT should be applied to qualifying expenditure. VAT is charged at the reduced rate of 5% on the supply of services and building materials for:

- The conversion of non-residential property into residential property

- The conversion of a residential property into a different number of residential units or changing the total number of dwellings

- The conversion of residential or non-residential property into a multiple occupancy dwelling (e.g. bed-sits or an HMO)

- The conversion of a care home etc. into a multiple occupancy dwelling

- The conversion of non-residential property or one or more residential properties into a care home, children's home, hospice etc. (where the services are supplied to the person who intends to use the property for that purpose)

- And the renovation or alteration of dwellings, multiple occupancy properties and care homes etc. that have been empty for three years or more.

VAT on Serviced Accommodation (SA)/Furnished Holiday Lets (FHL)

One last word on VAT is regarding SA and FHLs, where VAT would be chargeable once the level of turnover exceeds the annual VAT threshold, currently standing at £85,000. This means that VAT would need to be added to all SA/FHL rental charges once this level of turnover is reached. Or, to put it a different way, it is more likely to mean a reduced net rental income, as it's difficult to charge more than current market rates for the same rental accommodation, especially to non-business travellers.

One potential workaround here is to use the Tour Operators Margin Scheme (TOMS) if you are operating on an agency or rent-to-rent basis renting short-term and holiday let accommodation. Here, you would not be able to recover any input VAT but the output VAT would only be on your margin and not the full rental value. As you could offset the incoming rental or lease costs of the property, this could produce a significant saving on VAT, or more likely, your retained profits as a large-scale operator.

There are some conditions around the application of TOMS and it might not always be worthwhile – but it's a little-known VAT saving strategy if it fits your requirements.

TPV TIP: If buying a commercial building that is opted to tax, meaning the purchase price is subject to VAT, there are a couple of angles worth considering to avoid this VAT cost becoming an additional cost of acquisition. The buyer can also opt to tax and so can reclaim the VAT paid that way. However, if the building is sold as a Transfer of a Going Concern 'TOGC', meaning it is leased out for three years or more prior to the sale, then the purchase price and the subsequent rent is exempt from VAT.

Capital Allowances

You are entitled to claim capital allowances on qualifying fixtures and fittings in your property, if you are an owner of commercial property and subject to UK tax. Capital allowances apply whether you own the property as an investment or it is used in your trading business. The definition of commercial property could be quite broad to potentially include an HMO, serviced accommodation or property to be converted, for example.

Qualifying expenditure can arise on the acquisition of a building, construction of a new building, extension, alteration or refurbishment of an existing building, and leasehold improvements to a rented property. If you can imagine picking up a building and shaking it; the items that would come loose from the floors, walls and roof could be classed as allowable fixtures and fittings that could be claimable. This could include, lighting and electrical, air conditioning, heating and plumbing, and sanitary ware.

Reliefs will vary, so engaging with a specialist capital allowances assessor is a very sensible suggestion here, I would suggest. My general rule of thumb is that the extent of qualifying capital allowances should probably be upwards of £30,000 in value to make the time and expense of the claim exercise worthwhile. I found some of the information in this section from various articles on www.rsmuk.com, which specialises in capital allowance claims, so whilst this is not a review or recommendation for their work, you might want to start there to find out more information.

Stamp Duty Land Tax (SDLT)

SDLT in England and Northern Ireland and its equivalents of Land and Buildings Transaction Tax in Scotland and Land Transaction Tax in Wales, is often seen as an unavoidable cost of buying property. There are different SDLT rates for residential and non-residential property, both of which are based around applying a percentage against the purchase price in incremental rates on a stepped-level threshold basis.

I won't list out the various thresholds and tax rates here, as these are constantly changing and readily available from the www.gov.uk website. However, I do want to share some of the SDLT and equivalent tax savings strategies here by way of a signpost for you to look into.

Potential ways to save on SDLT and it's equivalents include:

Multiple Dwellings Relief – in essence, if you buy two properties in a linked transaction, you are able to elect to use the average purchase price for SDLT purposes rather than the individual purchase prices. This is most effective when the prices paid are different and importantly, span different SDLT thresholds.

Chattels – SDLT is not paid on certain items that are often included in a property purchase but are not part of the fabric of the building. However, they are often not specified, but if they were separately specified it could lead to a saving in SDLT as a result. Examples of a chattel include, carpets, curtains, free-standing furniture and white goods.

Non-Residential Rates – typically, SDLT attracts a lower rate for non-residential property compared to residential property. Therefore, if you can class your transaction as non-residential, then you could save money on SDLT. Examples where this could be possible include: six or more residential properties bought in a single transaction (e.g. blocks & portfolios), derelict property (not simply having no functioning bathroom or kitchen as some would have you believe!), commercial and 'mixed-use property', forests and agricultural land on a working farm, among others.

Property Traders – if you are flipping property, then in certain circumstances there is no SDLT to pay at all! Strange as it may seem, this depends on the status of the seller and not the buyer. Examples where this could apply include probate sales by the personal representatives of the deceased estate, when a chain has broken down or if the seller is relocating due to their employment.

First-Time Buyers (FTB) and Homeowners Moving Home – FTBs pay little or no SDLT when compared with other buyers. Of course, this can only happen once on their first home. Similarly, people buying their own home will avoid paying the 3% additional premium that property investors would typically have to pay. However, if you are genuinely able to claim to be a FTB or a homeowner moving home, then you can make some savings on SDLT.

TPV TIP: One FTB myth is that you cannot own an investment property before owning your own home if you want to avoid paying the 3% additional SDLT. In fact, if you were to buy your investment property through a limited company rather than your personal name, then HMRC guidance is that this would not remove your FTB status when you come to buy your own home. It's buried in the small print and not even many conveyancers know this; but it's a fact! Make sure it still applies if and when you choose to follow this approach.

I found an SDLT summary document produced by Sylvia Snowling from www.SDLT.Claims very useful in compiling this section. Once again, this is not a review or recommendation, so maybe reach out to her for more information.

Pension Contribution and Interest Relief

Often in property circles we tend to favour owning properties to regular pensions, I have found. However, there are ways in which they could work hand-in-hand. SSAS and SIPP pension funds can be utilised by the savvy property investor or developer in their property business, subject to certain conditions. This idea of using SSAS or SIPP pensions is itself not widely known and understood. In addition, contributions to a SSAS or SIPP, or earlier contributions made into occupational pension schemes that are later transferred into a SSAS or SSIP attract tax relief from the party making the contribution. This could be an individual or a company. Now, hold that thought for a moment...

So, imagine you now have a SSAS, which we also discuss in Chapter 5: Be Your Own Bank. Any personal or company contribution made to the SSAS attracts tax relief, which is free money from the taxman! Under the qualifying rules of a SSAS, you could access those funds to help fund your business, so the taxman could also become one of your funders in a round-about way. This is an example of leverage or using other people's money, 'OPM', you could say.

If you would like to know more on SSAS pensions, then I would highly recommend that you read the book *SSAS Pension Legacy* by Richard Parker.

When it comes to interest relief, the taxman allows us to earn.

Rent-A-Room Scheme (RARS)

This is an annual tax-free allowance for renting out space in your own home. Rental could be from a lodger literally renting a room in your home or it could be from renting out your entire home for periods of time when you are away, for example on holiday.

You can currently earn up to £7,500 per year tax-free under the RARS, which is basically free money. Obviously, there are still costs involved, not least of which might be sharing your home with people outside of your immediate family.

TPV TIP: RARS is a great way to dip your toe into becoming a landlord or serviced accommodation provider and get paid some tax-free cash by doing so. Robert Kiyosaki writes in *Rich Dad, Poor Dad* that your home is a liability rather than an asset, as it takes money out of your pocket each month. Well, RARS, along with other benefits like adding value and selling using Principle Residence Relief and the annual CGT allowance, allows you to turn at least part of your home into an asset using the rental income and Capital Gains Tax breaks available.

Personal Savings Allowance

There are two neat interest Income Tax offsets to identify here. The first is known as the Personal Savings Allowance (PSA), which allows any basic rate taxpayer to earn up to £1,000 per year in savings interest tax-free. This is reduced to £500 for higher rate taxpayers and nil for highest rate taxpayers. This would mean paying no income tax on £1,000/£500 per year in this case, depending on your tax bracket. That's the first one.

The second one is what's known as the 0% 'Starting Rate'. This is where the annual savings interest allowance is lifted to £5,000 a year if your earned income is below the personal allowance threshold. This would mean paying no income tax on £5,000 a year in this case.

So, how does this relate to property, you might ask?

The most obvious way is when you have lent money to your property business and could charge interest on the loan, whether in a company as a director's loan or to the property business if you are self-employed/partnership. The first £1,000 / £500 in interest income would be tax-free for basic rate / higher rate taxpayers. The first £5,000 in interest income would be tax-free for low-paid property operators.

You can probably imagine a scenario where these could be applied.

Dividends

It used to be the case that taking income from a company in the form of a dividend was extremely tax-efficient. That's no longer the case, especially as the annual tax-free dividend amount has been reduced from £5,000 to £2,000. However, £2,000 tax-free is still better than paying tax on that sum, so take it if it's there, I say!

Of course, we can start to layer different tax breaks and reliefs on top of one another to find the optimal cocktail for us to use, depending on our circumstances. However, taking the personal allowance, 0% Starter Rate and tax-free dividend allowance into account, we could extract around £19,500 per person, per year in tax-free earnings if my crude maths is correct. Add in the annual CGT allowance on the odd sale of a rental property and that's an additional £12,300 per person in capital gains before tax on top. That all said, remember my double disclaimer and do make your own checks though, won't you?

R&D Tax Credit

The UK government, through HMRC, offers R&D funding through an R&D tax credit scheme. This enables businesses to gain money off or relief from tax based on funds spent for R&D purposes. The scheme is fairly generous and offers a wide range of companies the opportunity to pay lower taxes based on the research and development that they do. One problem with the scheme, however, is that not all businesses realise that they qualify for this R&D funding.

R&D tax relief (we use this interchangeably with the term 'R&D tax credits') is available to limited companies (we'll just call these companies from this point on), in the UK. This means that it is not available to all businesses in the UK. Companies like sole proprietors, partnerships, or alternatively, unlimited companies can not access the R&D tax credit. The current tax rate for companies is 19%, and tax credit schemes are applied to the final tax burden. Overall, the benefit for companies investing in R&D is great – 33.5% of eligible expenditure that can be set off or taken as a tax credit.

What are the R&D tax credit schemes?

There are two types of schemes for differently sized businesses that allow organisations to gain R&D funding in the form of tax credits or offsets. There is an SME scheme and the RDEC scheme (the latter was formerly known as the 'large company scheme'). To qualify for the SME scheme, the company needs to meet certain requirements in terms of size and income. Specifically, the company should have fewer than 500 employees, and it must have either an annual turnover less than €100 million, or a balance sheet that is under €86 million. Companies that do not fit these criteria can claim under the RDEC scheme, but this would be significantly less generous (though still worth pursuing!).

How do you calculate R&D?

Companies often think that they have to be working in Silicon Valley or some other high-tech sort of business to be claiming R&D tax credits, but that simply isn't the case. UK government figures previously released suggest that those claiming tax relief come from a variety of different sectors, including companies working in the real estate industry. The important thing to remember is that research and development, under the HMRC classification is explained as follows:

"R&D for tax purposes takes place when a project seeks to achieve an advance in science or technology. The activities which directly contribute to achieving this advance in science or technology through the resolution of scientific or technological uncertainty are R&D."

Typically, you can approximate the R&D credit to be around 33% of your business qualifying expenditure. If you use contractors, this is usually reduced to around 20–25%.

What qualifies for R&D tax credits?

You could be creating new IT systems, doing basic research or creating functionality that is innovative, or you could be developing new products. You might be developing new manufacturing processes to develop products or services more efficiently or working on virtual reality advances.

Which property development activities and projects are eligible for R&D tax relief?

- Property developers work on innovations e.g. renewable and affordable energy materials

- Development project technical issue problem-solving, e.g. restricted site access or minimising local disruption

- Property developers researching eco-housing designs and materials

- Property developers researching affordable housing designs

- The conversion of properties from commercial to residential use

- Property developers working with listed buildings

- Property developers at the planning stage of ground-breaking or complex building design.

Property development firms can cut 130% of all R&D costs incurred from their annual profits, on top of the existing 100% deduction. This relief is also available to loss-making developers, who can claim back up to 14.5% of all surrenderable losses.

All of these types of activities may be considered research and development by HMRC. If you are not sure if you qualify it may be worth asking a specialist R&D Tax Advisor for help. Ultimately, the diversity of companies and products and services that qualify for R&D tax credits is large, and it is definitely worthwhile considering if you are doing R&D to reduce the tax you are paying.

Business Asset Disposal Relief 'BADR' (formerly known as Entrepreneur's Relief)

Eligibility

You may be able to pay a reduced rate of Capital Gains Tax when you sell (or 'dispose of') all or part of your business.

BADR means you'll pay tax at 10% on all gains on qualifying assets.

BADR is a tax relief available to trading or service companies and NOT to investment companies, so understanding this difference is important. An investment company buys and holds investments, including property investments (such as buy to let) over a long period of time. Of course, your company might be a mixture of both or may change its trading status at some point in time. Rather than attempt to explain the circumstances and rules here, I would suggest that if you are considering an asset or business disposal, that you speak to a suitably qualified tax accountant.

BADR allows a company to be closed or sold with a reduced rate of Capital Gains Tax 'CGT' of 10% to be paid on the net gains on the disposal of the company or assets concerned. BADR is subject to a £1m per person a lifetime limit, although the rates change from time to time, so do check.

This compares with the 20% CGT rate payable on the disposal of other capital assets (28% for residential property) alternative or paying 32.5% dividend tax to take out funds from the company for higher rate tax company owners.

BADR might be very compelling as a tax-saving strategy if you are considering selling, but hold that thought, as there may be a sting in the tail! You cannot restart in the same trade as the disposed of business for at least two years after disposing of the business or assets when claiming BADR. That might be fine if you have sold and are subject to a restrictive covenant, or should you wish to take a sabbatical or switch business interests. However, if you wish to continue or restart in the same trade, then you will lose this relief, so think it through.

TPV TIP: An alternative to claiming BADR could be to cease trading and take the profits out 'on the drip' instead. If you consider that you can take a minimal salary and pay no tax up to the annual personal allowance and then dividends up to the basic rate of tax threshold with a 7.5% personal tax deduction, it could be more tax efficient to gradually release the funds. The choice will depend on your personal circumstances, so take advice on this.

ISAs & IFISAs (collectively ISAs)

An Individual Savings Account (ISA) or the recently introduced Innovative Finance Individual Savings Account (IFISA) could offer additional tax breaks to property investors and developers under the right circumstances. One of the features of ISAs is that all interest, gains and profits realised within the 'ISA wrapper' become tax-free. At the time of writing in May 2021, the annual limit on how much you can invest into ISAs collectively is £20,000 per person.

There are two main ways in which we could look at benefitting from this tax-break. The first could be where we are saving up for a large expense, such as a deposit to buy a property. The interest or gains within the ISA would all be available without a tax deduction, which could save a fair chunk of your cash. If you happen to be a first-time buyer, then you might want to look into the so-called Lifetime ISA or 'LISA'. In the particular case of the LISA, the taxman will top up your savings by adding back some tax on top to further swell the pot. Do look into the rules and conditions on all ISAs, as there are certain limitations and restrictions to navigate.

Another way in which ISAs could apply to property people is as an alternative way of investing in property altogether – tax-free! Whilst I won't make any specific recommendations, it is possible to invest in property-related projects, be they rental investments and/or development projects. This could be a handy alternative to directly investing and managing a property project, which might be suitable for people looking for a more passive investment, wishing to diversify their property and non-property investing portfolio or even, in certain situations, to observe how a property project works from a safe distance, without having to commit hundreds of thousands of pounds.

As with many things tax-related, it can get complicated and usually comes with strings attached. So, do your own research and due diligence at every step to make sure that your money is safe and that you are not in breach of the rules leading to potential penalties.

Council Tax

If we rent a property out under a single Assured Shorthold Tenancy (AST), then it is usually the tenant who becomes responsible for paying Council Tax. However, there are certain situations when the owner of the property is or becomes responsible for paying Council Tax and sometimes that can add up when 'empty property premiums' get ratcheted up at 100% or even 200% in some cases.

Situations where the property owner will become liable to pay Council Tax, along with a few of the ways to mitigate the cost, are as follows:

Void periods – the owner becomes responsible for Council Tax between tenancies. So, besides minimising void periods, some (although increasingly fewer) councils do allow a short period of grace where no or a reduced rate of Council Tax could be payable. That said, reducing voids to begin with is the best way to save money here.

Exemptions – if you own an HMO, then often the Council Tax becomes the responsibility of the owner. However, students are exempt from paying

Council Tax, as long as all occupants are active students. So, make sure you claim for this exemption if that applies to you. A similar exemption applies to a single adult occupant of a property, where a reduction in Council Tax can apply. It's not that likely that the property owner would be responsible in this situation, but claim it if that's the case.

Switch to Business Rates – certain types of accommodation could be reclassified as non-domestic and be subject to business rates, rather than Council Tax. The most common example is a furnished holiday let or equivalent (e.g. serviced accommodation). In some parts of the country, business rates are lower than Council Tax … but not always! However, in certain sectors full or partial business rates relief is being offered as the country recovers from the coronavirus pandemic, so make sure you claim yours if this applies!

Reality Check

As with the previous chapter dealing with grants and soft loans, taxation is another area that is subject to government policy and therefore constant change. Please do check that the tax situation as described in this chapter is still current if and when you are looking to apply these tax-saving strategies as a way to help finance your property activities.

Equally, I would suggest retaining the services of a tax accountant and even a tax specialist if you are planning to reclaim certain tax credits, as with grants and soft loans. By engaging professional or expert support, tax doesn't have to be taxing, to coin a well-worn phrase!

Part Three

Creative
Financing
Strategies

Chapter Twelve

Options, Delayed Completion and Instalment Contracts

Introduction

The use of certain contractual arrangements can sometimes make a property funding arrangement look like finance, without there being a strict finance agreement in place. Option agreements, exchange with delayed completion and instalment contracts are examples of this. These all involve the owner of the property or land granting time to pay in some shape or form. This is my definition of finance actually: time to pay or 'terms'. These are variations on the Owner Financing strategies that we discuss in Chapter Thirteen, so you might want to cross-reference against that to understand the differences, which essentially boil down to the nature of the legal agreement.

Options, delayed completion and instalment contracts are great tools to have in your toolkit. Some investors or developers decide that they will pursue an options strategy, or perhaps a delayed completion or instalment contract strategy. However, as you will see, they will not always be applicable to the situation at hand. In my approach, I prefer to know that I have the tool there ready for when the right situation presents itself. Then, I focus on the circumstances and what the needs of the respective parties are, rather than try to force it into a situation where it might not be appropriate. Once we understand the needs and situation, our choice of tool is more likely to be accepted.

TPV TIP: Some of these contractual arrangements are more complex to explain and understand, so are less common. They are often best applied when the owner is a commercial operation/business or has a greater level of sophistication or more experience of these type of arrangements through their work, business or investment activities. It's not that they won't work outside of these bounds, it's more that the process could take longer to explain, with a lower success rate than with other more familiar arrangements.

Let's run through them now.

Option Agreements

What You Need To Know

An option agreement creates a right to buy on behalf of the person holding an option, but without the obligation to do so. There are two main types of option agreement: land/property options, used more frequently with vacant land or commercial property, and lease options, used more frequently with residential property.

Land and Property Options

An option agreement is where a deferred purchase is agreed between the vendor and the buyer. This is commonly used in cases where a buyer wants to secure their position on a piece of land or property pending obtaining planning permission to develop or change the use of that property, for example. It also allows the owner some assurance around the price to be paid, albeit in the future and at the buyer's discretion by way of the option agreement.

Lease Options

A lease option agreement is similar to a land option and has that deferred purchase right included within the arrangement too. In this case, the property is then 'leased' or rented to the would-be buyer until such time as the purchase option is exercised. Once the purchase price is paid, the title of the property is transferred to the buyer for the pre-agreed price that was struck in the option agreement.

The main difference between a lease option agreement and owner finance is essentially around legal ownership. With owner finance, the borrower usually takes on legal ownership of the property from the start of the arrangement and the finance is in the form of a loan or debt, secured against that property. With an option agreement, as the name suggests, ownership is an option and deferred until a later date. A lease arrangement or rental can be negotiated in the interim between when the arrangement begins and when the option is exercised to convert a pure option agreement into a lease option agreement.

Lease and land options are an excellent way to secure the right – but not the obligation – to buy a property or piece of land. Essentially the current owner's property is utilised or 'leveraged' as a creative way of 'financing' and controlling a property or piece of land, without having to buy it.

From a commercial point of view, lease and land options can also be very flexible. Advance payments, lease/rent payments, option fees, the final purchase price, option periods and even repair and maintenance responsibilities for the property can all be negotiated around the parties' circumstances, to arrive at a customised win-win outcome.

On the flip side, beyond people operating in the property sector or more sophisticated residential property owners, there's little awareness of option-style agreements, so they can be difficult to understand for many. As a result, they are not as commonplace in the residential property sector as they are in the commercial land and property sector.

Advantages and Benefits

There are several benefits that option agreements bring, to both the buyer and seller of a property:

- This strategy can really open up the market for both property investor/developer and owner, as it enables time to pay or 'terms' that may not be possible through a standard property purchase and finance alternative.

- Opens up deals that may have been otherwise restricted to more traditional buyers thus giving the seller a bigger number of potential buyers.

- Can be used as an interim finance source until more traditional finance can be arranged, thus ensuring the buyer doesn't lose out on a deal because of the time it can take to arrange formal finance.

- Options remove the risk on the buyer of certain future events not happening as expected, such as planning permission, market prices rising or finance approval.

- Terms can be very flexible and agreed around both parties' interests and circumstances.

Disadvantages and Risks

There are risks for both investor/developer and owner, as there are with any property-based contract:

- The option/lease option agreements are often more complicated than a standard purchase contract.

- An option agreement is not a definite commitment on the part of the option holder to proceed to purchase, so it may not be suitable to all owners.

- There is less awareness and 'legal case law' around these types of structures, which makes the legal position a little more fragile than with some other types of structure.

- A level of commercial awareness, understanding and representation is required and so it is best designed when the parties are more commercially aware and/or sophisticated with regard to financial arrangements.

Exchange With Delayed Completion Agreements

What You Need To Know

Exchange with delayed completion, also referred to as delayed completion or 'EDC', is a form of deferred property purchase agreement. Unlike with an option agreement, with delayed completion there is a clear and contractual commitment to complete the purchase as with a conventional property transaction. So, the buyer is 'on the hook' to coin a phrase.

What makes delayed completion particularly attractive is the extended deferral period between exchange and completion. With a conventional property transaction, the gap between exchange and completion is typically one or two weeks at most or none at all with a 'simultaneous exchange and completion'. However, with delayed completion, you can set whatever delay period works for the parties, from several weeks to a few months, or in some cases a year or more. Tax advice may need to be taken by the parties in order to understand whether any taxable event is triggered at exchange.

The parties would agree to a set delay period, let's say 12 months for argument's sake, and then agree on any special conditions that need to take place during the exchange period. An example of a special condition could be 'key access' which would allow the would-be buyer to enter into the property. The would-be buyer might want key access to undertake licensing, surveys, planning, marketing, renting, redecoration and even more involved works such as refurbishment, extension, conversion or even development activities. Permission from the current owner must, clearly, be received for any of the above.

TPV TIP: It is important to identify who would be responsible for any repairs, loss or damage during the delay period. I would always want to insure the property myself just to be sure. Do keep in mind that certain activities, especially in long-term, unoccupied properties, will usually lead to a restriction of insurance cover to 'FLEA perils' only (Fire, Lightning, Explosion and Aircraft impact).

Note this excludes risks like theft, 'wet perils' (e.g. flood) and 'hot works' (e.g. work with heat guns).

Delayed completion could be beneficial in cases where the property value can be increased during the delay period. This could be in cases of resale or flipping the property on. However, it could also be useful in cases where the buyer is retaining the property and could benefit from refinancing at a higher valuation after any changes of use, planning approval or improvement works have been completed.

TPV TIP: Make sure that you include a right of assignment provision in the sale agreement, which allows you the flexibility to substitute another buyer to 'step into your shoes' should you want to change your plans.

From an owner's point of view, they shouldn't have too much to lose either. If the buyer does not complete as contractually obligated, the owner could enforce the contract to compel the buyer to complete or alternatively retain ownership due to a breach of the contract by the buyer. In the latter case, the owner could retain any deposit paid on exchange and potentially claim for any loss incurred during the exchange period as well. It could be attractive to them in certain situations, such as where the property condition is uninhabitable, which might lead to a reduced sale value, as an example.

Of course, the parties might want to discuss whether the delay period comes with any adjustment in price to reflect the equivalent of interest or not. Personally, I tend to position things that the owner might get less with a conventional sale than I am offering and so I would not look to pay more in interest on top of that for the extended delay period, unless it was very long. Of course, in this situation, the owner has effectively become your bridging finance lender, so from an investor buyer's point of view, this should mean less cash is required and it would avoid the costs involved with bridging finance too.

TPV TIP: The owners most likely to accept an exchange with delayed completion arrangement are likely to be ones that do not need all of the money straight away and/or where they would get less money for their property. So, always ask this question before pitching: what are your plans after selling? If the answer does not imply that they will need to link their sale to another purchase, then you never know…

One variation on exchange with delayed completion worth mentioning here is what is called a 'conditional exchange contract'. Here the agreement is entered into with a legal exchange of contracts. However, the formal completion is then conditional on something specific taking place. The most common conditions are obtaining planning permission and fixing issues with the property or the title. The contract becomes binding once the condition is met rather than a pre-set period of time as with a regular exchange with delayed completion. This could be handy to reduce the risk to a buyer, whilst providing a degree of contractual certainty to the seller. Another way to think of this is to say the sale is 'subject to … ' whatever condition needs satisfying. Careful wording in the contract will be required, as will an understanding of what the consequences of the conditions not being met might be. This could include loss of deposit on the part of a buyer, so try and make that below the customary 5% to 10%, particularly if the condition is outside your control.

Advantages and Benefits

There are several benefits that exchange with delayed completion agreements bring to both the buyer and seller of a property:

- This strategy can help buyers get a fair price, especially for poor condition properties, whilst helping an investor/developer buyer avoid using all their own cash or expensive bridging finance.

- Allows a 'transformation event' to take place before an 'ownership transfer event', leading to a higher end-valuation in the case of either a resale or refinancing by the investor/developer buyer.

- It's based on what is already a very common property transaction, which should make it easier to explain and for owners to understand than with an option agreement for example.

- Provides greater certainty to owners that the sale will proceed as the contract is legally binding.

- The exchanged and delayed completion period is a matter to agree to suit both parties' interests and circumstances.

Disadvantages and Risks

There are risks for both investor/developer and owner, as there are with any property-based contract:

- By definition, the delayed completion period does mean that an owner will need to wait to get all of their money out of the property. This won't be that appealing if they need it for a linked transaction or other short-term requirement.

- Work undertaken during the period before completion could give rise to risks. If the buyer withdraws, then the seller might be left with a partially completed building project. Conversely, if the seller withdraws, the buyer might find it difficult to recover any costs incurred. The legal agreement should address these points carefully to help avoid them.

- Whilst technically any length of time could be negotiated between exchange and completion, it is more likely to suit situations of up to one year.

- Insurance can be complex and offered on restricted terms during the delayed completion period.

Instalment Contracts

What You Need To Know

An instalment contract is where a property purchase is paid for along the course of the contract period. Think of a hire purchase agreement for a car or an appliance and you get the picture. The various elements of the agreement can be discussed and agreed between the parties to suit their situation. The main elements include:

- Deposit or down payment.

- Regular or recurring payments.

- Any final payment or 'balloon' as it is often referred to.

This is the 'pay as you go' way of buying a property and, in theory at least, would allow for a very flexible and friendly way to acquire property without using cash or other forms of finance.

This type of arrangement is usually documented as a variation to the sale contract in a similar way to an exchange with delayed completion. However, I have personally used 'lease purchase' agreements, particularly in the USA, which is another term for an instalment contract. Legal completion of the purchase and sale, known as closing over there, should be recorded as a condition upon successful completion of the payments made under the lease purchase agreement.

Clearly, it is extremely advantageous for an incoming buyer to be able to pay for a property in instalments. However, it won't suit every owner due to the extended time usually required to complete the agreement. I have undertaken lease purchase agreements of 15 years, to illustrate the point. However, there is nothing stopping the buyer and seller agreeing to a shorter-term arrangement, usually where there would be a large balloon payment that might be similar to the amount of a mortgage the property is likely to generate at the time when it comes to be paid. So, a variation would be to set the contract up such that the equivalent of a deposit is paid over the contract term with a final balloon payment equivalent to a mortgage advance at the end.

In many ways, an instalment contract is a bit like the exchange with delayed completion from a legal point of view but it 'behaves' like a lease option agreement due to the regular recurring payments. The way that it is documented will dictate what the actual legal agreement is called. It could be an 'amended sale and purchase contract' or a 'lease purchase agreement'. The main distinction is that the sale is more certain with an instalment contract.

TPV TIP: Flipping this idea on its head a little – a developer who owns a property can sell it using an instalment contract, make a profit on their development work AND on the instalments. They might attract a premium on the instalments equivalent to an interest charge. Add in additional services, such as project management or lettings/property management, and there could be multiple streams of income from a single property sale available. Now put yourself in the shoes of that developer and consider offering this type of arrangement to potential buyers of your properties. An interesting concept to generate several layers of profit, isn't it?

Advantages and Benefits

There are several benefits that instalment contracts bring to both the buyer and seller of a property:

- As with many of the alternatives shared in this book, here is another example where payment over time can be constructed to the benefit of the parties.

- Payment by instalment could also be attractive to certain types of property owner, such as those who can wait for the money and see an opportunity to make an additional income stream(s) from the arrangement.

- As with delayed completion, it's based on what is already a very common property transaction, making it easier to explain and for owners to understand.

- Provides greater certainty to owners that the sale will proceed, as the contract is legally binding.

- The elements of the agreement, such as deposit, instalments and final 'balloon payment' can be flexed and agreed to suit both parties' interests and circumstances.

Disadvantages and Risks

There are risks for both investor/developer and owner, as there are with any property-based contract:

- The disadvantages and risks here are almost identical to those of delayed completion.

- There might need to be a longer period of time required to make the instalments affordable to a buyer.

- Potential for tax complications, resulting in a tax liability arising for an owner before having the funds to cover that cost.

- Not often found by looking on the typical property portals, where the expected intention is a conventional sale on the part of the owner.

Reality Check

You can probably see by now that there is a lot of similarity in terms of all the concepts and agreements discussed here, with payment over time being the common theme. What differs is the legal construct and the terms agreed between the parties.

When I talk to a property owner, I tend not to talk about options, delayed completion or instalment contracts at all. Instead, I try to have a conversation where I can ask some open-ended questions around their key drivers, circumstances and future intentions. Once I understand these, I might then be considering presenting one or another of these types of agreement after constructing a suitably 'financially-engineered' solution that I believe works for both parties. Equally, and as mentioned, the level of commercial awareness or financial sophistication on the part of the property owner can have a bearing on the likelihood of them both understanding and then agreeing to our non-traditional offer.

As a consequence of this process, it is usually better suited to situations where we can meet and discuss terms directly with property owners in person. That often means looking at 'off-market' properties and/or where there is a specific issue or opportunity with the property that might lend itself to making it a better outcome for both parties overall for bothering with this type of arrangement, rather than something more conventional.

Chapter Thirteen

Owner Financing

Introduction

I consider myself to be something of a creative problem solver. In fact, when a traditional sale, purchase and financing transaction seems to be a struggle is when I tend to come alive! Many investors get hung up on 'price' and seek the Holy Grail of securing a 'below market value' discount to lock in a profit on a deal. As do I.

However, there is more than one way to skin a cat as the saying goes. One alternative to a price negotiation is a 'terms negotiation'. Terms can trump price in many situations; let me illustrate…

Timing can help both parties of a transaction walk away happy, especially if one of them doesn't place a high value on the 'time value of money'.

The price paid might be such a focus for a seller due to a financial obligation or tax liability for example, that they can become entrenched as a result. Saying, "I'll pay your price, if you can give me some time to do X" can be a great conversation starter.

Not all vendors 'need' the proceeds of a sale on completion due to their personal circumstances. They might need some of the proceeds, rather than all and so if we take the time to understand and appreciate their situation, very often we can suggest something that will still work for them.

As with all forms of alternative or creative financing, they are merely tools in our toolbox. The trick is knowing when to use which tool for the job and that requires a more creative or consultative approach, dealing directly with vendors/owners and developers. Therefore, it is often the people skills that matters most – and is often the least worked on too. So, I will explain some of the ways in which we can use 'Vendor Finance' and option agreements, but keep in mind that this is only half of the story.

Owner financing typically comes in the form of vendor or developer financing, which are variations on a theme but with different motivations and drivers, as we shall now explore.

Vendor Finance

What You Need To Know

Vendor finance is a form of lending or deferred payment in which the owner of the property being sold (the vendor) lends money to the borrower (the buyer of the property) for the sole purpose of purchasing the vendor's property. Typically, vendor finance is in the form of a loan from the vendor, although it could also be in the form of instalment payments, which we cover more deeply in Chapter Twelve. The vendor would typically take or retain first charge on the property being bought by the borrower, until the loan is repaid or instalments completed.

There are two common options for vendor financing:

1. Vendor financing to generate a deposit: the vendor finances the deposit based on an agreed purchase price. This deposit will qualify the borrower for a mortgage on the remaining amount due on the property. The UK Government's *Help to Buy* scheme is perhaps the most common version of this arrangement.

2. Vendor financing of the whole purchase price: the vendor lends the entire value of the property to the borrower, thus enabling the purchase of the property. Or, as mentioned, the purchase could be made in instalments over an agreed period of time.

This strategy can be very useful if the borrower cannot raise the required funds through more traditional methods, particularly in economic conditions where traditional loans and mortgages are harder to acquire. Equally, many owners use it when price is an issue for them, such as an owner with low or negative equity. I tend to see the prevalence of vendor finance rise when market cycles place a strain either on lending in a 'credit crunch' or in a property market down turn where prices drop significantly, a 'correction' or a 'crash'.

The vendor may lend 'Vendor Finance' at a higher interest rate than would be offered by more traditional lenders. However, this can often be flexed dependent on the circumstances and market cycle at the time. There are no standard entry or exit fees, rather all fees will be negotiated on a deal-by-deal basis.

The vendor may charge interest on the loan or simply defer the payment. If the loan is deferred the vendor may seek to take an equity share in the property. It is the responsibility of both parties to ensure that the arrangement is understood and agreed to by all parties. It is advised that solicitors are involved to offer advice and a formal agreement documented.

The details covered within a vendor finance agreement must be detailed and clear. Details often covered by such an agreement include (but are not restricted to):

- What is the agreed purchase price?

- Who is liable for the property costs, taxes and other fees prior to the final payment being made?

- Are there any agent's or finder's fees associated with the purchase?

- What is the repayment plan, (i.e. instalments or lump sum)?

- What is the interest rate for the deal and what governs any changes to it (e.g. is it fixed or perhaps tied to the Bank of England base rate)?

- What happens if the deal breaks down (i.e. who is liable for what)?

- At which point of the deal and under what conditions does the borrower take control of the property?

- At which point of the deal and under what conditions does the borrower own the property?

Due to the fact that there are slightly more complicated legal requirements for this type of deal, the legal costs incurred will be more than for a typical buy-to-let mortgage. As a result, the legal work is best undertaken by a solicitor with commercial law or creative property strategies experience, rather than a conventional conveyancing solicitor. Ideally, a tax accountant should also advise on the tax position of the structure agreed. The exact cost of these professional fees will depend on the value of the deal and how complicated the vendor financing agreement is.

TPV TIP: An owner or vendor is more likely to be in a position to agree to some form of vendor financing if they have a strong financial position to begin with … in other words, if they do not 'need' the money straight away. So, try to establish their financial position, including whether the property has much debt secured on it and ask 'what are your plans' to gauge whether they are likely to depend on the proceeds of sale or not.

Advantages and Benefits

There are several benefits that vendor financing brings to both the buyer and seller of a property:

- This strategy can really open up the market for both property investor/developer and vendor as it enables financing that may not be possible through a standard method.

- Solves difficulties buyers face with low deposits, obtaining mortgage approvals and overcoming minor credit defaults.

- Opens up deals that may have been otherwise restricted to more traditional buyers thus giving the seller a bigger number of potential buyers.

- Often a quicker transaction than waiting on traditional lenders.

- Can be used as an interim funding source until more traditional lending can be arranged, thus ensuring the buyer doesn't lose out on a deal because of the time it can take to arrange formal lending.

- Terms can be very flexible and agreed around both parties' interests and circumstances.

Disadvantages and Risks

There are risks for both investor/developer and the vendor, as there are with any property-based contract:

- The vendor finance agreement is often more complicated than a standard purchase contract. All parties should carefully review the terms and conditions of the agreement and the buyer must ensure that they are able to meet the financial commitment.

- Buyers opting for this type of deal may suggest this is because they have limited access to the more traditional finance options. The vendor, therefore, must ensure that the agreement clearly lays out the re-payment terms and also satisfies them that the buyer has adequate means to pay.

- A level of commercial awareness, understanding and representation is required and so it is best designed when the parties are more commercially aware and/or sophisticated with regard to more complex financial arrangements.

Reality Check

These types of deal financing are not as common in the UK, unlike some other countries. Therefore, it is important that both parties understand the arrangement that has been agreed and that specialist property solicitors and advisors are used. Full details of the negotiated deal, between vendor and borrower, need to be carefully recorded and should be stored with your solicitor or accountant.

These types of deals are, however, very common in the USA, for example, and therefore there is plenty of documentation around on how these types of agreements can work.

Developer Finance

What You Need To Know

Developer vendor finance is a variation on the owner vendor finance strategy, where the owner of the property is a professional property developer rather than, say, an individual. Opportunities sometimes exist to acquire properties direct from the developer or builder with funding terms that incentivise an investor to make the purchase. This is different to the normal stage payments during a build phase where the full balance would be paid (or most of it) by the time the property is completed.

Developer vendor finance exists where funding is available on a property even after completion, although typically for a limited period only. It is not to be confused with development finance, where funding is offered to a developer to build properties.

A developer may choose to offer funding for a couple of reasons, but most likely these reasons all boil down to sales revenue or unit completion figures – in other words to meet sales targets. Whilst this is not a very common source of funding it can be a good way to acquire a property without the need for a conventional loan from a formal lender at the outset.

In some cases, it is also possible to get funding for the full purchase price of the property, especially if the property purchased is at a discount from its market value. Market value is often a tricky area however and any investors should satisfy themselves that any discount enjoyed is a genuine discount by comparing this to other sales on the development within a very recent time frame as well as other comparable sales in close proximity. The very fact that a discount exists could itself have an effect on the market value and this is a consideration if looking to refinance again later.

A developer cannot usually record a sale when they still have an interest in the legal title of the property; so either they understand that the actual sales revenue will be delayed, or they have another way to separate the funding from the sales division that works for them. They could also have a different short-term driver, such as unit sales, filling a development to encourage general public sales, or in some cases interest in management revenue post-completion. Whatever the situation and whilst exceptions do exist, it is likely that the developer finance will need settling within a short timescale and within a year typically; so a clear exit strategy for the investor is required. In other words, investors need to know how they will pay off the developer at the end of the term.

Settling of the developer funding will need to be through cash or another form of property funding, such as a buy-to-let mortgage for example.

Due to the nature of this type of funding and as with many non-mainstream financing arrangements this is likely to be an 'off-market transaction', meaning not publicly marketed. Therefore, access to these sorts of deals requires continued good relationships with developers and more hunting around than other discounted new-build development sales. It is also more likely that such funding will be available in times of low property demand and/or general credit availability.

Some of these deals are presented for overseas as well as UK properties and so great care needs to be taken to research fully what is being offered, by whom and why – due diligence is extremely important in such cases.

A quick word on 'off-plan purchases' here. Far more commonplace than developer financing is the practice of property developers offering payment terms with 'off-plan' properties. An off-plan property is where the agreement to purchase the property is made BEFORE it is built or completed.

Many developers look to pre-sell their developments, which helps them to fund their development costs. Often, a buyer can secure a property by paying a nominal deposit and then agree to some kind of progress payments along the build period. This is typically 12 to 24 months for most conversion or new-build development projects.

Note that these instalment payments cannot be mortgaged or financed in more traditional methods, such as bridging finance, and so they need to be paid in cash. Once the building is completed, the new owner can then look to raise a mortgage on the property or sell it to another buyer.

Spoiler alert … I am not a big fan of acquiring properties off-plan. There are so many risks involved, which I discuss on *The Property Voice Podcast* in an episode called '10 Reasons why I don't like off-plan property investment'. Here's a summary of those reasons…

1. Developer risk

2. Market shifts

3. Lender risk

4. Valuation risk

5. No rental income

6. No opportunity to add value

7. Time to repay developer premium

8. Build quality

9. Snagging issues

10. Snake oil sales people

OK, so that was all a bit negative and possibly slightly controversial, wasn't it? So, let's try to even things up with my ONE reason to like off-plan, new-build investment property.

When the Deal Stacks Up!

That boils down to two things in my view: 1) a juicy discount from a COMPLETED property rather than an off-plan or part-built property and/or 2) should developer finance be available.

I would suggest that you look up that podcast episode if you want to know more, although you have been warned!

TPV TIP: The most likely source of such opportunities is through developers driven by performance targets around their quarter and year-ends or when there has been a change in market conditions, such as a property market downturn, recession or credit crunch. Remember that developer finance relates to completed properties and not to off-plan or part-completed properties. However, some developers do offer staged payments during the development period as well.

Advantages and Benefits

Similarly to owner vendor finance deals there are some good benefits to investors who can find these types of deals:

- A good alternative to mainstream lender financing, typically on simple terms and fast to arrange.

- Usually lower entry and exit fees, and when combined with developer discounts can be very attractive commercially.

- Allows more rapid portfolio expansion.

Disadvantages and Risks

It is imperative to watch out for some of the risks of developer finance deals:

- It is harder to find these types of deals as they are typically only available off-market.

- Developer lending is typically short-term funding so an exit refinancing/sale strategy is required at outset.

- False discounts could affect resale/revaluation figures. It is also possible for discounted deals to affect future resale/revaluation if there is only a very short period between purchase and sale/ revaluation.

- In some cases, the availability of developer finance can mask other potential hidden problems. For example, a large concentration of investors may restrict lending options on the block or site, a lack of new build warranty or latent defects, unsatisfied planning conditions, etc.

- The opportunity for bogus operators to exist – watch out for sharks!

- Keep in mind that there are several 'hidden risks' of buying from a development, as outlined above. These include lender concentration risk and limits that prevent them from getting a traditional mortgage, which many people have no visibility of until it's too late.

Option Agreements

A quick word about lease and land options here, which were covered more fully in Chapter Twelve. You could say that a lease option or land option is another form of vendor or owner financing, as the property or land owner is granting some kind of time deferral for some or all of the payment to be made. I would agree that in the strictest definition these could be classed as other forms of owner financing. However, because they do not use a legal agreement in the form of a more traditional financing arrangement, it sits better as a Creative Strategy rather than Alternative Financing.

Reality Check

One of the best ways to find these deals is to make direct contact with a developer, particularly in the lead up to an important deadline like their year-end when they would be most receptive to such arrangements. It is likely that the best initial port of call will be a local development site where it's possible to sound out the likelihood of doing such a deal.

As this type of deal is generally 'off-market', access can sometimes be found via a third party such as a property deal sourcer, financial intermediary, bank/lender, receiver or other such 'middle man' that specialises in finding such opportunities. There are many such specific companies or individuals that can often be found via a web search or hanging out in the property communities generally, either online or offline.

Care should always be taken when working directly with developers or through an intermediary. Do proper due diligence on any parties that you may want to work with as this is an unregulated area of the market and so is open to miss-selling, bad practice or even deception and fraud if we are not too careful.

Chapter Fourteen

Assisted Sale

What You Need To Know

Funnily enough, an 'Assisted Sale' is a property sale that is assisted by someone else!

The assistance in question is provided by a third party. The assisted sale is performed under an agreement between a company or individual and a property owner to allow the owner to sell their property to a separate buyer based on the terms of the agreement.

This can be a great strategy resulting in a good price for a property as well as a profit opportunity for the investor providing the assisted sale. There is often a warm feeling of helping an owner out of what can be a tricky situation as well. There are three parties to the transaction:

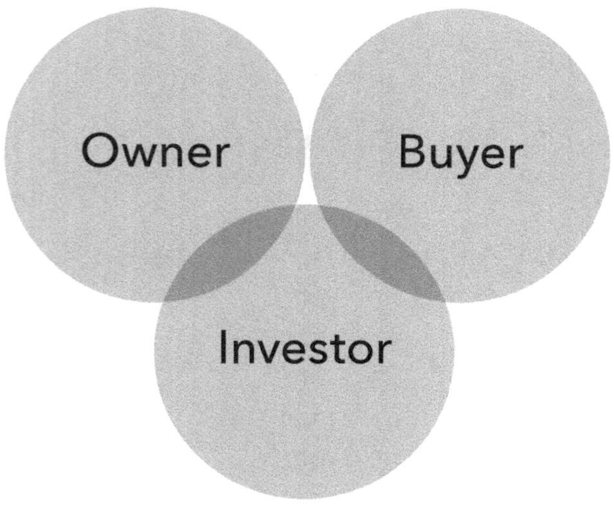

The principle of assisted sale is quite straightforward to grasp. A property owner or vendor is introduced to a buyer with the help and intervention of an investor, to use this language. Of course, this also sounds like traditional estate agency sales – and under some of the ways of approaching it, it could well be. However, the key differentiator with an assisted sale is that in this situation the role of the investor is significantly more than merely advertising a property for sale to attract and introduce a buyer.

The role of the investor here is to add value to the transaction over and beyond traditional sales agency. The best way to add value to the transaction is to add value to the property and/or the owner. Some examples of adding value include:

- Improving the appeal of the property with, light-touch presentation, de-cluttering, clean-up and then repackaging through better marketing or using an alternative sales channel. This is essentially sales agency but with a twist, which Phil Spencer often adopted in his *Secret Agent* TV series.

- Increasing the value of the property by undertaking works, such as repair and refurbishment or more significant development work (e.g. extension, loft conversion, garage conversion, etc.). This usually means bringing the investor's cash to the table in a kind of partnership with the owner. A variation is to help repurpose the property's market or appeal, such as into a holiday let or an HMO, for example.

- Adding value through 'paper-based methods' such as gaining planning permission, obtaining certificates of lawfulness for unapproved works, removing enforcement orders, title splitting, change of use classification, HMO licence, etc. This is a great way to bring a specialist knowledge and contacts profitably at minimal investment or expense.

- Removing problems that could give rise to a lower sale value, such as a short lease (where the remaining term is less than 80 years), property problems (e.g. Japanese knotweed, subsidence, lack of new build warranty, etc.) or title issues (e.g. 'ransom strips', unregistered land, removing/insuring against restrictive covenants, etc.).

- Fixing issues on the part of the owner, such as a lack of funds to undertake improvement works, a lack of understanding of how to position or where to present the property for sale, a lack of knowledge in how to overcome issues such as mortgage arrears, threats of repossession, probate and so on. Acting as a kind of consultant on behalf of the owner to negotiate or manoeuvre out of tricky or time-pressured situations.

As you can see, there are several scenarios in which this strategy can be worth looking at for both the investor and the owner.

An investor can act as a 'private estate agent' to either market the property or even to source another investor buyer directly. The assisted sale investor would then receive the agreed commission or fee based on the terms set out in the initial agreement. This is commonly known as 'deal sourcing' or 'deal packaging' and is a form of sales agency, so it does require the right credentials to operate as such. To legitimately operate as an estate agent or deal sourcer/packager, the following compliance requirements are required under the law:

- Registered with the Information Commissioner's Office for data protection.

- Registered with one of the three Government-approved a property ombudsman schemes.

- Have professional indemnity insurance in place.

- Registered for Anti-Money Laundering with HMRC.

- If you take on client funds in advance of payment being due, then you will need a separate Client Money Protection bank account to hold them separately.

- It is also advisable to have written terms of business, contracts and business policies.

Other scenarios could be where the investor becomes more active to help with improvement works or fix issues with the property or on the part of the vendor. This is more like a partnership arrangement and can be documented in a number of ways. The result here is more likely to be profit share based on the uplifted sale value of the property, which acts more like a joint venture agreement than a sales agency agreement.

Perhaps the best thing about this strategy is that it allows people to be as creative as they wish. There are many techniques that can add value to a property before sale, so it can showcase the skills and knowhow of the investor in a way that generates a fee or profit, without them needing to actually own and finance a property.

As I mentioned, the principle of assisted sale is quite easy to grasp. However, the more complicated aspect, beyond the 'work' of increasing the value, is how to document the arrangement in a way that protects all parties. There are three main ways to document an assisted sale: an agency contract, an assignable option agreement/sale agreement or some sort of joint venture/partnership agreement.

Assisted Sale Through an Agency Agreement

This is an agreement that grants the investor (acting as an agent) the right to market the property on behalf of the vendor. The best form of agency for the investor is both exclusive and with a long time frame. However, it is also essential that any agency arrangement is fair, reasonable and ethical to the owner. A long-term exclusivity arrangement would not be a good idea where the owner is facing significant time or financial pressure and penalties, for example.

A sales agency can be easily drafted in one to two pages and signed by the parties. This creates a 'lockout' or exclusivity arrangement, which then allows the investor to reveal the precise method in which they will market the property for sale to achieve a higher value. The reward to the investor in this case is typically in the form of a fixed fee or variable commission based on the end sale value that is realised.

As with a traditional sales agency, the investor would usually present their fee/commission invoice to the solicitors acting for the owner to be paid out of the sale proceeds upon distribution. It is therefore important that the agreement stipulates this very clearly and that any fee/commission is paid prior to distribution of the funds to the owner. A variation could be that the vendor pays this fee directly to the investor. Finally, of course, could be a mix-and-match approach if there is a fixed component and a variable 'success fee'.

TPV TIP: Agency is similar to the business of deal sourcing as mentioned. However, you don't necessarily need to become a full-time deal sourcer in order to use this strategy. Think of it as one of those Allen keys you might have in your toolbox that might only be used once every few years to tighten that Ikea chest of drawers that has come loose. The right tool for the right job at the right time.

Assisted Sale Through an Assignable Option/ Sale Agreement

This agreement allows the investor to control the property and gain the right to sell the property at any point during the option period or prior to completion of the sale agreement. Some important elements to this type of agreement include:

- Control – through a Power of Attorney agreement, allowing the investor the ability to 'step into the owner's shoes'.

- Permissions – agreement for 'key access' and to carry out works to the property if required.

- Assignment – allowing the investor to sell the option or the property on to a third party.

- Reward – clearly documenting how the investor will be paid for their work.

- Deadlock – often ignored, it is wise to include some reference to how disputes will be resolved, without going to court!

Unfortunately, an assignment contract can sometimes also be a double-edged sword.

On the plus side it is a fundamental part of making an assisted sale possible and it also allows the *property to be controlled* by the investor *without change of ownership*. That means that when a buyer purchases the property, there will be no issues with the '6-month rule' imposed by many mortgage lenders, as the vendor did not transfer ownership to the investor.

However, the downsides are that the uplift produced from the work carried out by the investor would have to be sold off as the option fee to a new buyer or the proceeds have to be split between different parties. This can be illustrated with the example below:

- An investor has an agreed purchase price of £100K (current market value).

- The investor undertakes a refurbishment at a cost of £20K.

- The new market value of property is now £150K.

- The investor sells the property on to buyer for £150K.

- £100K goes to the vendor with £50k going to the investor.

This can limit the number of potential buyers due to the greater cash outlay for the buyer involved in this transaction, if it were an option. Equally, as an assignable sale, the terms would need to be disclosed to the buyer's solicitors (and in turn any lender), who may query and potentially object to the transaction and the splits. It could all be acceptable, especially if the property is being sold for it's 'fair market value' but it is more complicated and can give rise to a risk of the sale collapsing, if not too careful.

> **TPV TIP:** It is always advisable that both parties in a transaction are legally represented in order to help smooth the process of 'the legals' should you find yourself negotiating an assignable option or sale agreement. Have your own 'pool of recommended solicitors' on hand ready to suggest to your property owner counter party. Where do you find them? Ask your own solicitor for a list of the best solicitors that they work with regularly and have a list ready to share. These will then be independent, recommended and should understand the complexities of the arrangement at hand.

Assisted Sale Through Joint Venture/ Partnership Agreement with Owner

An assisted sale can also be structured as a Joint Venture (JV) or Partnership Agreement. Here a drawn-up agreement sets out the schedule of works to be carried out by the investor (if any) and the profit-split amounts or percentages between owner and investor.

The agreement will also outline who will pay for legal fees, estate agent fees and any other associated costs. Such an agreement will usually outline a time frame in order to sell the property and will include an provision for extending that period, if need be. It is often the case that the property equity split created by the JV or partnership is documented in a separate 'Declaration/Deed of Trust' agreement (DoT). A DoT sets out the 'beneficial ownership' of a property, which is different to the 'legal ownership', which is recorded at HM Land Registry.

We've all heard the old saying, "Marry in haste, repent at leisure." It's the same with joint ventures, if they're not done correctly! Like any other type of property deal, it is essential to perform due diligence on the people you will be working with and ensure that all legal documentation is drawn up and reviewed by a good solicitor. All these different conditions should be fully discussed and worst case scenarios considered *before* entering into a joint venture. The JV/Partnership Agreement will therefore likely run to many pages and cost money to document but is worthwhile to get it right and prevent problems later.

As with an option or assignable sale agreement, to create ease and protection for the investor, a power of attorney can be requested from the owner to oversee control of the sale of the property. If the investor does not require that level of control, a simpler lockout agreement may do. A lockout agreement gives exclusive rights of sale of the property for a set period of time to the investor, similar to that of an agency agreement.

Joint venture agreements can work better than options, as a conventional sale can be undertaken and the investor doesn't have to sell on the right to buy the property as they would in an option arrangement. But on the flip side, it does not offer the investor the backup of being able to buy the property should the sale not proceed in the allocated time frame, unless this provision is included with the JV/Partnership Agreement.

TPV TIP: Given that a joint venture or partnership arrangement is a close tie-up under what can be a lengthy and complex property project, it is best reserved for when you are working with two categories of people. The first are close contacts, including friends, family and work/business associates, where a higher level of trust is likely. The second is with more 'sophisticated owners', such as business owners, high-net-worth investors and fellow property investors, where a higher level of commercial understanding of the arrangement is more likely.

Advantages and Benefits

Using assisted sales as a property strategy has the follow advantages:

- There are many ways of structuring an agreement, which can offer flexible and creative solutions to difficult situations.

- Creativity adopted within the strategy can unveil many opportunities for property investors to generate a profit.

- Controlling a property in this way requires no mortgage or finance of the property on the property investor's part.

- The strategy can sometimes be implemented with minimal expenditure with selective added value methods.

Disadvantages and Risks

Assisted sales, while being a great creative strategy, can also present the following disadvantages:

- A property may not sell within the agency/option/joint venture/partnership period, leaving the investor out of pocket or without pay, potentially.

- The investor may have no option but be forced to purchase the property themselves if there are difficulties with the sale process and if they have significant funds tied up in the property.

- Whilst the principle of assisted sale is easy to grasp, the documentation can appear quite daunting, especially for everyday and non-sophisticated owners. This can result in a lot of time, energy and potential legal fees invested that may not come to fruition if the owner backs out.

- A poor legal agreement could result in losses to the investor unless the agreement has been drafted correctly.

Reality Check

The two biggest challenges with an assisted sale are *finding a suitable deal and then convincing an owner to proceed with it*. These types of deals are typically found off-market and involve liaising direct with owners who may be in difficult situations. To find such deals it is important to have a good network, with lots of different channels, and be prepared to do a lot of canvassing of property owners. I recall an investor friend of mine that was pursuing this strategy exclusively for a period of around two years. He had several nibbles but absolutely no bites and so ended up abandoning this approach. Therefore, I would not suggest going all-in with this one.

Owners can be wary of the structure and complexity of an assisted sale. Not many people have heard of them and this often creates fear and uncertainty. Assisted sales are sometimes suggested by banks and are often viewed with suspicion.

As with all financing strategies, they are a tool to have available in our toolbox to be used for the right job, which I know I keep repeating. However, it's true! It is much better to act as a consultant that has access to all of these tools, applying them to the right job when it comes around, rather than blindly following a single strategy. It's like carrying a hammer and only looking for where to bang a nail in a wall.

However, if you are an investor that is 'knowledge rich' yet 'cash poor', an assisted sale strategy can be a great way of marrying your know-how to an owner's asset in a way that creates a win-win outcome to both parties.

Chapter Fifteen

Rent to Rent

What You Need To Know

Rent to Rent (R2R) is a property investment strategy that allows people to enjoy property rental income without actually owning the property themselves. The investor rents the property from its owner, typically an owner-occupier or an existing landlord, and then rents or sublets it on to tenants, or guests in the case of short-term accommodation. Hence Rent to Rent!

Usually, the sublet arrangement takes the form of a commercial agreement or commercial lease rather than an Assured Shorthold Tenancy (AST), as the investor won't be living in the property. Once an agreement has been signed with the owner, the investor will then rent out the property to tenants under AST agreements or under a licence agreement in the case of short-term guests. Another variation of R2R involves the owner agreeing to sell the property at a future date via a purchase option or exchange with delayed completion. This is actually combining two separate strategies; R2R and a lease option or exchange with delayed completion agreement, to form a new 'hybrid' between either of the two.

R2R is what you might call an 'arbitrage model'. Arbitrage is buying/renting in one market and selling/renting in a different market to create a margin or profit between the two.

During the writing of this book, I became the co-owner of a Rent-to-Rent business, in fact. The business is called Capital Living, which is a co-living provider in London that has been established for 12 years. It uses a

'Peace of Mind' rental model for property owners to provide quality shared accommodation for young professionals.. The business currently manages over 40 properties and 250+ member tenancies and is looking to further expand. Within the book bonus section is a case study of a recent property acquisition that I worked on personally, you can see how to structure such a property deal yourself too, if you'd like. For more information on this business please visit www.capitalliving.co.uk.

The key to successful R2R is to make sure that you can make enough margin or profit between the rent you pay to the owner and the rental income you receive from the tenants or guests – not forgetting costs and voids. The most common ways of ensuring a profit are:

1. Discount – agree enough of a discount on the market rent to pay to the owner, whilst collecting the higher market rent from the tenant found.

2. Division – converting the property into either a multi-room (divide up the space) or short-term rental letting arrangement (divide up the time).

The rewards of high occupancy generally mean a higher overall rent than would be achieved by the equivalent single let rental value.

TPV TIP: The 'golden rule' when it comes to models such as R2R is the occupancy rate. Achieve high levels of occupancy and the model works like a dream. Achieve lower levels of occupancy and it can turn into your worst nightmare! Many inexperienced R2R operators overestimate their occupancy rates and underestimate their costs – don't be one of those.

The benefits for the owner of R2R include:

1. Certainty and reduced risk – having certainty of rental payments (by amount and timing).

2. Hands-free – reduced time, input and hassle by passing over the management of the property to a third party.

3. Reduced cost – potential to pass over upgrade, repair and maintenance costs to a third party; although smart R2R operators will leave most of these with the owner. However, avoiding voids and management charges is another way to save cost.

4. Passive value-add – potential to increase the value of the property with minimal effort.

R2R could appeal to 'tired landlords' looking to reduce their day-to-day involvement in managing a property, or as a stepping stone to exit their business. R2R could also appeal to homeowners that want / need to move, have limited or no equity, or who want or need to retain an investment but without the hassle of managing it.

Considerations

Finance

Many (but not all) owners have a mortgage or other form of finance secured against the property. It's important to understand what is allowed under the terms of the mortgage and to make sure that the owner gets the relevant permissions *before* entering into an R2R arrangement.

Insurance

Along the same lines as finance, you need to understand the insurance situation at the property and notify the insurers to enter into a R2R agreement under certain circumstances, such as short-term letting, for example.

Licensing

Certain types of letting arrangements require approvals, consents and licences, e.g. HMO (multi-room letting) or Selective/Mandatory licensing or Short-Term Letting in certain cities/. This can vary depending on the property, location and tenancy/occupancy type; therefore, it is essential that all such consents are in place. In particular, you need to make sure that the property owner is protected from fines and regulatory hassle, as they will be at least equally liable here. In recent years, councils have massively tightened up HMO regulation – so make sure that you know the rules and abide by them.

There are also plenty of areas where an HMO is not going to be given planning permission – no matter what. In particular, councils are actively looking to stop student 'ghetto' areas – which are often quite visible and unpopular with local residents – and want to disperse student HMOs more widely, as a result. Also, considerations like parking may come into play during decision-making. For example, that large Victorian terraced house that would make a great HMO could automatically be rejected for an HMO licence, because it only offers on-street parking in an already congested location. The moral of this story is to be very careful if you're looking to do R2R using a strategy that requires some sort of licence or planning approval. Get expert advice, speak to the planning department and network with other local landlords to find out more about the situation in the local area.

Maintenance and Repairs

It is vital that an agreement is reached as to how these will be managed, at what frequency and who will be responsible for them, including payment. There are several levels of repair and maintenance to consider: wear and tear, damage, general repairs to contents, repairs and maintenance of functional systems (e.g. central heating) and the 'fabric of the building' (roof, walls, windows, etc.).

It can be very appealing to a landlord or property owner if you offer to cover maintenance and repairs, so they don't need to worry about them. It's common and indeed advisable, for Rent to Rent investors will limit the extent of the repairs they'll cover, so they might include everything right up to boiler replacement, say, but draw the line at anything structural, for example.

TPV TIP: There is always a trade-off I find. Here, too, if an owner wants us to cover repairs and maintenance, then there has to be a trade-off in the rent payable. Similarly, we might want to make some alterations or adaptations to suit our intended purpose, such as adding a stud wall to split a room to create two rentable bedrooms. Just do your sums to work out your return on investment. As a bonus tip – the longer the agreement-term, the better the chances of recovering any up-front investment, but also the higher the chances of repairs and maintenance as well.

Upgrades and Renovation

When it comes to upgrades and renovation, all parties involved must understand how the property will be changed, what the associated costs will be and who will be paying for the work.

As with licensing there are certain changes to a property that require planning, building control and other consents or approvals. It is essential that these all regulations are understood, and the responsibility for approval agreed and fully documented.

Inspections

From the current owner's point of view, whilst it is tempting to leave the management of the property entirely to someone else (i.e. the R2R operator), in reality the owner will still be liable for much of what happens inside the property, like criminal activity for example. As a result, regular inspections are recommended to check on such things, or at least ask for some photographic or video footage periodically.

Tenant/Occupier Issues

As the property will be sublet under an AST or licence agreement, the owner essentially allows a third party access and occupation rights to their property. Some of these are both regulated and legally controlled. Owner and operator should carefully consider matters like illegal occupation, arrears, voids, damage, evictions etc., and make sure that everyone's clear on who is legally responsible for what. This should be documented in the agreement. Things like tenancy deposits and rent collection should be thought through too, especially if tenant has paid the investor, but the operator fails to pay the owner.

Financial Risk

A Rent-to-Rent agreement is a financial arrangement as well as a management one and so the respective financial position of the parties needs consideration. For example, what is the mortgage situation of the owner – could there be a default or repossession looming, which could threaten the operator's income stream? How about the operator – what is their financial standing, track record and credit position, could they go bankrupt or be put in a tough financial position leading to them suddenly disappearing with or without owner and tenant/occupier funds? What tenant referencing will be put in place to ensure that decent tenants who can reliably pay the rent occupy the property?

End of the Arrangement/Property Return

The timing and terms of the end of the arrangement should be made clear – when, in what condition, converted back to a single dwelling, etc. – all need thinking through and discussing.

> **TPV TIP:** Having an inventory and schedule of condition at both the start and end of the arrangement, along with clear terms around wear and tear, damage and the general property condition, such as decorating, can help to keep any potential disagreement to a minimum.

General Responsibilities

There will no doubt be other responsibilities to think about when the requirements of at least three direct parties (owner, operator & occupiers) and several indirect parties (lender, insurer, local authority, etc.) need to be taken into consideration. It makes sense to give enough time to scrutinising and discussing everyone's needs and documenting the decisions that are made regarding them.

Documentation

I'd strongly advise that all terms and conditions are drawn up into a formal commercial/management agreement or lease by a solicitor. In addition to the commercial agreement or lease, it could also be helpful to have a Power of Attorney in place if certain actions are required to be undertaken by the operator as a part of their responsibility. Both owner and operator should also have their own legal representation to ensure proper protection and independent advice.

Commercial Drivers

When it comes to R2R, there are several commercial or economic drivers or 'levers' that you can pull. These levers can make a lot of difference in the financial or operational performance. They are as follows:

Deposits – there could be two types of deposit: one paid by the operator to the owner and the others paid by the occupants to the operator. In theory, these will cancel each other out. However, keep in mind that you typically need to pay any deposit to the owner before collecting them from the occupants. Equally, you cannot usually retain the deposits paid by occupants yourself as they need to be deposited into a protected deposit scheme or client money protection account, so there is a genuine cash outlay with deposits to the operator. Better still, try to avoid paying the owner a deposit, offer a reduced deposit or even ask to have some or all of it returned 'for good behaviour' after a test period to protect your cash outlay. There are also deposit insurance schemes so in lieu of paying a deposit you can take out an insurance policy for an amount equivalent to the deposit requested. They are very affordable and can make a big difference to cashflow.

Payment Terms – rent is usually always paid in advance either way. However, if you can negotiate with the owner for payment in arrears, variable payments based on occupancy or even an escalating rental payment arrangement, then you can protect your cash and/or profit position as an operator. Equally, the length of the lease with the owner will directly affect your return on investment. The golden rule is longer is better; I suggest a five-year term but certainly not less than three years to give yourself time. Equally, conditional break clauses can be a good way of giving the owner peace of mind that they can exit if you are not meeting your obligations but it also gives the operator certainty to continue if they are meeting their obligations. It also gives the owner time to get used to a completely passive and hassle-free income – few want to go back to self-managing or traditional agent models once they've enjoyed the peace of mind and certainty that a professional R2R operator brings.

Property Set Up – there are a couple of characteristics of setting up a R2R property that can impact your returns. The first is up-front costs, such as furniture, updating the property and even some internal reconfiguration. The second is filling the place, where the gap between taking on the property and filling it with tenants creates a cashflow and profit drag. Try to avoid or defer some of these costs if you can. Some owners will cover them, some can be spread over time, such as furniture leasing and then try to have a pre-marketing period before formally taking on the property. 'First month free' is a common agreement to reach with the owner to allow for furnishing, marketing, viewings and filling prior to any incoming rent being possible. Although this may be surprising to the operator, it's important to remember that owners are used to voids, so if it is going to be the last void they have for three to ten years, usually they are OK with that!

Occupant and Property Management – an unhappy tenant or guest could potentially destroy your business if not too careful. Imagine a disruptive or anti-social tenant in an HMO upsetting all the other tenants who then leave, or a disgruntled guest in a serviced apartment leaving a bad review and you get the picture. Equally, issues with the property like repairs, if not dealt with, can lead to tenants leaving. In this case, having a clear agreement and a good relationship with the owner is paramount. Equally, remember that operating a R2R is a hands-on job at heart and so it comes with the need to be on call 24/7/365 potentially. Whilst it's not immediately apparent that these could cost money, they can do indirectly. Also, as an R2R operator, you have the same legal, ethical and moral obligations as an owner or traditional letting or managing agent. You must take all fair and reasonable measures to ensure you are providing a safe and compliant living environment.

Margin – whilst in theory you can make a R2R work with a single let property, the richer pickings will come from where you can arbitrage the rent as previously mentioned. If you can pay the owner as if the property were a single let and charge the occupants as a multi or short-term let arrangement, you will create the largest margin. Equally, don't forget those operating costs that can eat your margin, almost without noticing, such as repairs and maintenance, wear and tear or damage, voids/unoccupancy, bills and council tax, compliance and regulatory fees, call-out service, marketing and so on. Also, make sure that you value your own time to make sure you are adequately compensated. Keep in mind that sourcing agents will often show the profit on a property if it is self-managed. It is rarely disclosed that self-managing the properties has a literal cost in terms of travel expenses and subsistence but also cost of the operator's time. If the operator doesn't account for these they will find themselves trapped in a business with potentially great headline revenue figures but actually not paying them any business profit.

TPV TIP: A business is only a business if you can replace yourself in it and still make a profit! So, aim to cover all your costs and the equivalent of paying someone else to manage your R2R property on your behalf and still make a profit. If you decide to operate it yourself, then at least work out your 'effective hourly rate' and don't undervalue yourself by paying a low wage just to say you are 'in business' – as you aren't, unless you can take a reasonable profit from the business. However, if you are looking to earn a living through property, then many people starting out with low capital consider R2R as a good way to get going.

Advantages and Benefits

Advantages of the rent-to-rent strategy to the operator include:

- There is no mortgage, no deposit and no property ownership needed by the operator to generate an income from this strategy. It's a property finance strategy that uses a commercial agreement structure to mimic a financing arrangement, without it actually being one.

- If used correctly it can be a high cash flowing strategy, especially if it is 'arbitraged' such as converting a single let converted to a higher rent multi-let or serviced accommodation, for example.

- It allows the operator to control property and generate an income stream from it without a limit on funds available, credit rating, lending criteria etc. In most other strategies, property investors and developers will encounter these barriers at one point or another.

- Perhaps the 'Holy Grail' is R2R with an option to purchase at a sensible pre-agreed price; this would then convert a purely 'income strategy' into a 'wealth strategy' instead.

Disadvantages and Risks

Disadvantages of the rent-to-rent strategy include:

- There are risks involved for all parties: operator, owner and possibly, also for the occupants and so adequate protection, assurance and an ethical approach is strongly advised.

- The sector is unregulated and therefore open to abuse as with some high-profile news stories of late.

- There is limited understanding and awareness of all the responsibilities and requirements and this could leave the parties involved open to legal action, fraud, financial consequences and a host of other implications if things were to go wrong.

- The model is simple, but not easy! It's difficult to convince some property owners to go with this model. There can be disagreement, misunderstanding or ignorance that can lead to the margin between rent in and rent out being eroded. Finally, it's a very hands-on model and would not suit people that are 'time poor' or don't enjoy working as an operator of people and properties.

Reality Check

There are two real life challenges that property investors or R2R operators should be aware of if contemplating using this strategy.

Rent-to-Rent deals are often difficult to find because not everyone understands the underlying theory. Because it's not a standard rental arrangement, Rent-to-Rent can be viewed with suspicion by less 'sophisticated' owners. Therefore, the people most likely to agree to renting out a property on an R2R basis are probably landlords, people in negative equity that need to move on, or owners of property looking for a guaranteed, yet hassle-free income stream or who have limited time or interest to manage their properties any longer. It can also pay to target what I call 'sticky properties'. These are properties that have stuck on the rental or even sales market for some time. In fact, if you see a property listed as for sale and also for rent, this could be a good target to approach.

Alternative or non-traditional types of property can also be a clue to a potential R2R opportunity, such as commercial buildings, guest houses/B&Bs and nursing homes (although change of use consent may also be required). As these are already commercial properties, the owner is likely to be more open to a pitch for R2R.

This is an unregulated market and so care should be taken when dealing with people, be they sourcing companies, trainers or advisors (gurus). A simple Google search will reveal many that operate in this field, and like any aspect of property investing it is vital to undertake thorough due diligence on the people and entities that we deal with.

However, for people with limited capital to get started in property and/or with challenges securing more traditional finance, R2R can be a great way to get involved in the property market. R2R operators are leveraging off other people's assets with what is an income strategy. If some of the proceeds can be diverted into deposits on more traditional purchases it can be converted into a wealth strategy instead. Equally, add in an option to purchase on an R2R property and inflation could reduce the effective deposit required to buy the property in a few years' time. Alternatively, if you can negotiate an exchange with delayed completion agreement, and then 'arbitrage the valuation' between a single-let and an investment valuation as with an HMO for example, then you can 'force the valuation' to reduce your level of deposit and allow time to prove it.

A little twist for those of you that have read this chapter thinking, 'I have a little bit of capital, say £25k to £50k, but I don't have the time and know-how to give R2R a go', then, why not consider acting as an Angel Investor or as a way to 'earn and learn' at an arm's length into somebody else's R2R business instead? You could negotiate a fixed return or a percentage share of the profits, potentially. Keep in mind, though, that your operator partner will effectively be heavily employed in running the R2R business and so they do need to be properly compensated and rewarded also.

Chapter Sixteen

Best of The Rest – Another Dozen Property Finance Strategies

Life is like a giant smorgasbord of more delicious alternatives than you can ever hope to taste. So you have to reject having some things you want in order to get other things you want more."

Ray Dalio

What You Need To Know

As we come towards the end of this book on property finance, there were a few remaining property finance strategies that I had accumulated and wanted to share with you. There are more to them than I will cover here; suffice to say that this is more of a signpost to some of these less familiar approaches to financing your property activities … just to have in your property finance toolbox.

Some of these strategies might work at different times in the property cycle. For example, the idea that a bank would offer 100% finance on a purchase might seem like a crazy idea to those that understand how bankers usually think, as I do. However, that's exactly how I managed to obtain a nice three-bedroom apartment in the Algarve soon after the global financial crisis. So, don't necessarily dismiss all of these potential concepts straight-away, just because it might not be possible right now. Instead, keep them in mind, as one day the property cycle will turn once again, making the timing more suitable to consider some of these.

Feel free to research further around any of the dozen more random property financing methods that follow, therefore. Also, do keep in mind that many of these alternative strategies are advanced, specialised or come from alternative business sectors that could be applied to your property activities in a creative way.

1. Adverse Possession

This strategy is basically squatting! Did you know that you can legally claim a property or piece of land as your own after occupying and possessing it for a certain period of time, even without owning legal title? Yes, adverse possession allows squatters legal rights to claim full legal title to land and property. You do need to be patient, as you have to wait 12 years before a legal title can be registered in the squatter's name.

Here is an extract from the www.gov.uk website on the subject:

Where land is unregistered a squatter can acquire title by their adverse possession over a period of time. This is through a combination of the positive effect of the adverse possession giving them title and the negative effect of the Limitation Act 1980 which extinguishes the documentary or paper title (section 17 of the Limitation Act 1980).

Under the law as it was prior to the coming into effect of the Land Registration Act 2002 on 13 October 2003, the provisions of the Limitation Act 1980 applied in the same manner to registered land as unregistered land except that the estate of the registered proprietor.

Since the introduction of the Land Registration Act 2002, there are different rules that apply to registered and unregistered land. In either case, "certain things will need to be proven in order to legally take over the title". Here are some of the essentials that need to apply for adverse possession to be proven, again courtesy of HM Government.

You must show that:

- The squatter has factual possession of the land.

- The squatter has the necessary intention to possess the land.

- The squatter's possession is without the owner's consent.

- All of the above have been true of the squatter and any predecessors through whom the squatter claims for at least 12 years prior to the date of the application.

Many of the cases of adverse possession come about by what we might call neighbourly disputes around boundary lines where one neighbour pinches a bit of the next door's garden, for example. However, I recall a case where a friend of mine had a piece of land in what you might call a 'brownfield area'. It was open and unoccupied for many years having been inherited from a relative. One day, he drove past the plot and noticed that a fence had been erected around the plot; that's factual possession by the way.

My friend sought legal advice and it became clear that they had to legally evict the squatter and reclaim possession of the land as their own, or risk losing it after 12 years. They did that and later decided to sell the plot to create a McDonalds! Had they not taken this action, then the squatter would have been able to legally claim the plot as their own after 12 years had elapsed and then sell it to McDonalds themselves!

TPV TIP: Adverse possession is what you might call a slow burner when it comes to property strategies! Claim an empty property or piece of land, occupy it and then wait 12 years to assign the proper legal title to yourself. As you might imagine, there are a number of pitfalls to this approach. However, you could legitimately occupy without payment, potentially claim a rent or equivalent from a tenant during the occupancy period and then one day your ship could come in with the paper title in hand. But don't hold your breath…

2. Assignable Off-Plan Contracts

This is one of those strategies that seems to be prevalent at a certain stage in the property cycle. Back in the mid-to-late noughties, the property market was in the 'mania stage' of the property cycle. You couldn't avoid people talking about property and how they were making loads of money as house prices were literally going through the roof. People started to come up with ingenious ways to finance their activities and one of these was assignable off-plan contracts.

During the late noughties, house building was booming. If you looked at the skyline of any major cityscape then all you could see was cranes, as blocks of apartments were going up at great speed. Many of these apartments were offered for sale on an 'off-plan basis', which meant that you committed to buy them before they were built, usually by paying a small deposit. Many of these contracts contained a 'right of assignment' provision, which meant you could legally assign the contract to someone else – or resell it in other words. As prices were rising at breakneck speed, it was possible to buy an off-plan property and also resell it during the 12–24 month build period and make a profit due to the significant rises in property prices during this time. Sometimes, off-plan properties were assigned more than once during this time, with each seller pocketing a profit during their holding period.

Whilst it sounds great, it has a significant potential drawback. If the market shifts downwards, then it's akin to trying to catch a falling knife! Add into the mix a credit crunch, a glut of samey-looking apartment blocks that people did not, fundamentally, want to live in and you have the perfect storm to be left holding the proverbial baby. So, it's one of those strategies where timing is everything you might say. Acquire and flip on the contract during a fast-rising property market but don't be left with a potentially worthless obligation to buy an apartment should the tide turn against you, is all.

3. Shared Ownership

Shared ownership is a government-backed scheme of home ownership. Therefore, it's not exactly suitable as an investment strategy as such. However, when you consider how capital intensive property ownership is, then a saving on buying your own home could give rise to additional capital being made available for alternative investment purposes instead.

Combined with low deposit mortgage schemes for homeowner buyers, shared ownership could be one of those strategies that allows people to gain a foothold on the housing ladder and acquire a stake in their own home, whilst enabling additional opportunities to profit through property in an alternative way.

Shared ownership is essentially a scheme where you part buy and part rent a property, usually in conjunction with a housing association. In fact, my own daughter asked me about this exact thing. She is currently renting and saving for a deposit to buy her first home. She sent me a link to a property where she could buy a 25% share for around £70,000, which meant the property was worth £280,000. She could theoretically get a 95% mortgage on her £70,000 share for just £3,500 in this example.

Sadly, as a student right now, she does not have the earnings to support the mortgage application, which would also need to demonstrate affordability of both the mortgage and rent components of the shared ownership arrangement. But you can't fault her logic for considering it! Maybe, once she graduates and takes her first or second job for this one…

However, if she could secure the mortgage and acquire the property, it had a second bedroom which, subject to the terms of her shared ownership agreement, she could rent out under the government's Rent-A-Room Scheme. This could give her up to £7,500 per year in tax-free income to help support her mortgage and rental costs. Not a bad return on a £3,500 cash investment, hey?

4. Revolving Credit Facility

I was chatting to a listener of *The Property Voice Podcast*. In essence, they had managed to accumulate a significant number of properties over the past 7–8 years. They felt a little bit stuck, as they had significant growth plans but didn't have piles of cash lying around any more, as it was always invested into buying the next buy-to-let property. They were therefore 'asset rich yet cash poor', relatively speaking, of course. What they didn't realise was, that even though at something like 60% loan to value on average across their portfolio, they could potentially access some of the equity above this level for further investment purposes.

Enter the 'Revolving Credit Facility' (RCF). Whilst an RCF could vary from provider to provider, of which there are not so many, in essence it looks as follows: the RCF provider will provide a facility or 'line of credit' at a value above the mortgage or first charge of anything up to 95% of the property value. They will want a second charge to secure their position, so keep that in mind both in terms of your own risk profile but also in that the first charge-holder will need to give their consent to this being put in place. There will be a set-up fee to pay and then interest once the funds are actually used, although not usually when the facility is set up. For this reason, it is often referred to as a 'hunting licence', as it allows you to have the certainty of having funds available to go hunting for that bargain property that has to be snapped up in double-quick time.

In the case of the podcast listener, he had a portfolio valued in the region of £2.5m with outstanding mortgages of around £1.5m. If he wanted to, he could potentially create an RCF of around £875k to go hunting with. Clearly, this creates additional debt secured on the equity contained within the existing portfolio, so decide how you will invest those funds wisely and make sure you can repay the RCF, which should ideally be for a temporary period only.

TPV TIP: An RCF or 'hunting licence' is a great tool to have at your disposal. Consider what I like to call 'bluebird deals' that you rarely see, but just have to take when you do see them. Those deep discounts or other ways to add value and repay much, if not all, of the investment you sink into them. If you happen to have significant equity in your existing portfolio, then speak to a decent broker about setting up an RCF just in case. Just ask me and I will tell you which broker gave me this idea, although all is revealed in the Book Bonuses.

5. Leveraging Alternative Assets

When it comes to property finance, we often think of lending or debt that is secured on the property we wish to acquire or invest in. However, there are ways in which you can secure borrowing against a range of other assets. This is also known as 'cross-collateralisation', which is where part of a loan is secured on another asset that is not the same one being acquired. This other asset could be another property, but it could also be another type of asset altogether. Equally, rather than cross-collateralising, which links the two assets being secured to the same loan or acquisition, it could also be arranged on a separate and standalone basis by certain lenders.

I am aware of certain lenders that will consider taking security over classic cars, valuable art, second homes (including overseas homes), precious metals, gems and jewellery, fine wine and now even cryptocurrency. Basically, anything that can be valued and for which there is an established resale market could be used as an asset to raise borrowing against.

TPV TIP: This is similar in concept to a modern day pawnbroker, I guess you might say. So, just in the case of the pawnbroker, you do need to make sure that you have a very clear exit plan in order to repay any debt secured against these valuable and often sentimental assets if you want to make sure you get them back again!

6. Home Equity Release

A variation on a theme here in some respects, as the concept is still to use an alternative asset as security for lending that can be used in another property transaction. The reason for listing this one separately is that there is a rarely available mortgage product called an offset mortgage where this could be utilised to provide additional capital for property investment and lending purposes. Besides the offset mortgage, you could consider a remortgage, further advance or a second-charge loan to release equity for investment purposes.

Given the fact that you are accessing equity in your own home, this also means reducing the level of equity you have and also paying more money in interest for your day-to-day living costs. For these reasons, I tend to favour the temporary use of equity in your own home with a short-term repayment, rather than a more permanent arrangement that increases your long-term home mortgage and cost of living. That said, some people are 'home equity rich yet investment cash poor' so to speak and if this will allow you to invest at a higher rate of return than the cheapest cost of finance you are ever likely to have, then it's something to consider.

In addition to an offset mortgage, another temporary use of home equity for property investment purposes could be to provide security in the form of equity in your home to a bridging finance lender. I have in the past acquired a property with 100% funding, or none of my own cash, by providing a second charge to my home to a bridging lender to top up the lending on an investment property purchase. In my case, I made sure that I would have enough upside profit once I completed the project to repay the second charge bridging loan secured on my home. A variation could have been to agree a further advance with my existing home loan lender or a remortgage at a higher loan-to-value but these would have led to more permanent debts secured on my home, which I did not want to do.

7. Arbitrage the Valuation

What is a property worth? The common response is what someone is willing to pay for it. However, when it comes to property finance, that's not always true. There are usually two outside parties that dictate what a property is worth when it comes to property finance, particularly regarding lending. These parties are the finance provider, often a lender and the valuer, often a surveyor. What they say, and in particular what the valuer says, is gospel when it comes to property finance. So, keep that in mind whether buying or selling property – whilst a buyer and seller of a property may agree on a price, its value for finance purposes is dictated by the lender to some extent and the valuer to a very significant extent. Get used to the phrase 'valuer's opinion', which is rarely overturned.

That said, one way to increase the amount you can raise against a property is dependent on the *type* of valuation that is undertaken. My property buddy, Damien Fogg, is also a RICS Chartered Building Surveyor. He wrote a guest blog post on property valuations for *The Property Voice* website, which turns out to be one of the most popular blogs on the site … but don't tell him that or his ego will grow even bigger. 😉 In that blog post, Damien outlines the five most common methods of valuing real estate property. Here is an extract:

There are five methods of property valuation that are generally recognised globally.

1. Comparative method
   - Comparing the property value with similar properties sold or on the market nearby.

   - For most residential investors this may be the only method you will experience.

2. Investment method
   - Uses discounted cash flow techniques or yield calculations to establish value through the income-producing nature of the asset.

- This method is often used in commercial valuations, notably including some HMO valuations.

3. **Residual method**
   - This is used to establish the valuation of development sites.
   - Uses the final gross development value, the cost of developing the land and the 'developer profit' to assign a balancing or residual value for the site.

4. **Profits method**
   - Used more as a valuation for a business premises, such as hotels and cinemas; it's often expressed as a multiple of annual profit or income in some instances on what is termed a 'going concern basis'.

5. **Replacement cost method**
   - This is generally reserved for buildings with little comparable evidence, such as churches, schools, etc.
   - The cost of the land and the cost to rebuild the structure are the basis of the valuation.
   - For some property developers there will be a need to understand the Residual method of property valuation and the replacement cost method of valuation.

Let's focus on the first two for a moment: the comparative and investment methods. The comparative method is what most of us are used to – it's the how-much-did-next-door-sell-for type of method. You look up recent sales and sometimes on-the-market properties to gauge a property's value by comparing it to these. However, with an investment property, you can also value it based on the income (or rent) that it generates, as an alternative.

A standard buy-to-let is very unlikely to be valued on an investment basis, as it more closely resembles a regular home than an investment property. This is because come time to sell, the likely buyers will include regular homeowners as well as investors. However, for properties that don't fully resemble a regular home, the valuation can often be gauged based on it's income instead. The most obvious example is a commercial property, which is based on yield expectations, with certain adjustments. However, there are some properties that could fall somewhere between these two examples of regular residential and commercial properties. These could include houses of multiple occupation (HMO), serviced accommodation or mixed-use properties, for example.

Arbitrage is typically where you buy something in one market and resell it in another one. A common example is buying a property at an auction, which is often frequented by investors and developers or 'professional buyers', and then reselling it into the open market via a regular estate agent, which is often frequented by regular homeowners or 'amateur buyers'. That's one method of applying arbitrage to potentially gain on the different values expectations between the professionals and the amateurs.

However, a similar approach to arbitrage could also apply to the type of valuation. Here, you could buy from an 'amateur seller' and then have the property revalued by a 'professional valuer', clearly as long as it is recognised as an investment. This usually requires some type of conversion project to transform the property from a regular home into a recognisable investment instead.

Another way to arbitrage the valuation is to defy gravity. What I mean by this is to do something that is extremely difficult to do. In the world of property finance and valuations, one of the seeming 'laws of physics' that cannot be broken is that of lending against the purchase price, regardless of a higher property valuation. Those times when we bag ourselves a property at 'below market value', only to have the smile wiped from our face when the valuer and lender conspire to limit the lending to the lower of the market value OR the purchase price on acquisition.

Well, there are some lenders, particularly bridging lenders, that will consider lending against the higher open market value upon acquisition instead. Now, imagine lending based on, say, a 20% higher valuation compared to what you are paying for the property and you are in effect defying the laws of gravity, so to speak. If you find a lender prepared to do this, then you can reduce the level of your own cash required to fund the deal and that really should put that smile back on your face.

TPV TIP: Use the idea of valuation arbitrage alongside other financing methods for optimal 'financial engineering'. For example, you could buy a large residential home using bridging finance. Then, convert it into an HMO that clearly looks different to a regular home, such as having ensuite bathroom in every bedroom, including what was a lounge or dining room. Then, have it revalued for a commercial loan upon completion using the investment valuation method. Depending on a number of factors, this investment valuation could come in higher than an equivalent comparative method valuation, which would look at regular residential properties to arrive at the valuation. I often find that this works best in areas with high yield, than lower yielding locations, as a bonus tip.

---

8. Supplier Credit & Loans

This could be useful when looking at how to fund the works cost for a project. There are two different angles that could be possible here, with one more frequent than the other.

In the case of suppliers, sometimes you can agree trade terms with them. Here you get given a trade account credit limit, which would allow you to buy goods, materials or services on extended payment terms. Whilst terms vary, they would typically be set as 30 days in arrears. Sometimes, a slightly more generous, payment by the end of the month following the month of invoice provide up to 60 days of credit. You can also potentially agree similar terms with builders and contractors. Taking 30–60 days to pay a supplier might not sound like it could save you a lot in terms of cashflow and cost of credit, but it all adds up!

As a little twist, I have also had the luxury of paying for larger ticket items such as windows, furniture and such like using supplier or vendor financing. This can be arranged directly with the supplier or by their appointed finance provider. Sometimes, but not always, there is a charge for credit, either as a premium by paying by card or an interest charge for spreading the payment out over time. So, do the sums to see if this cost of finance is worth it to you in terms of the financing returns you will get by deferring payment.

TPV TIP: If you combine a supplier trade account with, say, 45 days average credit terms, using the pay at the end of the month of invoice method, along with payment via a credit card, you can get between 30 and 90 days free credit. If you are undertaking a quick refurbishment project, this could save you having to use your own cash for materials costs for this period of time, which could lead to a significant cashflow advantage. Equally, getting a payment plan on, say, furniture for an HMO or serviced accommodation property would allow the payments to be aligned to the income over time rather than paid out up-front. Neat, hey?

---

9. Business Acquisition Structures

This is an indirect method of finance and so won't suit that many situations, so feel free to skim this section if it starts to become a little foggy. Here, the idea is to use some of the alternatives found in business acquisition or operations financing to provide additional property finance options, under the right circumstances. An example could be commercial loans, which might value a business based on its revenues or profitability. This could potentially be combined with, or enhanced by, any property the business owns.

Other examples taking us down a different path of alternative business finance include asset finance (lending secured against non-property fixtures and fittings), invoice discounting/factoring (advance funding of sales invoices), subscription income advances (specialist finance against monthly recurring income receipts) along with a bank overdraft/ unsecured loan.

You may wish to consider these sorts of options if looking to acquire a business as a 'going concern'. The reason for mentioning this as a property finance strategy is in case you want to add value to property that sits inside an existing business. Think of a shop where you might want to develop the 'uppers' into flats, or a business that has some land or an unutilised building that could be redeveloped to realise a value uplift as examples to consider here.

10. Debt Servicing via Power of Attorney

Here's a neat one. Instead of buying a property and then looking at how to finance it, why not defer the legal acquisition and simply take over any existing debt liability and payments instead? Clearly, this would need the support and agreement of both the current owner and/or the current lender(s) in order to succeed. Equally, the power of attorney would allow you to act in the place of the owner/borrower so that you can undertake whatever type of recovery or value-adding action you might wish to take.

This strategy is often used where the owner or borrower has found themselves in financial difficulty, although before formal repossession has taken place, ideally. Our job would be to satisfy any lender that agreeing to us stepping into the shoes of the owner/borrower would result in a better outcome for them rather than the repossession alternative. In some ways, this strategy is similar to an assisted sale, along with obtaining the lender's consent, so make sure you check out that chapter along with this section to better understand the strategy.

TPV TIP: This type of financing solution could be a better outcome for an owner in financial difficulty given the fact that repossession results in a complete loss of control, usually extremely high costs, often along with a diminished resale value. So, it can be what you might call a win-win-win outcome. It does need a very professional and I would strongly suggest an ethical approach that considers the best outcome for the owner/borrower, along with almost perfect timing!

---

11. Mortgage Host & Guarantees

OK, this one could be somewhat controversial, so bear with me here!

Starting with the least controversial approach, if you find yourself in a position where you would find it difficult to qualify for lending, then obtaining a third-party guarantor to back you could potentially open up more property finance opportunities to you. Of course, the point of a guarantor is that they would stand in your shoes if you defaulted on the loan, so make sure you do not default on the loan! At the same time, consider the position you might be placing a guarantor in and think carefully whether that's the best thing for them on balance.

There are essentially two types of guarantor that you could look at here. The first is the common one of a director's or shareholder's guarantee that you might be asked to provide if you seek lending through a limited company, for example. In fact, it is quite difficult to get a loan for a company without this type of guarantee, unless you have an established, profitable trading history or significant net assets that the lender could take into consideration. A variation could be to provide a cross-company guarantee from another company owned by the same people as the loan application. This would allow the lender to take into consideration the additional security offered under the guarantee and might change a no to a yes, or at least reduce the cost of the finance terms offered.

The second type of guarantee comes from what is usually a more 'unconnected third party', such as a family member or business partner. Here the third party would help the lender to underwrite and approve the lending by way of their guarantee that supports the proposed borrower. Just take care not to place an unsuspecting or unsophisticated person into a potentially compromised position here, I would add.

In terms of controversial approaches, there are perhaps not many as controversial as that of the 'mortgage host'. A mortgage host is where one party agrees to act as the borrower on behalf of another party who may not qualify for lending on their own. It goes a step further than a guarantee as it places the mortgage host as the sole party responsible for the debt liability, which is more risk and responsibility than with a guarantee.

The controversy comes from two places in essence: non-disclosure to the lenders and the detrimental treatment of the mortgage host. Most lenders would prohibit the idea of mortgage hosting that is not disclosed to them under their terms and conditions, so I don't recommend you do that and so do look to disclose your arrangement. There's nothing wrong with a family member taking on a loan on the part of their relative under the right situations, such as a parent taking on a mortgage for their child to live away from home at university, say. Equally, in a business partnership, such as a joint venture, one party may take on the responsibility and liability for a loan on behalf of the partnership. The partnership or joint venture should be disclosed to the lender, however. Both of these options involve a transparent disclosure, which removes the controversy with the lenders.

What is not acceptable is where there is deception, fraud or downright manipulation or abuse of the mortgage host. There have sadly been cases where someone was paid a nominal sum to 'front' a mortgage application by an undisclosed party to the lender, only to later find themselves left high and dry by the person paying that fee. Even if the intention is a good one, it is not acceptable under any circumstances to place innocent, ignorant or otherwise vulnerable people in a position where the risk and liability of debts from a third party could fall on their shoulders.

TPV TIP: When considering providing a guarantee, try and negotiate one with a fixed amount rather than an open-ended indemnity. This will at least place a cap on your liability should the unexpected worse case happen with it being called in.

---

12. Conditional Exchange

This is an alternative to an Exchange with Delayed Completion (EDC) agreement, which we discussed in Chapter Twelve, so revisit that chapter to refresh your memory there.

With EDC the variable is usually simply one of time, where the gap between exchange and completion of contracts is set to a certain time period. In the case of a conditional exchange, completion on acquiring property or a piece of land after exchange is linked to a certain pre-set condition instead of a set period of time. Examples of this could be obtaining planning permission, removing a restrictive covenant, obtaining vacant possession, fixing a structural issue, or removing a legal liability such as an attachment liability order.

In fact, the party that undertakes the resolution of the conditions could be the current owner, us as the incoming owner, or a combination of the two. The benefit of this type of contractual agreement is that it provides a bit more certainty to the parties with an 'as long as this happens, then we will definitely complete on the transaction' outcome. However, it also allows that certainty to offset any risk or abortive cost of 'fixing the problem'. As a result, it's also another kind of vendor finance you might say.

TPV TIP: This type of strategy usually works best with either a 'sticky property', where the owner is struggling to sell due to a problem that needs fixing and/or where there is too much risk associated with achieving a certain outcome, such as planning approval. In other words, it is one that requires both a level of expertise to fix the problem and also a good level of co-operation between the buyer and seller, which comes out of cultivating the relationship and fully explaining the circumstances and risks.

Advantages and Benefits

There are several advantages that come with these additional property finance strategies:

- Less reliance on traditional forms of property finance.

- Combining property strategies with property finance strategies for a more holistic commercial or 'financial engineering' solution.

- A greater level of creative, commercial or consultative property finance solutions in the toolkit that can be applied to the right situation and timing, turning a definite no into a possible maybe or a yes at times.

Disadvantages and Risks

There are also several disadvantages with these additional property finance strategies:

- There are often limited opportunities to utilise them, further restricted by the stage in the property cycle.

- They can be complex or more sophisticated to deploy or understand by the current owner, so require an advanced level of knowledge, professional support and great skill in dealing with sometimes less sophisticated people.

- They can sometimes be controversial in that they could place vulnerable people at risk or be in contravention with lender policies leading to potential unintended consequences and exposure, if not correctly applied.

Reality Check

Whilst I wanted to share another dozen property financing strategies in this final content chapter, they are not without complexity and risk.

As you will have picked up throughout, there could be limited opportunity to deploy these strategies. Even if we do find the right situation to do so, they need to be carefully applied to avoid placing either ourselves or others into a potentially difficult position. For these reasons, I suggest these strategies are used in very specific circumstances and timing. I would highly advise seeking professional advice, including accountants and tax advisors, solicitors and finance brokers on your team.

That all being said, as you will have also detected throughout, I have myself, or know of others who have, used many, if not all, of these alternative and more creative property finance strategies in the right situation.

Summing Up

If, like me, you like the idea of being a 'financial engineer', with plenty of tools in your toolbox ready to deploy for the right job at the right time, then I am sure you found this chapter illuminating. Remember that by the time you have read this book you will have at least 50 property finance strategies that you could apply to any given situation, which is quite likely a considerable number more than when you started.

Part Four

Bringing It All Together

Chapter Seventeen

Money Mindset

You can have all the knowledge and skills in the world, but if your [money] 'blueprint' isn't set for success, you're financially doomed.

T. Harv Eker

It's impossible ... unless?

Darren Hardy

Get ready, as this chapter is going to be quite a different one! Many of the people that I work with have not really come across the idea of 'money mindset', let alone considered how it plays out in their property finance journey. However, I would encourage you to maintain an open mind and join me here as we unravel the main concepts. Then, you will potentially have a greater awareness and understanding of how your own thoughts around money could be playing out with your results around money when it comes to investing in property and property finance.

What You Need To Know

Call it what you want – money mindset, money blueprint, money DNA, money blocks, sacred money types and so on – but our thoughts towards *and* relationship with money plays a massive part in how we can bring many of the ideas and concepts outlined in this book to life for us personally.

Some time ago, I realised that I had some limiting beliefs, financial triggers and repeating patterns when it came to money matters. These did not always serve me as well as I would have liked. As a result of this greater awareness, I have been on something of a quest to understand my own money mindset over recent years. Great credit must be given to Sue Whittle, who became a Certified Money Coach, and used me as a bit of a guinea pig to road test her now expanded coaching capabilities. In fact, Sue also works alongside me to deliver *The Property Voice Apprentice Programme*, which specifically includes an opportunity for the participants to explore their money mindset. It really is that foundational to our success in this business of property and also property finance.

Our money mindset is how we think about money and just like all thoughts, they have an impact on our behaviour, actions and, ultimately, our results. Our thoughts and beliefs are the 'roots' and our results and outcomes are the 'fruits'.

> *If you really want to change your fruits,*
> *then you first have to change your roots.*

The Conscious and Unconscious Mind

Our mind consists of both the conscious mind, but also the unconscious mind.

Interestingly, it is the unconscious (or subconscious) mind that is the more powerful one, as it makes us do things on autopilot, seemingly without thinking or control over our words, behaviour and actions. If you ever take a familiar journey somewhere, sometimes you arrive with very little conscious awareness or recollection of all you saw along the way.

Did you know that we have over 30,000 thoughts every single day? Of course, we are not conscious of each and every individual thought, otherwise we would quite literally be overwhelmed to the point of brain-freeze. So, our unconscious mind is the one that makes most of these decisions for us; mostly based on our ingrained beliefs, learned behaviours, social and environmental influences, habits and rituals, our emotions and even our ancestral animal instincts.

Daniel Kahneman, in the book *Thinking Fast and Slow*, describes the idea of our unconscious thoughts driving our behaviour as 'Type 1 Thinking'. He describes the more conscious thoughts, where we make considered and deliberate decisions as 'Type 2 Thinking'. What we need is more Type 2 Thinking to deliberately take control of our thoughts and emotions. This will help to ensure that we make good choices and considered decisions, instead of instinctive or impulsive ones, when it comes to money matters. However, we cannot take control of over 30,000 thoughts a day, so we need to develop some kind of system combining principles, rules, habits or 'heuristics' that help us to practise healthy thinking leading to better outcomes, at least in money matters.

Before we can get to that place, we need to check on our beliefs, values and ideology. After all, it is our beliefs, values and ideology that drive our thoughts and emotions. It is our thoughts and emotions that drive our behaviour and actions. It is our behaviour and actions that drive our results and outcomes.

Ergo, we need to start with our beliefs around money if we wish to change our results around money.

Beliefs, Values & Ideology → Thoughts & Emotions → Behaviour & Actions → Results & Outcomes

Your beliefs become your thoughts,
Your thoughts become your words,
Your words become your actions,
Your actions become your habits,
Your habits become your values,
Your values become your destiny.

Mahatma Gandhi

However, we can start to take control and begin to reprogramme our unconscious thoughts, leading ultimately to better results and outcomes. One of the simplest ways is to plant conscious thoughts into our unconscious mind. A few simple ways to do this include practising affirmations, visualisations and posing questions for the unconscious mind to work on. There is emerging research and anecdotal evidence to support how the words and imagery that we take into our unconscious mind influences our thoughts and so our results, ultimately. Just look at the advertising industry and you can see how that can play out.

My wife and I are big followers of the Olympics. I recall watching many an athlete close their eyes and 'rehearse their perfect race' in their mind before their big moment. However, they are not merely rehearsing this for the first time in an Olympic final but probably for the thousandth time over the preceding four years! It's the repetition and positive reinforcement that counts. So, why not positively 'brain cleanse' or reprogramme yourself with good thoughts and positive images of your chosen results and outcomes through affirmation and visualisation?

Another tool that I like to use is that of posing a question, problem or challenge to my unconscious mind. This is best done before you go to sleep and can be enhanced by journalling your thoughts: framing them as a question. Your unconscious mind really likes a challenge and will go to work on solving this problem, literally whilst you sleep. You can also build this idea into a morning routine to help you become aware of what it is you need, keeping it front and centre in your conscious thoughts during the day. That's a powerful combination of using both the conscious and unconscious mind right there.

The Money Archetypes

An archetype in psychological terms is a representation of a recurring theme or pattern. There are different types of archetype categorisations, which might interest you to look up and research more widely, although here we will focus on the Money Archetypes. Here they are, along with a quick summary:

- **The Innocent** – takes an ostrich-like approach to money, often burying their head in the sand. Naive and almost childlike when it comes to money matters. Characteristics: trusting, financially dependent, non-confrontational, feels powerless, represses feelings and beliefs, seeks security, feeling fearful or anxious (internally), happy-go-lucky (externally), indecisive.

- **The Victim** – living in the past, blaming others for their financial woes and expecting others to fix them. Characteristics: seeks to be rescued, lives in the past, resentful, unforgiving, addictive, lives out self-fulfilling prophecy, feels powerless, financially irresponsible, highly emotional (melancholy or angry), prone to blame others.

- **The Warrior** – sets out to conquer the world of money; seen as successful business people and investors and often make their own financial decisions. Characteristics: financially successful, confident, calculating, generous, rescuer, wise, discerning, goal-oriented, disciplined, competitive, loyal, driven, powerful.

- **The Martyr** – too busy taking care of others' needs to fully take care of their own. Characteristics: critical and judgemental, perfectionist, resentful, passive-aggressive, compassionate, wise, disappointed, self-sacrificing, caretaker, secretive, long-suffering, manipulative, controlling.

- **The Fool** – plays by different rules, often gambling or looking for shortcuts to financial success but can lose on that dice roll too. Characteristics: optimistic, overly-generous, happy-go-lucky, adventurous, lives for today, impetuous, financially irresponsible, undisciplined, restless.

- **The Creator/Artist** – living a spiritual or artistic life, often having a love-hate relationship with money and perhaps their guilt pushes money away from them at times. Characteristics: detached, non-materialistic, loner, seeker of truth, internally motivated, passive, spiritual, restless.

- **The Tyrant** – uses money to control and manipulate people, events or circumstances – think of the Netflix series *Billions*. Characteristics: controlling, unforgiving, rigid, prone to rage or violence, highly materialistic, oppressive, critical and judgemental, fearful, manipulative.

- **The Magician** – the ideal money type, using the best of the material and spiritual worlds to transform and manifest their financial reality. Characteristics: powerful, optimistic, confident, compassionate, detached, open to flow, financially balanced, transforms reality, tells the truth, lives in the present, fluid, loving, generous, trusting, vibrant, conscious, wise, spiritual.

The Money Archetypes are excerpted from the book *Money Magic* by Deborah Price along with a document called *The Eight Money Types* available from The Money Coaching Institute. Copyright 2001 © used with permission.

Now that you have an idea of the Money Archetypes, allow me tell you a few short personal stories that helped to form a part of my own money mindset, which might help you appreciate how deeply rooted some of your own thinking might be.

One of my earliest memories around money was that I used to literally find money in the street! I would be out walking and just find money; mostly coins, sometimes the odd note and one time even a bundle of cash! This was a positive influence on my money mindset, which has stuck with me – if ever I need to find money, I know that I can. That's part of the 'magician' at work in me.

Over the past decade or so, I have become quite shrewd as an investor, I would say. I can literally look at an investment proposition and size it up in outline terms in next to no time. I am good with numbers and understand the drivers that can influence an investment, both good and bad. This is not meant as a brag, it's simply how my mind now works, I am happy to say. However, considering the fact that I am now in my mid-fifties, having studied, trained and worked in both accountancy and financial services and run my own businesses for over three decades, in addition to a solid twelve years and counting in property, that may not come as too much of a surprise to you. This would be my 'warrior' revealing itself. Although, I would say that this warrior-thinking has developed over time with a lot of hard work, practice, often forced diligence and some trial and error thrown in. This is a 'learned behaviour' for me, therefore.

On the other hand, I seem to have had occasions when bad things have happened around money too. For example, around fifteen years ago I was charmed by the combination of fast growth in the Asian economies and China in particular, helped along by an IFA who liked to sail close to the wind, let's say. I ended up placing the vast majority of my pension investment into Chinese growth funds in what I now call a 'rolling the dice move' with my then inadequate pension fund. It started very well, with double-digit growth. But come the global financial crisis, and whilst the whole world suffered, China seemed to suffer more than many and went into reverse for a period, along with my pension fund! There's more I could share but this illustrates the 'fool' that could sometimes be at work in my financial affairs and with my money mindset.

As Sue Whittle likes to put it, imagine you are driving a Winnebago, which is one of those very large recreational vehicles that you can both travel and live in. Now, in that Winnebago you have up to eight people, some are up at the front bench-like seat driving, navigating or just there to influence where you go and what you do along the journey. Some are in the back or the boot, you know they are there but they don't bother you too much and just come out occasionally. The rest are in and around the middle and chime in now and again as you move along your journey. These people are like the influences in our money mindset: who is up front, driving, navigating or influencing your thoughts and relationships around money? In my case, it seems to be the 'magician' as the driver, the 'warrior' as the navigator, which is a very good combination, along with the 'fool' – which I am sure you can tell purely from the name is not such a good influence to have up in the front seat with me!

So now you understand what was going on in my Winnebago, don't you?! You see, we all have these money archetypes playing a part in where our own

Winnebago is heading. Some money archetypes are helpful, many are not so much. In my own case, the Magician and Warrior would be doing just fine, only for the Fool to now and again cause us to take a dead-end turn or stop to pick up a stray! Fortunately, with the help of Sue, I have been working on improving my own money mindset; in particular to put the Fool in the boot!

Perhaps my little stories make a little more sense now. If you'd like to take the Money Archetypes quiz to find out who is in the front seat of your Winnebago, then I would suggest that you connect with Sue Whittle and ask her how to do that: https://www.linkedin.com/in/suzanwhittle/

By now, you might start to see how all of these different elements around our money mindset add up and play out in our life. Our early childhood influences start to shape our attitudes and beliefs around money. Then, we start to make our own financial decisions, influenced by our environment and then our learning and real-life experiences. Without being completely conscious about our attitude and relationship towards money, it starts to play out a kind of movie script that gets repeated time and time again. Just like watching an old movie, we know how it will end.

I can clearly see these triggers and repeating patterns play out the movie of my own life. Sure, the movie might get a bit of a makeover, or might even be turned into a sequel. However, just as the three *Hangover* movies follow a very similar pattern, so too does our movie sequels follow a familiar pattern. In order to change the end of our movie or make a new plot, we would need to change the lead character and how they play out their role. This is the idea of the next section of this chapter, to consider how we can change the lead character in our own money mindset movie.

How To Control, Influence and Change Our Money Mindset

Just as our thoughts in general play a part in our behaviour and actions. so too do our thoughts and beliefs around money. Understanding what our personal money archetypes are is a significant part of unblocking the flow of money towards us. In fact, those two words 'block' and 'flow' give us some real insights into what is going on beneath the surface.

The best place to start with changing our beliefs, values and ideology around money is to better understand them in the first place. Here are my top tips of how best to do that.

To understand and reprogramme our money belief, values and ideology system, I recommend the following steps

- Take the Money Archetype Quiz as mentioned above to see who is driving your Winnebago (contact Sue Whittle via the link above).

- I would also strongly suggest getting in touch with your core values – those 3–6 things that make us who we really are. You will find a couple of resources to do that in Appendix 2.*

- Read the money mindset books listed in Appendix 2.*

- Build in affirmations, visualisations, journalling and conscious/unconscious problem-solving challenges into your morning and evening routines.*

- Write down your money mindset plan, including investment principles, due diligence checks and your Type 2 decision-making criteria.**

- Consider getting some money mindset coaching for a 'reset' and external intervention in your thoughts and relationship around money.

*   See the Appendices for further reading and resources around these ideas.

**   I use checklists and have investment or buying criteria in my property business – you can get copies of these in the Book Bonuses.

Now, I realise that a lot of this chapter relates to things largely unseen, somewhat intangible or even esoteric. I also appreciate that as I am taking you deeper into the topic, some of these concepts might sit better with you than others. I often say that we should use the 'supermarket approach' when it comes to books and other forms of learning material – including my own!

So, take what you need from this chapter, and in fact this entire book, just as you might when you go shopping at the supermarket. However, before you leave anything behind, perhaps give some of these ideas a chance or even a 30-day trial. What do you say? The reason that I suggest this is that I have done this myself and have found great results from doing so.

Now that I have nicely primed you to receive more or leave some ideas behind, here comes the final dimension in our money mindset…which might just blow your mind!

The Collective Mind

Besides our conscious and unconscious minds that we covered earlier, there is a third mind that I would like to mention: the 'Collective Mind'.

The collective mind is the combination of all of our unconscious minds or every person on the planet. Many believe that we are all connected by an unseen level of energy – a hidden force if you like. Imagine having a conscious or unconscious thought and that thought being transmitted as energy to the collective mind of all seven billion people on the planet.

OK, so I appreciate that this might perhaps be starting to all sound a little bit stretched for some. However, I can tell you that I have found this to be increasingly true on many an occasion.

For example, I recently reset a personal limiting belief around the size of property projects and business opportunities that I could get involved with. Honestly, I did not know how I would do this but I simply set myself the challenge or 'problem' of doing property deals in the £1m to £10m value range instead of £0.5m to £1m range, where I had become settled. That's an example of me reprogramming my own thoughts.

However, in what might seem a bizarre twist of fate, I started to receive larger opportunities AND then also the means to achieve them financially. I would be having a random conversation with someone and they would say something like "I know this investor that is looking to park £2.5m, do you have anything of that sort of size that they could get involved with?". Err, I didn't think so but suddenly now I do! That's an illustration of how putting a thought as energy out there into the universe, allowed other people to pick up on the signal and unconsciously bring the opportunities and the means back to the sender of that signal.

OK, so this is a book primarily about the solid, hard world of property finance and not the softer, less tangible worlds of psychology or spirituality. Or is it? If you find yourself wondering why you are not getting the breaks, the deals, the yeses to your bids and the right property finance to support your goals and objectives, then perhaps the answer lies within … and that sentence was meant to have a dual meaning. 😉

Needless to say, I will leave it there for now, if only as a seed for you to allow it to take root in your unconscious mind. I sincerely hope that it does take root and that it is watered and cultivated into the juicy fruit of financial success, allowing you to realise your plans, goals and dreams in property through the property finance tools and channels outlined in this book – along with a very healthy money mindset. After all, what have you got to lose by trying?

TPV TIP: Keep an open, receptive and active perspective around the topic of money mindset – it could literally change your destiny! Remember, "it's impossible … unless?".

Appendix 1

Books and Further Resources Around Money Mindset

Specific to the concept of Money Mindset

- *Money Magic* – Deborah L. Price

- *Secrets of The Millionaire Mind* – T. Harv Eker

- *The Soul of Money* – Lynne Twist

Some great books on mindset and values, generally

- *Growth Mindset* – Dr Carol Dweck

- *Thinking Fast and Slow* – Daniel Kahneman

- *The Chimp Paradox* – Professor Steve Peters

- *The Values Factor* – Dr John Demartini

- *What Matters Most: The Power of Living Your Values* – Hyrum W. Smith

Some more great books on money, investment linked to mindset

- *The Richest Man in Babylon* – George Samuel Clason

- *Rich Dad, Poor Dad* – Robert Kiyosaki

- *Think and Grow Rich* – Napoleon Hill

- *What I Learned Losing a Million Dollars* – Jim Paul & Brendan Moynihan

- *Seven Strategies for Wealth and Happiness* – Jim Rohn

- *Principles* – Ray Dalio

- *Get Rich, Lucky Bitch* – Denise Duffield-Thomas

Some resources around visualisation, affirmations and journalling

Visualisation

- Visualization Techniques to Affirm Your Desired Outcomes: A Step-by-Step Guide from Jack Canfield

- How Vision Boards Work & How To Make A Powerful One For Yourself: Sarah Regan writing for MBG Mindfulness

- MindMovies App

Affirmations

- 5 Steps to Make Affirmations Work for You: Ronald Alexander Ph.D. in Psychology Today

- *What to Say When You Talk to Yourself* – Shad Helmstetter (Book)

- ThinkUp Affirmations App

Journalling

- The Journaling Deconstruction: Robin Sharma

- The Bullet Journal Method

- Five-Minute Journal App

<h1 style="text-align:center">Chapter Eighteen</h1>

<h1 style="text-align:center">Property Financing Strategy
and Review</h1>

What You Need To Know

Now that we have covered 50+ different types of property finance through-out this book, it is time to pull it all together into a personalised Property Finance Strategy. We should have both a 'strategy' and a 'plan'. We need both of these to support our goals and objectives, which will be subject to change as we progress along our property journey. I like to use the term 'fix and flex' in this context. We do need to fix our goals, plans and strategy in order to have a solid sense of direction in order to make progress. However, times change and so do we, so we also need to have some flexibility to fine-tune or alter course along the way too.

In this wrap-up chapter, I plan to cover the following key themes of our Property Finance Strategy and Plan:

1. The stage we are at in our property journey

2. The different types of property cycle

3. The different types of property finance

4. The principles that can guide us to make effective property finance decisions

5. There is some additional bonus material if you'd like to dig a little deeper.

The process we go through might look something a little like this, although some of the steps overlap and are interrelated.

1. The stage we are at in our property journey

The 4Es of our Property Journey

a. Enter

b. Expand

c. Establish

d. Exit.

There are four clear phases in our portfolio journey, each marked out by different facets and characteristics. For example, our focus in the Enter phase will be mostly about strategy selection, education and getting our starting investment funds together, whereas in the exit phase, we will more likely be concerned with issues such as tax planning, legacy and asset realisation.

The Enter Phase

During this Enter phase of our portfolio development, by definition we don't yet have a portfolio and so the focus will be on getting started. As a result, we will have a focus on identifying which property investment and property finance strategy we should follow. This can be very daunting and overwhelming, especially when you consider that there are at least 50 different property strategies and as you have seen from this book, a similar number of property finance strategies too.

It would be easy to feel a little overwhelmed and confused if we had to choose from over 30 different property and/or property finance strategies. For this reason, I usually advise focusing on one or at most two strategies initially.

There are also the new, hot or in vogue property strategies of course. If you go to some of the property meetings and events you will hear about many of these. However, this does not mean that they are suitable for all, or indeed possible for the aspiring property investor.

At the Enter phase there will most likely be some form of scarcity and / or limitation. It could be limited funds, limited knowledge or limited skills. Finance is a big barrier to entry to starting with many property strategies, such as large deposits plus fees being required for traditional buy-to-let.

This is partly why certain other strategies, such as rent-to-rent to name but one, have emerged, which often require far less upfront investment to get started. The trade-off is likely to be time here though, so if you are in full-time employment, or have a business, this may not be a viable option to pursue, even if you wanted to.

Then, of course, there is the knowledge and skills gap, so we will have a focus on learning and development to understand more about the options and how to decide on our best way forward. This book, along with other learning resources, is available to assist us here. However, it can be very confusing, overwhelming – and even a little bit scary to be honest.

Deciding on the right property strategy and so property finance strategy will vary from person to person. In my opinion, it should be linked with our long-term goals and purpose. We should not start with strategy at all, but with our goals, vision and purpose. If we know what we are looking to achieve in life, not just out of property, and by when, we will have a better idea of what direction or strategies are likely to get us there in the best way.

In addition to our goals, vision and purpose, we should also consider our skills, resources, capabilities and even lifestyle preferences, before we decide on a chosen strategy. Certain strategies will be suitable for some investors, whilst others will not be. It will depend on our aims, time availability, resources and, crucially, our lifestyle preferences as well.

Needless to say, the Enter phase can actually be quite quick, unless we determine that we need to start saving up for a few years, before we get going. However, there is also another risk that we may face at this stage: procrastination. We may get so overwhelmed with all the information and be so well prepared for our new property investing journey that we fail to take any action. Therefore, this could mean that we fail to progress into or beyond the Enter phase if we fall into this procrastination or perfectionism trap. If this sounds like you, then consider getting some external support in this respect.

The Expand Phase

The second phase in the portfolio journey is the Expand phase.

Once we have started out on our property journey, we may wish to expand the portfolio beyond the first property, if that is relevant to reaching our desired goals. For some people, having a single investment property could be sufficient to realise all we ever need from property. This could mean that the Expand phase never happens and instead the focus would be either on the Establish and/or Exit Phases.

However, many of the people that I speak to are looking to grow their portfolio, even if it means with just one or two more properties. For some, it could mean lots more properties or different income streams to support or even replace our employment income potentially.

One of the characteristics in this Expand phase is likely to be a lack of expansion funds, especially if we sank our life savings into our first property. There could be a significant threat to our property business here too – a lack of liquid cash resources.

Often when we start in property, we end up sinking everything into the first or second BTL deal and, at the same time, our profitability will typically be at the lowest point in the first five years. If something were to go wrong with our first properties, such as a boiler breakdown, an interest rate rise or an absconding tenant, then we could be under severe pressure. Therefore, we can be quite vulnerable at this stage if we do not have an adequate buffer in place to protect against these shocks. It is wise therefore to keep some contingency funds aside just in case, despite how tempting it may be to throw caution to the wind and simply go all in instead.

There is also a risk of frustration setting in here. We may have been all pumped up and full of enthusiasm after deciding on what direction we want to take. We are likely to have ploughed headlong into our first property investment project, only to find ourselves stuck as we try to repeat the process with our next investment. For example, we may need to save up another deposit.

It is helpful to ready ourselves for this potential dip in our property journey. This could at the simplest level be a case of preparing ourselves mentally for a wait between property investments. Alternatively, it may mean seeking out alternative property finance strategies that will allow us to keep going instead.

For example, in my own case, I adopted this idea of recycling my cash by adding value to properties to release most of my initial investment funds from a project to put into the next one. This can accelerate the rate of expansion, but it is just one way of doing this. In terms of property finance, this combines bridging finance at the 'project phase' with a BTL or commercial mortgage upon completion. Then, I have adopted some of the alternative or creative property finance strategies to enable me to continue to add to my portfolio, which at the time of writing extends to 75 rental units.

In terms of our thinking at this stage, we could lose focus and get distracted or even disheartened. Equally, we could be more exposed to risk by having a lack of cash or higher debt levels. So, we should be careful and make some deliberate plans if we are to avoid some of the potential pitfalls that could arise here.

In the context of property finance, it is more about raising finance for growth at this stage. By now, we will be aware of a wide array of different traditional, alternative and creative property finance strategies that will enable us to grow and scale. It is often quite an eye-opener to the people that I mentor when they realise that they don't necessarily need to save up those 25% deposits plus all the other associated buying and/or improvement costs every few years or so. There are plenty of alternatives that can mean we can grow and scale much more rapidly.

The Establish Phase

During the Establish phase of our portfolio journey, we are likely to have a portfolio that we may be largely content with. Whilst we may still wish to grow and continue our acquisition of properties, we may be focused on what I like to call a 'rinse and repeat model'. We have probably worked out a preferred strategy and method of progressing and so it is a case of continuing to do the same thing repeatedly.

Here then, our focus may shift away from strategy selection but into scalability, debt management and diversification of risk. Starting with scalability, we may be concerned with systems, procedures and portfolio management generally. In terms of mindset here, it is all about staying calm, resilient but also agile as the market shifts, maintaining a long-term, balanced judgement and staying current with our knowledge to avoid becoming stale, or getting caught out.

To maintain sustainability, it is all about protecting what we have already and so this often means deleveraging, balancing out the risks in the portfolio and having plenty of cash reserves around. In Appendix 2, I refer to 'making our portfolio bulletproof', which is available as a Book Bonus. I suggest that you check that out if you are at this point in time with your property journey.

In the meantime, I often like to get my teeth into a 'Portfolio Review' with the people that I support in their property journey. The portfolio review can be quite a roller-coaster for some. My view of a sustainable portfolio involves making provisions for all costs and needs in our portfolio over time. This includes an adequate provision for all costs but also voids, repairs and longer-term replacements, plus updates/upgrades of our properties. Many people overlook the fact that over the sometimes decades-long holding period of an investment property we will need to redecorate and recarpet, undertake an update or upgrade of electrical and plumbing/heating systems and make provision for more significant updating to the property structure with windows, doors, roof replacement, etc.

In fact, I often talk about the need to have three separate pots if we plan to live off our property income: one to live on, one for repairs and replacement and a third for future growth. However, the good news with a portfolio review is that there is often real gold to be found in our portfolio. This gold translates into what I like to call the 3Rs: repurpose, release and redeploy. This is where we convert the 'reds' and 'ambers' in our portfolio into 'greens'. I really get a real kick out of showing people how they can upgrade the returns on their portfolio!

The Exit Phase

The final phase of our 4E Model is the Exit phase. I am talking about the portfolio here, rather than any individual properties. For many people, there is no exit, aside from our own departure from this world. That though is still an exit and will lead to a liquidation or transfer event of the portfolio, for sure.

There are alternatives to this, however, such as merely living off the fruits of the portfolio, for example by selling off individual properties over an extended time period, living off the rental income or further equity release through extending the debt. It could also mean handing down properties in the family in a controlled and planned way, selling the portfolio, or potentially setting up some kind of lasting legacy wealth fund or trust for the benefit of our chosen beneficiaries, or our chosen good causes.

It may seem odd then that some of these options mean retaining assets and others disposing of them, or that some may imply reduced debt levels, whilst others may look to extend borrowing. The fact is, that it will very much depend on individual circumstances as to which approach is considered best.

Ideally, we will have thought about all this when we started out, or soon after. However, I rather suspect that many won't have thought about things too early. Hence exit planning is often more likely to take place towards the end of the property journey, rather than at the beginning, for many.

However, perhaps with the exception of investors with net assets below the inheritance tax threshold with a will in place, it would be wise to seek professional advice sooner rather than later. Seeking out professional advice from a specialist wealth advisor or estate planner is therefore well worth considering before getting too close to the Exit phase, as it could be too late to significantly alter the landscape and direction once too far down the track.

The dominant thoughts at the Exit phase are likely to be legacy, philanthropy, enjoying the fruits and how best to keep our tax bill down! In terms of sustainability, we are often preoccupied with timing and phasing issues, asset management and wealth protection and potentially using our privileged position for the benefit of others.

In my own case, I am building towards setting up a Foundation that will hold a large part of my property assets. This will support some causes that mean a lot to me in terms of housing, entrepreneurship, learning and poverty, which of course spells HELP. My original objective when I got started was to fix a hole in my pension. Then it was about financial freedom and choice. This next phase of my own personal journey in developing the

Foundation highlights quite well how we each progress and develop as we grow. Or fix and flex as I mentioned earlier.

Now that we have a general understanding of where we are in our property journey, we can consider the different types of property cycle and these relate to our property finance strategy.

2. The different types of property cycle

I intend to keep this section brief to provide some awareness and context as to how our property finance strategy is influenced by these different cycles, without delving into further detail. There is also some further reading available in the Book Bonuses section.

Property Cycles

- The Property Market Cycle – is how house prices and rents move over time. There are highs and lows, booms and busts, especially in the house price market. These tend to follow some of the economic, credit cycles and housing affordability metrics for the most part. The rental market tends to track wage inflation but is also influenced and impacted by economic factors. Over the long-term, the trend line is definitely up. However, there are some clear cycles that repeat, meaning there are periods where prices and rents will stagnate or even fall as well.

- The Property Investment Lifecycle – a cradle to grave view of how a property moves through its own cycle. The steps are: property search and acquisition, property finance, improvement works, project exit and ongoing property management. There's more to this available in the mini-series of articles available through the Book Bonuses.

- Portfolio Cycle – if the property market cycle is a *macro view* and the property investment cycle is a *micro view*, then the portfolio cycle is a *midi view* if you like. It considers a collection of different properties over an extended period of time of ownership, stating with growth and acquisition, through to consolidation and finally to exit. This is how we started this chapter, in essence.

Our property finance strategy will inevitably be influenced by all of these different cycles. Some are internal considerations and some are external factors. Ideally, we need to maintain a watch on what is going on at an individual deal level, our own portfolio level and then a market level. This will help to ensure that we are making decisions in a broader context, without closing ourselves off to wider considerations and their implications.

3. The different types of property finance

A quick recap of what we have covered throughout this book.

- **Institutional finance** – this is what most people think of when they think about property finance and includes buy-to-let mortgages and commercial loans, bridging finance and development finance and to a lesser extent, consumer finance.

- **Alternative finance** – starts to take us into less familiar territory and, includes sources such as crowdfunding, peer-to-peer lending, friends and family, becoming our own bank and broker, private finance, including joint ventures and then bonds, shares & mezzanine finance iand finally grants and soft loans.

- **Creative finance** – we have certain methods of financing our property acquisitions that might not at first glance seem like a property finance source at all. But not in my book! These could include property and land options, sublease or rent-to-rent structures, 100% vendor, developer and bank finance, assisted sales, instalment contracts and exchange with delayed completion, along with the wide array we saw in the 'Best of The Rest' chapter, including: adverse possession, assignable off-plan contracts and valuation arbitrage.

We have covered over 50+ different sub-types of property finance that might be open to us to choose from!

4. The principles that can guide us to make effective property finance decisions

Here are some general principles that will help us to have a solid property finance strategy.

- **Be aligned** – it is important to choose the right property finance method to match our investment project and indeed our chosen goals, property strategy and available resources – (time, know-how and, of course, money. This correctly suggests undertaking short-term projects using cash, bridging or development finance and longer-term projects with the right type of property finance, such as BTL mortgages or commercial loans. Of course, add into the mix some of the alternative and creative methods of property finance and we have many options. Even so, this simply means matching the right property finance to the right project.

- **Be methodical** – regardless of which property finance method we decide upon, if we follow the principles of undertaking a methodical process along with an 'investment case approach', then it will help to guide us to the best solution. We shall walk through the process shortly, but this is all about adopting a logical and analytical approach to our property finance and wider property investment needs, with less emphasis on emotion and personal bias.

- **Be prepared** – we need to makes ourselves 'bankable', 'investible' and 'finance-ready' in advance, taking care of all the necessary details well before the time comes. This includes checking credit files, bank statements, HMRC tax return info, source of deposits and so on. It also goes further than this to prepare a solid and well-thought-out property investment case. The point of this is to increase the scope and extent of available property finance sources available to us, which opens up more competitive offerings, whilst also helping to improve our chances of successfully securing our chosen property finance.

When speaking of a methodical approach to property finance above, I developed what I like to call the '5Ps Property Financing Process'. Here it is:

1. **People** – is not necessarily individuals, but it can be. People means either the provider of the property finance that we are looking to use, such as a bank or JV partner, or alternatively, who we need to go through to access them, such as a broker or crowdfunding/P2P platform.

2. **Process** – yes, it is sort of a process within a process but, often with property, things that seem simple and straightforward have several layers to make them more complex than they may first appear! Here we mean the steps we need to take to get us all the way through to taking control of the property we are looking to acquire or control. As well as the obvious step of dealing with the finance provider and giving them all that they need to be able to approve the finance, it could also extend to legal steps, such as conveyancing, contract drafting and negotiation, arranging insurance, due diligence checks and so on. Think of it as an in-depth application process with several related tasks to work through. I have shared some of my own steps in the due diligence checklist in the Book Bonuses.

3. **Pennies** – Yep, it's a massive cheat with the 'P' here, but it is all about the money itself. However, this aspect also includes the terms of the finance, such as loan-to-value levels, fees, early redemption penalties, interest rates, repayment term, capital/interest-only repayment and so on. I like to use the concept of 'Total Cost of Finance' whenever I am looking at a property finance proposition. I prefer to use a time frame of around 5–10 years, rather than say the full 25 years of a mortgage

and add up ALL of the costs linked to the property finance. This takes some of the guesswork out of factors that could be decades away, if they happen at all. This ensures that we take into consideration what a lot of people tend to overlook – renewing property finance facilities over the short to medium term, and all the costs associated with doing that not just the basic interest rate. Just to illustrate, if we take out two-year fixed rate mortgages at a fee of £1,000 each time, then we will have spent £5,000 over a ten-year period, which might outweigh the apparent reduced interest rate saving of that short-term fix compared to two 5-year fixed rate renewals.

4. **Property** – the property we are acquiring is our asset and this asset will be used as security to underwrite both our investment and also our financial commitment to repay any finance provider. Does it stack up? For example, is it built on a flood plain that may hamper its future saleability or insurability? How easy or costly will it be to maintain or are there some major capital expenses looming, such as roof, windows, central heating replacement and so on? Does it have the required legal protection in place, such as a long remaining lease term, or legal access to the property from the street? Are there any other risks around the property that could undermine our investment and ability to repay the finance, such as knotweed, industrial waste, subsidence?

5. **Performance** – is all about the numbers. What sort of returns will this property finance help us to generate? Key performance indicators, or 'KPI's, could include such measures as: annual cashflow and profit, return on investment (ROI), our leverage factor (i.e. utilising other people's money), payback period (time to get our original cash investment back) and the total cost of financing, for example. If we don't have some idea of what a decent investment looks like for us, then we can't judge whether it is worthwhile to us or not. Equally, different types of property finance may give rise to different metrics to us. For example, if we didn't have to put a deposit down we may be able to tolerate lower cashflow.

This is an overview of the general principles to consider; what matters most is to tailor these to our own needs and formulate our own specific property finance principles. These will mean we will have our own personalised process that incorporates what is important to us individually. It will also enable us to have a frame of reference upon which we can make sound judgements and decisions, rather than being swayed by what is on someone else's agenda.

Concluding Thoughts

We can formulate our property finance strategy by working through each of the steps outlined above and deciding what works best for us, allowing for some flexibility. This enables us to have a clearly defined, personalised property finance strategy; also one that can be varied depending on the nature of our views, objectives and plans.

I am not suggesting that you adopt the same property finance strategy as me. Your approach, goals, plans and circumstances will no doubt be unique to you. However, if we sit down once a year and evaluate our views on the subject, we should be able to come up with a pretty decent property finance strategy that will aid us to continue to achieve our overall property goals, plans and objectives.

I have put together a handy Property Finance Strategy checklist and flowchart, which is available as a Book Bonus ... by now you will know how to find the book bonuses but just in case, here's the link again www.thepropertyvoice.net/property-finance-my-book-bonuses

Appendix 2

Further Reading and Resources

Within the Book Bonuses, you can find expanded versions of the following additional resources.

BTL Finance Strategy

Why we should have a strategy regarding our buy-to-let finance is so that we have some guidelines to fall back upon to assist our planning and long-term goals. Having a strategy means we know what we intend to do and can articulate this to other people – in particular mortgage advisors and lenders. If we know what our strategy is, then we have a degree of certainty and predictability in our decision-making and implementation that we can rely upon without having to waste countless hours deliberating.

To identify our finance strategy, we need to evaluate a number of considerations, following a five-step process as follows:

1. Our overall property investment strategy, plans and goals

2. Our plans for each individual property

3. Our view on interest rates and credit conditions

4. Our view on the current and mid-term housing market

5. Our attitude to risk.

Check out the Book Bonuses to read more about my own BTL Finance Strategy.

Making Our Portfolio Bulletproof

*Only when the tide goes out do you discover who's
been swimming naked.*

Warren Buffett

Here are some of the major causes of a recession, along with their significant consequence:

- High Interest Rates (e.g. 1973, 1980 & 1990) – High cost of borrowing

- High Inflation (e.g. 1973 & 1980) – Lack of affordability of housing/rents

- Currency Shocks (e.g. 1990) – Devaluation of assets

- Lack of Liquidity/Credit Crunch (e.g. 2008) – Lack of financing

- Regional/Global Shocks (e.g. 1919, 1930, 1939, 1973 & 2020) – Reduced economic activity in general (and or all of the above!)

In the article available through the Book Bonuses, I outline some of the common threats to our portfolio, along with some of the Primary Defences (PD) and Secondary Defences (SD). As a taster, here is a 20-point checklist to address controllable actions over both the short term and longer term.

The main thing we can look to do, is to make a plan to address how we go about making our property portfolio bulletproof to these apparent Black Swan events, which seem to come around with alarming regularity …

The Property Investment Lifecycle

I wrote a mini-series of articles called 'The Property Investment Lifecycle', which is available as a Book Bonus. There is one stage dedicated to property finance as you will see.

Here is an overview of the five components.

Property Investment Lifecycle Stage	Overview
Search & Acquisition	Six of the common ways to source investment properties. Follow either the 'Outward In' or the 'Inward Out' approach to search, selection and due diligence.
Property Finance	A bite-sized view of property financing as was the case for this article, including the Key Principles and 5P process outlined in this chapter.
Undertaking Improvement Works	Refurbishment and renovation, conversion and extension, development and reconstruction or repairs and maintenance – we got it covered. Includes many of my 'Golden Rules' and a nifty works cost estimation table.
Project Exit	There are five ways to exit a project, one of which you definitely DON'T want. This section explains them all for you, including the 'TRACK' mnemonic to give some extra guidance.
Property Management	There are three main ways to manage a property that you plan to hold: self- manage, outsource and 'insource' – all laid out neatly for you.

Wrap Up and Next Steps

Wow, we have covered a lot of ground in this book! I won't repeat what has already been said here. However, you might find the summary table of the 50+ property finance strategies – and where you can find them – helpful as an appendix to this chapter.

Don't forget to grab your book bonuses, which will include any new property finance strategies that I come across along the way, including one or two that came too late to be included in the book before publishing! Here's a reminder of where to go to find them one last time: www.thepropertyvoice.net/property-finance-my-book-bonuses

What's Next?

I did not invent any of these property finance strategies, even if I have applied many myself. However, I did collate them here for you to include in your shiny new property finance toolbox. It would give me great pleasure to hear how you take these tools and apply them in your own property investment and development activities. So, do tell me, and perhaps tell others too using the hashtag #thepropertyvoice in your social media channel of choice.

DON'T FORGET to pay it forward as I mentioned in the Introduction. If you gift your copy of this book to another investor, then I will gladly replace your copy with a PDF version with pleasure, just drop me a line admin@thepropertyvoice.net.

Finally, from me, whilst knowledge is great to have, what really gets me excited is applied and determined action based on that knowledge. To that end, this is my final call to action…

Go and do some property deals and put into practice one, some or many of the property finance strategies that have been outlined in this book. Would you do that, not for me but for yourself along with who and what matters most to you?

Thank you for joining me on this journey into the world of property finance. If I can support you in any way, please do get in contact and start a conversation – I do like to have conversations about property and property finance!

Ciao ciao

Richard Brown
The Property Voice

Appendix 3

Summary of the 50+ Property Finance Strategies

Finance Type	Category	Ch. Ref	Ch. No.	Summary
Buy-to-Let Mortgage	Institutional	Buy-to-Let	1	A loan against residential rental property for individuals and companies.
Commercial Mortgage/ Loan	Institutional	Buy-to-Let	1 Bonus	A mortgage for non-residential property or property with a commercial use even when occupied by residents (e.g. HMOs).
Personal Loans	Institutional	Consumer Finance	2	Loans in an individual's name, usually unsecured against property (2–7 years).
Credit Cards	Institutional	Consumer Finance	2	Credit cards in an individual's name either with short-term credit terms or 0% interest over an extended term (6–18 months).
Trade Accounts	Institutional	Consumer Finance	2	Credit terms offered by trade merchants and suppliers that grant short-term spending on extended repayment terms (30–60 days).

Finance Type	Category	Ch. Ref	Ch. No.	Summary
Bridging Finance	Institutional	Bridging Finance	3	A short-term secured loan (3–24 months) to 'bridge' the gap between property acquisition and exiting the bridge (sale/refinance).
Auction Finance	Institutional	Bridging Finance	3	A variation of a bridging loan specifically designed to fund an auction purchase after the auction (15–45 days typically).
Second-Charge Loan	Institutional	Bridging Finance	3	A short-term loan or bridge to fund property acquisition or work secured against a second property or behind a first-charge mortgage.
Light Refurbishment	Institutional	Development Finance	4	A hybrid product that allows some minor improvement work (<15% of purchase price) to be done before occupation.
Heavy Refurbishment	Institutional	Development Finance	4	A hybrid product that allows some significant improvement work (15% to 40% of purchase price typically) to be done before occupation.
Development Finance	Institutional	Development Finance	4	Lending to convert or build on property or land. Can fund development work alone or acquisition and development work combined.
Savings and Bonuses	Alternative	Be Your Own Bank or Broker	5	Setting money aside from your regular and 'windfall' income.

Finance Type	Category	Ch. Ref	Ch. No.	Summary
Garage/Loft Clearance	Alternative	Be Your Own Bank or Broker	5	Selling unneeded items to raise funds to invest.
Alternative Income Streams	Alternative	Be Your Own Bank or Broker	5	Undertaking overtime, starting a second job or starting a 'side hustle' or additional business to help fund investing.
Equity Release	Alternative	Be Your Own Bank or Broker	5	Taking out a loan on a property to release some of the value locked in to further invest.
Second Charge/ Further Advance	Alternative	Be Your Own Bank or Broker	5	Additional lending secured against an existing property.
Alternative Asset Refinancing	Alternative	Be Your Own Bank or Broker	5	Using alternative types as asset as security for a loan (e.g. art/antiques, classic cars, fine wine and other types of investment).
Pensions	Alternative	Be Your Own Bank or Broker	5	Accessing your old or sometimes current pension funds to use for investment purposes.
Intercompany Loans/Profit Extraction	Alternative	Be Your Own Bank or Broker	5	Using funds accumulated with a separate business for property investment purposes.
Director/ Shareholder Loans	Alternative	Be Your Own Bank or Broker	5	Accessing funds personally on a temporary basis to fund short-term property projects.
Friends & Family	Alternative	Be Your Own Bank or Broker	6	Gifts, loans, equity and property contributions from close connections that can support your property finance requirements.

Finance Type	Category	Ch. Ref	Ch. No.	Summary
Joint Names Purchase	Alternative	Friends and Family Finance	6	Buying a property in combination with a friend or family member.
Silent Investment	Alternative	Friends and Family Finance	6	Investing in a property transaction without appearing on the Land Registry deeds.
Gifted Investment	Alternative	Friends and Family Finance	6	Raising funds from a donor on a gifted basis.
Peer-to-peer (P2P)	Alternative	Be Your Own Bank or Broker	7	Going direct to peer-to-peer platforms to raise debt finance.
Crowd-funding	Alternative	Crowdfunding and P2P	7	Going direct to crowd-funding platforms to raise equity finance.
Private Finance	Alternative	Private Finance and Joint Ventures	8	Loan contributions from private individuals and small businesses, trusts or investment/pension funds for property investment.
Joint Ventures	Alternative	Private Finance and Joint Ventures	8	Equity contributions from private individuals and small businesses, trusts or investment/pension funds for property investment.
Property Bonds	Alternative	Bonds, Shares and Mezzanine Finance	9	Using a bond, which is a form of loan to provide an additional layer of finance, especially for development companies.
Shares	Alternative	Bonds, Shares and Mezzanine Finance	9	Issuing shares in a company to raise equity finance.

Finance Type	Category	Ch. Ref	Ch. No.	Summary
Mezzanine	Alternative	Bonds, Shares and Mezzanine Finance	9	A hybrid of debt and equity to provide a 'middle layer' of finance between acquisition finance and equity finance.
Grants	Alternative	Grants and Soft Loans	10	An award of money that does not need to be repaid (subject to conditions) to help fund a property project.
Soft Loans	Alternative	Grants and Soft Loans	10	A loan with less stringent underwriting and/or conditions due to support to a lender from government.
Tax Reliefs and Credits	Alternative	Tax Reliefs and Credits	11	Financial contribution in the form of tax breaks, such as a rebate, offset or deferral to improve the financing of properties.
Options	Creative	Options, Delayed Completion and Instalment Contracts	12	The right but not the obligation to acquire a property or piece of land at some point in the future.
Delayed Completion	Creative	Options, Delayed Completion and Instalment Contracts	12	A contractual commitment to acquire a property or piece of land with a longer delay between exchanging contracts and completion.
Instalment Contracts	Creative	Options, Delayed Completion and Instalment Contracts	12	A contractual commitment to acquire a property or piece of land with payments over time.

Finance Type	Category	Ch. Ref	Ch. No.	Summary
Vendor Finance	Creative	Owner Finance	13	A form of financing where the current property owner becomes the provider of finance or time to pay rather than a separate entity.
Developer Finance	Creative	Owner Finance	13	A form of financing where the property developer becomes the provider of finance or time to pay rather than a separate entity.
Assisted Sale	Creative	Assisted Sale	14	An agreement to add value and participate in any gain made with a property sale via a commercial agreement with the property owner.
Rent-to-Rent	Creative	Rent-to-Rent	15	An agreement that allows us to profit from a property's incoming rent by sub-leasing it from the owner at a lower level of outgoing rent.
Adverse Possession	Creative	Best of the Rest	16	Legal squatting! Claiming ownership of empty or abandoned land or property through legal means.
Assignable Off-Plan Contracts	Creative	Best of the Rest	16	Agreeing to buy a property before it's built then realising a gain by assigning that right to a third party.
Shared Ownership	Creative	Best of the Rest	16	A government-backed scheme where a housing association becomes co-owner of a property to reduce the financial outlay.

Finance Type	Category	Ch. Ref	Ch. No.	Summary
Revolving Credit Facility	Creative	Best of the Rest	16	An agreement with a lender to provide funding for future property acquisitions, usually secured against existing property assets.
Leveraging Alternative Assets	Creative	Best of the Rest	16	Lending secured against assets other than property to raise funds, such as antiques, classic cars, fine wine and even cryptocurrency.
Home Equity Release	Creative	Best of the Rest	16	Raising funds to invest in property from the equity within your own home, either by financing or sale of the property.
Arbitrage the Valuation	Creative	Best of the Rest	16	Realising additional finance by changing the method of valuing a property for lending purposes.
Supplier Credit and Loans	Creative	Best of the Rest	16	Obtaining extended payment terms from suppliers, contractors and trades to allow more time to pay for goods and materials.
Business Acquisition Structures	Creative	Best of the Rest	16	Using alternative general business finance; includes asset finance, invoice discounting, advanced subscriptions and overdraft.
Debt-Servicing via Power of Attorney	Creative	Best of the Rest	16	An agreement with a property owner and their lender to take over the repayments of their loan to control and add value to a property.

Finance Type	Category	Ch. Ref	Ch. No.	Summary
Mortgage Host and Guarantee	Creative	Best of the Rest	16	An agreement with a third-party to support lending in cases where the investor may not otherwise qualify.
Conditional Exchange	Creative	Best of the Rest	16	An contractual agreement that allows us to acquire a property provided a certain event or condition takes place (e.g. planning consent).

Contacts

Email: admin@thepropertyvoice.net
Web: www.thepropertyvoice.net
Linked In: https://www.linkedin.com/in/richardwjbrown/
Insta: https://www.instagram.com/thepropertyvoice/
Twitter: https://twitter.com/PropertyVoiceUK
Facebook: https://www.facebook.com/thepropertyvoice

You can also find over 300 episodes of *The Property Voice Podcast* on your podcast feed of choice and me as a regular columnist in *Your Property Network* (YPN) Magazine. I have also written the books *Property Investor Toolkit* and *#PropTech* for your information.